Learn QuickBooks 6

KATHERINE MURRAY

A Division of Prima Publishing

© 1998 by Prima Publishing. All rights reserved. No part of this book may be reproduced or transmitted in any form or by any means, electronic or mechanical, including photocopying, recording, or by any information storage or retrieval system without written permission from Prima Publishing, except for the inclusion of brief quotations in a review.

A division of Prima Publishing

Prima Publishing and colophon are registered trademarks of Prima Communications, Inc. In a Weekend is a trademark of Prima Publishing, a division of Prima Communications, Inc., Rocklin, California 95677.

Publisher: Matthew H. Carleson
Managing Editor: Dan J. Foster
Acquisitions Editor: Jenny L. Watson
Project Editor: Kevin W. Ferns
Technical Reviewer: Bo Williams
Copy Editor: Robert Campbell
Interior Layout: Jimmie Young
Cover Design: Prima Design Team
Indexer: Katherine Stimson

Intuit, QuickBooks, QuickBooks Pro, and TurboTax are registered trademarks and/or registered service marks of Intuit, Inc.

Important: If you have problems installing or running QuickBooks 6.0, go to Intuit's Web site at www.intuit.com. Prima Publishing cannot provide software support.

Prima Publishing and the author have attempted throughout this book to distinguish proprietary trademarks from descriptive terms by following the capitalization style used by the manufacturer.

Information contained in this book has been obtained by Prima Publishing from sources believed to be reliable. However, because of the possibility of human or mechanical error by our sources, Prima Publishing, or others, the Publisher does not guarantee the accuracy, adequacy, or completeness of any information and is not responsible for any errors or omissions or the results obtained from the use of such information. Readers should be particularly aware of the fact that the Internet is an ever-changing entity. Some facts may have changed since this book went to press.

ISBN: 0-7615-1384-1
Library of Congress Catalog Card Number: 98-66465
Printed in the United States of America
98 99 00 01 02 DD 10 9 8 7 6 5 4 3 2 1

Learn QuickBooks® 6

Send Us Your Comments:

To comment on this book or any other Prima Tech title, visit Prima's reader response page on the Web at **www.primapublishing.com/comments**.

How to Order:

For information on quantity discounts, contact the publisher: Prima Publishing, P.O. Box 1260BK, Rocklin, CA 95677-1260; (916) 632-4400. On your letterhead, include information concerning the intended use of the books and the number of books you wish to purchase. For individual orders, turn to the back of this book for more information, or visit Prima's Web site at **www.primapublishing.com**.

*To Chris, my organic other half.
Smiles and love.*

CONTENTS AT A GLANCE

Introduction xviii

FRIDAY EVENING
Getting Started with QuickBooks 1

SATURDAY MORNING
Tracking and Recording Sales 73

SATURDAY AFTERNOON
Writing the Check: Paying for Goods and Services 115

SATURDAY EVENING
Keeping Track of Inventory and Managing Payroll 151

SUNDAY MORNING
Tracking Results: Reporting Your Financial Data 205

SUNDAY AFTERNOON
Online Banking with QuickBooks **241**

SUNDAY EVENING
Organizing Tax Information **283**

Appendix A   Installing QuickBooks 6.0 317

Appendix B   QuickBooks Pro 323

Glossary 325

Index 329

CONTENTS

Introduction xviii

FRIDAY EVENING
Getting Started with QuickBooks 1
Starting Out: The EasyStep Interview 4
Entering Your Company Information 6
Choosing Your Company Preferences 10
Starting with the Start Date 14
Setting Up Income and Expenses 15
Entering Income Details 17
Entering Opening Balances 21
Setting Up Payroll 27
Choosing Menu Items 38
Finding Out What's Next 39
Take a Break 39
Touring the QuickBooks Navigator 39
Exploring the Screen 42
Reviewing the Menu Bar 42
Using the Navigator 44
Getting Help 50
Checking Out the Help Index 51
How Do I? and Qcards 51
How QuickBooks Can Help in Your Industry 53
Good Advisors Are Worth Their Weight in Gold 55

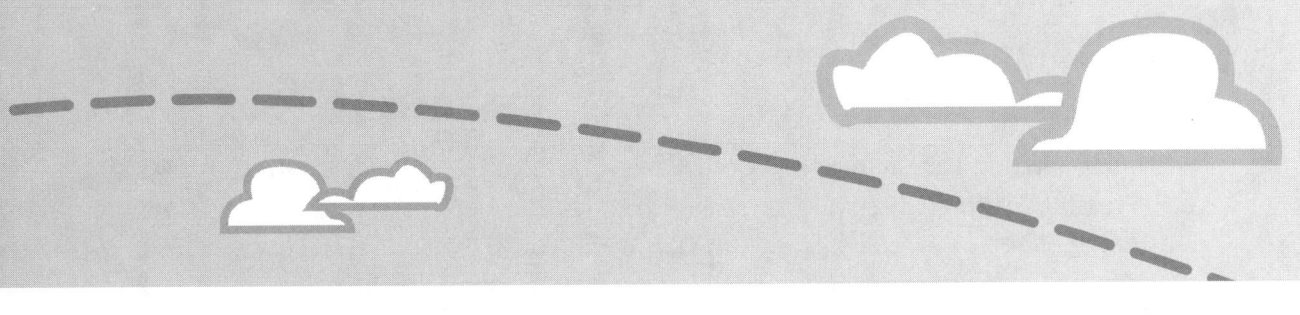

Online Help	57
Take a Break	57
Backing Up Your Data	58
Understanding the Chart of Accounts	59
Taking a Look at the Chart of Accounts	59
Working with Accounts	60
Lots of Lists	64
Setting Up Your Checkbook	66
Displaying the Register	66
Entering a Check	68
Entering Past Transactions	70
Closing the Register	70
Exiting QuickBooks	71
What's Next?	71

SATURDAY MORNING
Tracking and Recording Sales 73

Setting Up Customer Information	76
Starting Out with Customer Info	76
Adding Customers	77
Adding Jobs	83
Editing Customer Information	86
Creating Invoices	90
Figuring Finance Charges	94
How QuickBooks Figures Finance Charges	94
Setting Up Finance Charges	95
Assessing Finance Charges	96

Contents

Printing Mailing Labels and Invoices 97
    Creating Mailing Labels 98
Aligning Labels 101
    Printing Invoices 103
Take a Break 106
Recording Payments 106
    Receiving Payments from Your Invoices 106
    Entering Cash Sales 108
Making Deposits 110
Using Credit Memos 111
Checking the Customer Register 112
What's Next? 114

SATURDAY AFTERNOON
Writing the Check: Paying for Goods and Services 115

What Do You Write Checks For? 117
    Getting Checks 117
    There Are Other Ways to Pay 118
Getting Ready to Pay Bills 118
Two Ways to Pay Bills 118
Adding a New Vendor to Your List 119
Writing Checks 121
    Printing a Single Check 123
    Entering Check Transactions 124
    Adding Vendors As You Go 126
    Splitting Transactions 128
    Editing Transactions 129
    Voiding Checks 130
Getting a Reminder 131
Balancing Your Checkbook 132
What If You Need an Adjustment? 134
Take a Break 135
Creating a Bill System with QuickBooks 136
Entering Bills 137
Creating Purchase Orders 139

Receiving Goods 140
    Receiving Goods First, Bill Later 141
    Receiving Goods and the Bill Together 142
    Receiving the Bill 143
Paying Bills 145
What about Accounts Payable? 147
Editing Bill Payments 148
Deleting Bill Payments 149
What's Next? 149

SATURDAY EVENING
Keeping Track of Inventory and Managing Payroll 151

Inventory with QuickBooks 153
What Does Inventory Look Like? 154
Turning on the Inventory Features 155
Creating Inventory Accounts 156
Adding Inventory Items 159
    Setting Up Items for Later 163
    Setting Up Custom Inventory Fields 163
Working with Inventory 164
    Taking Inventory 165
A Quick Inventory QuickReport 166
    Adjusting Inventory Information 169
    Selling Stock 171
    Ordering Stock 172
    Reordering Reminders 173
    Receiving Items into Inventory 173
    Analyzing Your Data Using Inventory Reports 174
    What's Your Inventory Worth? 175
    Getting a Detailed Report 176
    Printing a Stock Report 177
    Reporting Vendor Status 177
Take a Break 178
Payroll with QuickBooks 178
    Turning on Payroll Features 179

Contents

- Choosing Your Payroll Preferences 179
- What Do You Need to Set Up Payroll? 180
- Entering Employee Information 181
  - Adding an Employee 183
  - Changing Employee Information 186
  - Entering Year-to-Date Amounts 187
  - Keeping Track of Payroll Expenses 190
  - Taking the Duh Out of Deductions 191
- Payday! A Step-by-Step Process 193
- Paying Your Liabilities 197
- A Payroll Tax Form Primer 198
  - Creating the 941 199
  - Creating the 940 200
  - W-2s Made Simple 201
- What's Next? 203

SUNDAY MORNING

Tracking Results: Reporting Your Financial Data 205

- When Do You Need a Report? 208
  - Checking Out Available Reports 208
  - Where Do You Find Reports? 209
- Choosing the Right Report 212
- Creating, Previewing, and Printing a Simple Report 214
  - Checking Out the Report Window 217
  - QuickReports On the Fly 222
- Project Reports You Can Create 223
  - Producing a Profit and Loss Statement 224
  - Printing Your Balance Sheet 225
  - Printing a Phone List 226
  - Creating a Sales Report 227
  - Producing a Price List 228
- Take a Break 229
- Formatting Your Report 229
  - Changing Number Display 230
  - Changing the Font 231

Working with Report Filters	232
Filtering Ideas	233
Applying Filters	233
Memorizing Reports	235
Saving a Memorized Report	235
Using a Memorized Report	236
Creating Custom Reports	236
Adding Graphs	238
Modifying the Graph	238
What's Next?	240

SUNDAY AFTERNOON
Online Banking with QuickBooks 241

Understanding Online Banking	244
What Can You Do with Online Banking?	244
Online Basics	244
Issues and Worries about Online Banking	246
What about Security?	247
What You Need to Get Started	248
Talking to Your Bank	250
Setting Up QuickBooks for Online Banking	250
Starting Out with Online Banking	251
Getting an Internet Connection	253
Finding a Bank Online	253
Applying for Online Services	256
Enabling Your Accounts	259
Who Will You Pay Online?	262
Using Online Banking	263
Writing a Check	263
Paying Bills Online	265
Working with the Register	266
Sending Transactions Online	267
Scheduling Your Payments	269
Transferring Funds Online	270
Sending Online Messages	272

Getting Help with Online Banking 272
Take a Break 273
Using the Payroll Service 274
Using the QuickBooks Updates Service 276
Getting New Tax Tables 278
Using Your Web Resources (Intuit Web Sites) 280
What's Next? 281

SUNDAY EVENING

Organizing Tax Information 283

    Finding Out about Journal Entries 286
    Handling Business Taxes 287
        Setting Up for Business Taxes 288
        What's Your Tax Form? 289
        Checking Tax Line Assignments 290
        Assigning a Tax Line to an Account 291
        Verifying Account Totals 293
        Modifying the Income Tax Summary Report 294
        Finding Sales Income Amounts 294
        Determining Your Total Purchases 297
        Filling Out Additional Forms 298
        Preparing Your Tax Forms 299
        Exporting Tax Information to a Tax Program 300
    Take a Break 300
    Reporting Payroll Taxes 300
        The Payroll Process Revisited 301
        Creating Payroll Subaccounts 301
        Payroll Reports: An Overview 303
    Working with Sales Tax 303
        Turning On Sales Tax 304
        Setting Up Sales Tax 305
    Identifying Taxable Items 307
        Recording a Tax Item 307
        Paying Sales Tax 308

Creating a Sales Tax Report 310
Using the Accountant's Review 311
    Working with the Accountant's Copy 313
    Merging the Accountant's Data 313
What's Next? 315

APPENDIX A
Installing QuickBooks 6.0 317
    What Do You Need to Install QuickBooks? 318
    Getting Ready to Install 318
    Simple Installation 319
    Reinstalling QuickBooks 321
    About Upgrades 321

APPENDIX B
QuickBooks Pro 323
    Program Highlights 323
    What Do You Need to Run QuickBooks Pro? 324
    Program Availability 324

Glossary 325
Index 329

ACKNOWLEDGMENTS

Although writing itself can sometimes be a solo gig, publishing a book requires the collaboration of a community of talented people. I'd like to specifically thank the great people at Prima who have taken this book from its raw text and turned it into an in-your-hands product.

Thanks to Jenny Watson, the acquisitions editor, who is bright, inventive, and energetic. She's always great to work with and inspires me to *make those deadlines*. Thanks to Kevin Ferns, the project editor, who shepherded the project and kept track of all the pieces flying hither and yon through author review. Thanks also to Bo Williams, the technical editor, who tested all the keystrokes you'll be using in this book to make sure I didn't scramble my directions or capture the wrong screens. Thanks to Robert Campbell, the copy editor, who painstakingly read through page after page of manuscript and compared all the illustrations to net out all the typos and confusing run-ons (rather like this one) I tend to include in my draft manuscripts.

And finally, a big Thank You to my family. To the kids—Kelly, Christopher, and Cameron—who gave up lots of trips to the pool and sometimes dealt with a grumpy, sleep-deprived Mom as she pushed toward meeting her deadlines for this book. And to Chris, for all the late nights we were up working together and for way you have filled my life with music, art, good books, food, wine, and the constant reminder that there *is* life beyond computer books.

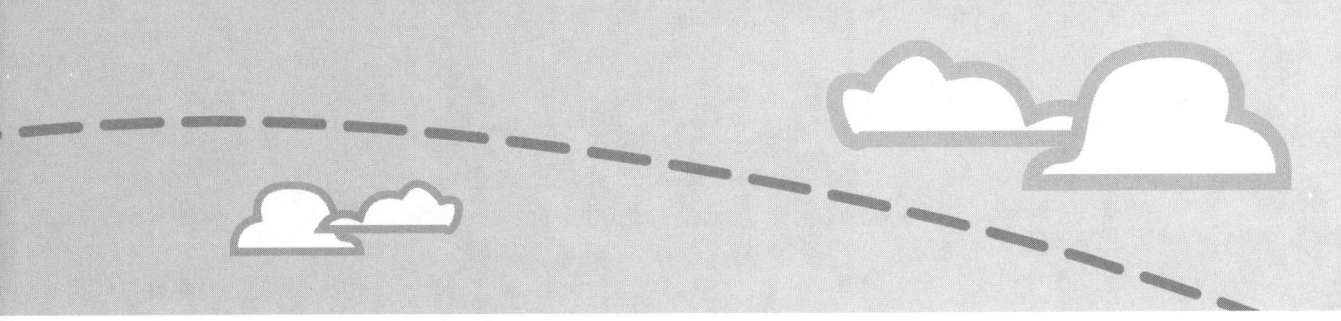

ABOUT THE AUTHOR

Katherine Murray is an old-timer in the ranks of computer book authors. Since she began writing books in 1987, Katherine has published well over 40 computer books for a variety of publishers. For the last 10 years, she has worked from home in her own business, reVisions Plus, Inc., which specializes in writing and publishing services for publishers and nonprofit organizations (**www.revisionsplus.com**). Katherine writes books on a variety of topics from parenting to PCs, and keeps her business organized using QuickBooks.

On the "fun" side of life, Katherine is the work-at-home mother of three (Kelly, age 17, Christopher, age 10, and Cameron, age 5), and the caretaker of Edgar-the-Dog and Maya-the-Cat. In her spare time, she enjoys writing plays, playing the guitar, and trying new recipes (the messier, the better).

INTRODUCTION

Hello! And welcome to a book that may change the way you do business forever. Have you been suffering from that vague, undefinable feeling of doom that awakens many business owners at 3:00 A.M.? Do you feel your stress level go up every time you even *think* about your accountant? Well, QuickBooks, from Intuit, is the bestselling software for small business in the world—if ever a program was made for you, this one is it. And *Learn QuickBooks 6 In a Weekend* is the book that will help you get from there to here—from the late-night business-owner sweats to feeling more in control of your business and your business data—in one weekend.

What This Book Is About

First and foremost, this book is about how you can learn your way around the QuickBooks 6.0 program and get your business organized in the process. A unique feature of this book is the time-based format. Not only will you learn the basic skills QuickBooks has to offer, but you'll do it in a set of seven work sessions arranged over a single weekend. This means you'll be able to set—and meet—a specific goal, an ability that is important to us as business owners with little (and dwindling) amounts of free time.

As a business owner myself, and a QuickBooks user for the last four years, I have organized the work sessions in *Learn QuickBooks 6 In a Weekend* to

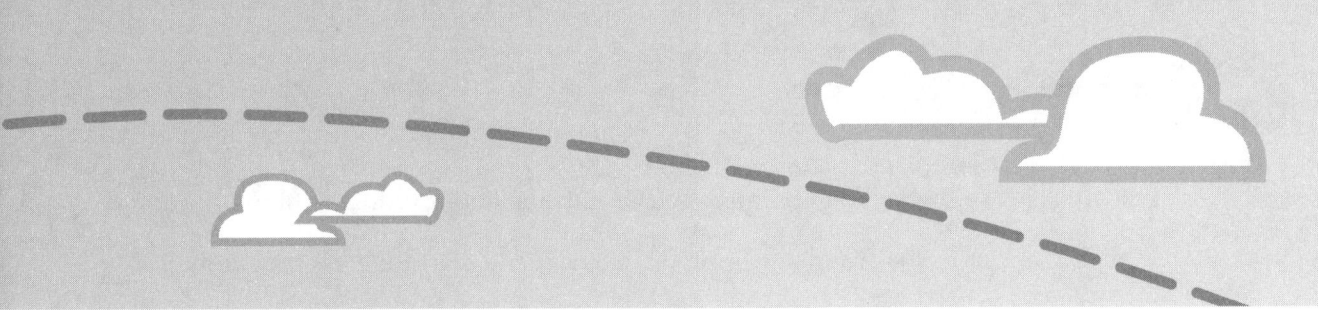

cover all of the most important and helpful aspects of the QuickBooks program. Specifically, you will learn to:

- Set up your company and accounts
- Track and record your sales
- Write, print, and manage your checks
- Keep track of inventory and handle payroll
- Create and print reports showing your financial picture
- Set up and use online banking features
- Organize your tax information and prepare data for your accountant

Who Should Read This Book

If you are responsible for handing business data and you are faced with the challenge of learning QuickBooks, this book is for you. You don't have to be a business owner; you don't need to be a math major. In fact, QuickBooks is designed to be easy to understand and use no matter *what* your background is. If any of the following items apply to you, you will find *Learn QuickBooks 6 In a Weekend* is just what you've been looking for:

- You are the owner of a small business.
- You are learning how to manage business data.
- You want to organize your business sales and inventory.
- You need to computerize your payroll.

- You are interested in learning about online banking.
- You have limited time to spend learning new programs.
- You want to be able to produce reports based on your financial data.
- You want to be able to print checks.
- You are tired of typing the same information on various forms repeatedly.
- You want to be able to learn simple accounting practices.

What You Need to Begin

First things first. You'll need to have QuickBooks 6.0 installed on your computer before you can begin working with your business data. If you haven't yet installed QuickBooks, turn to Appendix A now and follow the instructions listed there. It's a simple process and should take you less than 15 minutes. When you've installed the program, return to this point and assemble the other necessary items:

- Your last checking account statement for the account you want to use, along with any cancelled checks
- The current check register for your business accounts
- Your savings and credit card statements
- Your current employee information
- Your current sales and inventory data
- The invoice you currently use
- Copies of bills you pay on a regular basis
- The unpaid balances for both your customers and vendors
- Information on any outstanding loans

- Your last few years' completed tax returns
- Transactions you need to record in QuickBooks (including invoices, deposits, checks, and the like)
- Any other information you use now to keep track of your business data

How This Book Is Organized

Friday Evening: Getting Started with QuickBooks introduces you to all the basic features of this terrific program and helps you get started organizing your business. You learn to start your company QuickBooks file, go through the EasyStep Interview process, and begin making choices about the best ways to organize your business data. Before you can do much with the program features, you need to know your way around on the screen: One portion of the Friday work session involves exploring the various screen elements and learning to navigate menus, toolbars, and quick keys. You discover the Chart of Accounts and explore a list of lists, which track all kinds of business information from products to employees to payables. Finally, you learn to set up your checkbook so that it is ready for the Saturday session and to enter the past transactions you need to make your checkbook current.

Saturday Morning: Tracking and Recording Sales takes a look at your first priority after initially setting things up: making sales. After you have provided your service or sold your product, how do you invoice your customer? In this session, you learn to create an effective invoice, one that gives you all the data you need in a well-organized layout that's easy for the customer to understand. Once you have the invoice, you are ready for mass mailings—with QuickBooks' Mail Merge feature, you can easily send many invoices in many different directions. In the second half of this session, you learn how to handle payments—from cash sales to deposits to troubleshooting techniques.

Saturday Afternoon: Writing the Check: Paying for Goods and Services tackles the next big business concern. Once you invoice the customer and receive payment, how do you handle your *own* bills? In this session, you learn to set up vendors on your list. You find out how to automate bills you pay monthly, cutting down on the list of items you need to remember to do and allowing QuickBooks to handle the routine transactions for you. You learn the ten tips for an effective bill-paying system and see how QuickBooks fits with your old Accounts Payable system. You discover how to write, edit, and delete checks in QuickBooks and reconcile your checking account. Finally, you learn how to handle the sales tax in your transactions.

Saturday Evening: Keeping Track of Inventory and Managing Payroll takes you through the process of setting up a business inventory. How do you handle the goods you purchase? How do you track your products? This session shows you how to set up an inventory system and manage the data flow, recording the purchases you make and keeping track of sales accurately. You discover how to create and use purchase orders and modify them to adapt to your changing needs. The second half of this session involves payroll. You learn to set up your payroll system in QuickBooks while avoiding the Four Payroll Don'ts. You navigate the necessities by tracking your employee information, paying employees, handling quarterly payroll returns, submitting annual payroll returns (or preparing them for your accountant), and working with state returns as well.

Sunday Morning: Tracking Results: Reporting Your Financial Data teaches you to show off your business data in a colorful and easy-to-understand format. Reports and graphs can show at a glance what pages of numbers cannot: business trends, highs and lows, and areas of special performance. By learning to create and print reports, you discover how to show others at a glance how your business is doing—something that can be valuable when you are talking with prospective clients, investors, or contractors. You learn about the basic reports from balance sheets to profit-and-loss, and you discover QuickReports, for those times when you want a simple snapshot on the fly. Although QuickBooks includes a number of preset reports you can create easily, you may want to design and print your own custom reports: In this session, you learn to do just that. Finally, you discover how to create and print graphs—in black and white or in color—to help communicate your business information in an inviting and memorable way.

Sunday Afternoon: Online Banking with QuickBooks reaches into the realm of the Internet by showing you how to set up your business to do banking online. First you learn about the security issues—is online banking secure and how do you know? Next you find out about the basics of online payment and discover how to do an online fund transfer. You find out how to work with credit card transactions—both incoming and outgoing—in this session, and discover how to get software updates for your QuickBooks management system by downloading the files you need from the Web.

Sunday Evening: Organizing Tax Information moves into the tax realm. What kinds of reports do you need to have ready? Where do you get the necessary forms? This session helps you get your tax information together and prepare it in a form even a tax preparer could love. You also discover how to use the QuickBooks Accountant's Review, which summarizes your business tax information for your tax advisor.

The book finishes up with two appendixes and a glossary. Appendix A covers QuickBooks installation features, and Appendix B spotlights features of QuickBooks Pro that go beyond the standard QuickBooks features. The glossary provides definitions of terms introduced throughout the book.

Special Features of This Book

Learn QuickBooks 6 In a Weekend includes a number of special features that alert you to extra information in your work sessions:

Tips give you shortcuts and hints about how to use QuickBooks most effectively.

Cautions alert you to tricky or complicated procedures or spotlight times when you should get clarification from your financial expert.

 **Notes** give you additional information that complements the process at hand.

 **Find It Onlines** provide Web addresses to which you can go for more information on the current topic.

 **Buzzwords** give you quick, to-the-point definitions of terms introduced in the text.

Taking Charge of Your Business the QuickBooks Way

You probably already feel those night sweats slipping away, right? The days of disorganized business data and panicked trips to the accountant's office are drawing to a close. Armed with QuickBooks version 6.0 and *Learn QuickBooks 6 In a Weekend*, you are well on your way to making sense of your business data and running your company more productively and efficiently than you ever have before.

FRIDAY EVENING

Getting Started with QuickBooks

- ✹ Starting Out: The EasyStep Interview
- ✹ Touring the QuickBooks Navigator
- ✹ Backing Up Your Data
- ✹ Understanding the Chart of Accounts
- ✹ Setting Up Your Checkbook

Ready to begin your weekend work session with QuickBooks? Hopefully you have had a good dinner, played with the kids, and relaxed a bit, and now you are ready to turn to the computer to learn how to get your business information organized so that everything works more smoothly with less headache and hassle.

This first session takes you through the basic introductory information about QuickBooks and walks you through the EasyStep Interview, which gathers information about your business and helps you create the necessary accounts and lists.

So slip your favorite musical CD into the drive, get comfortable, and prepare to learn how to:

- Set up your business using the EasyStep Interview
- Learn about the QuickBooks Navigator and important screen elements
- Explore the business resources available to you
- Understand your Chart of Accounts
- Learn about lists
- Set up your checkbook

The first segment of this session gets you busy working with the QuickBooks EasyStep Interview, so if you haven't started QuickBooks, do so now.

Locate the QuickBooks icon on your desktop and double-click on it. Or if you elected *not* to add the icon on your desktop, you can start QuickBooks by opening the Start menu, pointing to Programs, pointing to QuickBooks, and selecting QuickBooks for Windows.

Starting Out: The EasyStep Interview

If this is the first time you've started QuickBooks, the EasyStep Interview will begin automatically. If you have worked with QuickBooks before, the file for your existing company will open on the screen. If this is the case for you, close your company file by opening the File menu and choosing Close Company. Then open the File menu a second time and choose EasyStep Interview.

Figure 1.1 shows the first screen of the EasyStep Interview. The purpose of the interview is to help you provide the information QuickBooks needs to create your company accounts. Don't worry—it's not as stressful as an audit, but it is a detailed and fairly elaborate procedure. Click on Next to start the process. Then just sit back and hit the answers out of the park as QuickBooks pitches them to you.

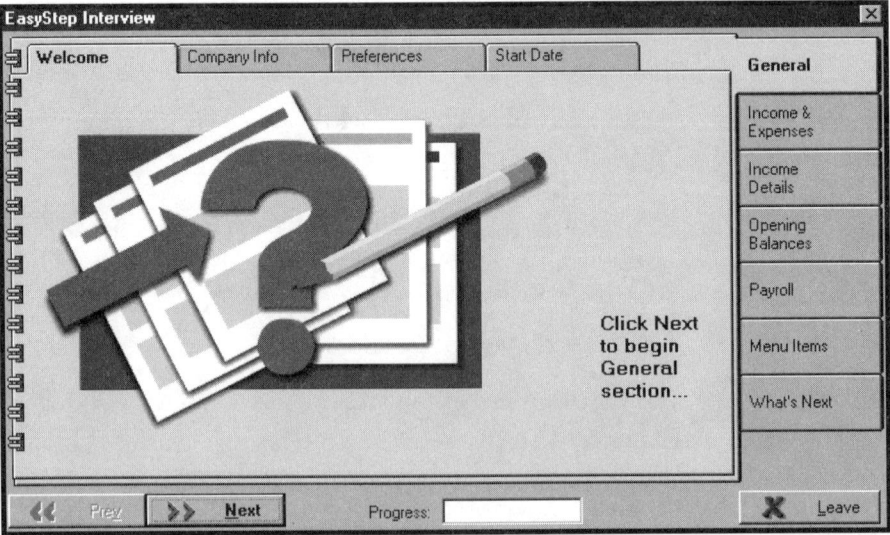

Figure 1.1

The EasyStep Interview walks you through a series of questions and then sets up your company accounts.

FRIDAY EVENING   Getting Started with QuickBooks   5

PREPARATIONS: WHAT DO YOU NEED FOR THE EASYSTEP INTERVIEW?

Here's a grocery list of items you need to have for questions QuickBooks will ask you during the EasyStep Interview. You don't need to have everything on this list, but the process will go faster (and you won't have to do any guessing) if you have these items handy:

- Your Federal ID number
- Information on sales tax you pay, if applicable
- Payroll information, including number of employees and all employee data
- Information on how you track your projects
- The date you want to begin tracking data in QuickBooks (known as your *Start Date*)
- Information on any unique income or expense accounts you need to create
- Data on the different ways you receive income
- Opening balances for your checking and savings accounts
- Outstanding loan information
- A current balance sheet
- Information on your customers and vendors, including current balances owed

The first question QuickBooks asks you is whether you are upgrading from another Intuit product. If you are a Quicken user or you used an earlier version of QuickBooks, click on the option that applies to you. If you are a new user, leave that third option selected. Click on Next. The following screen gives you the option of skipping the interview. Click on Next to continue.

 Because the EasyStep Interview begins automatically the first time you start QuickBooks, the program gives you the choice of opting out of the interview if you want to.

The next screen in the EasyStep Interview explains the buttons you use to navigate through the interview. Click on Next to move forward, Prev to move back, or Leave to exit the interview.

TIP You can complete the EasyStep Interview at any time. If you decide to exit the interview by clicking on Leave before you have completed it, you can resume the interview at a later time by opening the File menu and choosing EasyStep Interview.

The remaining three screens explain how the interview will proceed and alert you to the warning symbol displayed when answers you give cannot easily be changed. Watch for this symbol:

When you see this symbol, remember that your answers are important and cannot easily be modified. Double-check the information before you respond so that you know it's as accurate as possible.

Entering Your Company Information

The next tab of the EasyStep Interview begins the Company Info section. You will be asked for your business name and address, the type of business you run, your Federal ID number, and the type of data management tasks you need to manage with QuickBooks. When you click on Next, a screen appears asking for your Company Name and Legal Name (see Figure 1.2). Enter the information and click on Next to continue. If you want to see how to open more than one business in QuickBooks, click on the More button in the lower right corner of the screen.

NOTE Although you might think Company Name and Legal Name are the same thing, this isn't always the case. You can operate your business under one name, such as Astec Enterprises, but legally set it up under another name (AST, Inc.). You may see this referred to as a DBA ("doing business as") company.

FRIDAY EVENING **Getting Started with QuickBooks** 7

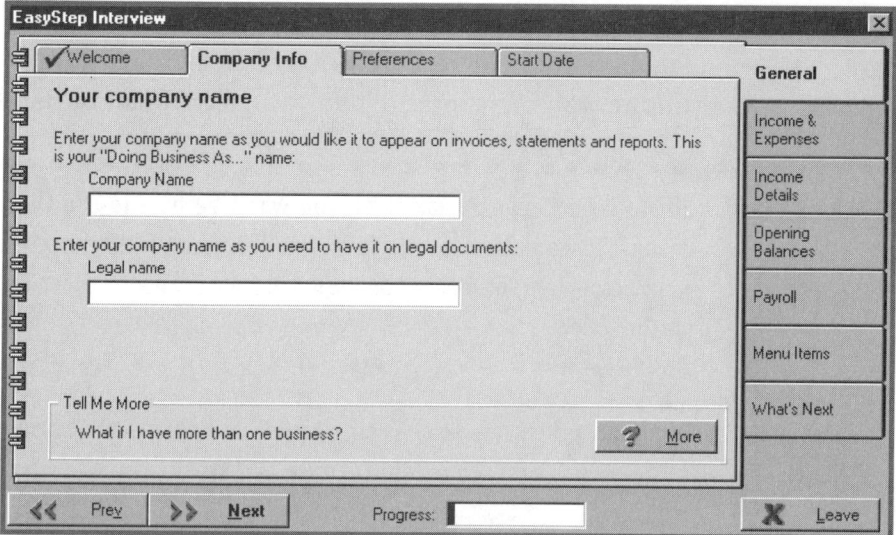

Figure 1.2

The Company Info section gathers information about your company and your business data needs.

 TIP If you have more than one company, do you file separate returns for the companies? If so, set up each company as an individual company by using the File menu's New Company option. If you file one tax return for both (or all) companies, you can set up the multiple companies with one EasyStep Interview.

The next stop asks you to supply address information. Click in the blanks, type your info, and click on Next. You are asked for your Federal ID number (you'll have one only if your business is incorporated), as well as your fiscal year and your tax year. Enter the information that is appropriate for your business; then click on Next.

 Your *Federal ID number* is a number assigned to your business by the Federal government. Your *fiscal year* and *tax year* are the twelve-month periods during which you track your financial information and tax liabilities, respectively. (For more complete definitions of these terms, see the Glossary.)

The next screen asks which income tax form you use for your business. If you have your last year's return, get the number from that form. If you are unsure, you can contact either your accountant or the IRS.

CAUTION If you do not select a tax form, you won't be able to use QuickBooks' tax reporting feature. Try to determine the form you need—by looking up last year's forms, asking your accountant, or looking online—before you choose Other/None and continue with the Interview.

FIND IT ONLINE You can go to the IRS Web site to find out more about the tax forms you can use in your business. Browse the site at **www.irsustreas.gov**.

The next page asks you to choose the type of business you are operating. You find a wide variety of company types from which you can choose. If you don't see one that fits your business, choose something on the list that is similar to what you do. Click on Next to continue. The next screen tells you about the tips you will see scattered throughout the interview and reminds you to check out QuickBooks and Your Industry in the Help menu after you complete the EasyStep Interview. Click on Next.

Creating Your Company File

You are ready to create your QuickBooks company file. Click on Next again. The Save As dialog box appears, prompting you to enter a file name for the company you will track in QuickBooks. The Company Name you specified earlier in the interview will be displayed in the File Name text box. Change it if necessary; then click on OK.

Choosing Business Accounts

The next screen helps you determine what kind of accounts you will set up for your business. QuickBooks displays a number of preset accounts (see Figure 1.3), and you can opt to use the accounts provided or change the accounts to fit your business needs. If you want to use the accounts QuickBooks has provided, click on Yes; if you want to change the accounts,

FRIDAY EVENING Getting Started with QuickBooks

> ### A Sample Business: The Write Company
>
> The company I use for examples throughout this book is a fictitious service-based company called The Write Company. This company is a small business, employing only three people, that offers writing, editing, and publishing services to corporate clients. In addition to the writing service The Write Company offers, it offers training for companies on how to create vision statements, produce annual reports, and improve traditional business communications. In recent months, it has begun offering a self-published set of manuals and three videos along with its training courses. It will use QuickBooks' inventory and sales tax–tracking features to help organize this newest area of the business.

click on No. If the accounts shown are close to the ones you need, it's easiest to go ahead and use the accounts QuickBooks provides and then modify them later. Click on Next to continue.

The next screen asks you how many people will have access to your QuickBooks company. If you are the only person allowed to work with the files, enter **1**. After you specify the number of people, click on Next. The next screen plugs QuickBooks Pro, which offers a multiuser version of

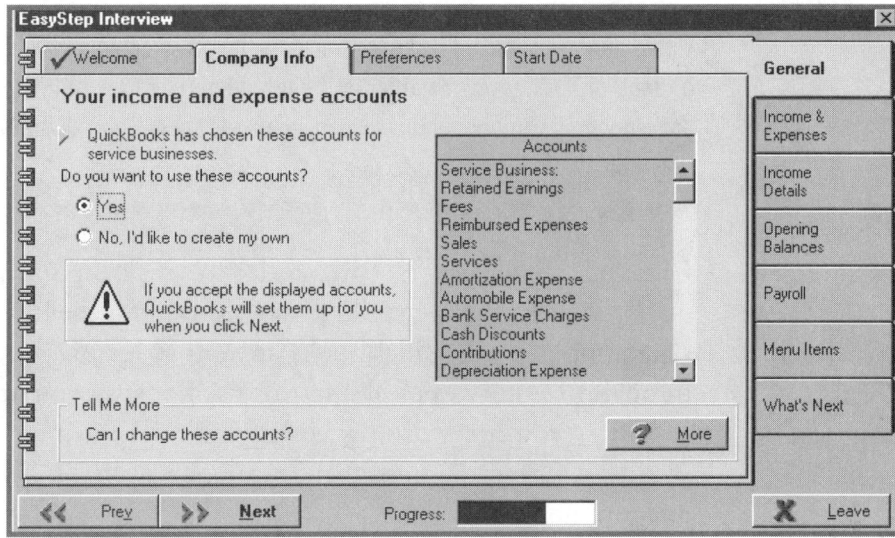

Figure 1.3

QuickBooks sets up accounts for you automatically, based on the type of business you selected earlier in the Interview. You can change the categories as needed.

QuickBooks. If you want to be able to allow several people to access your QuickBooks data *at the same time*, you may want to explore the Pro option. Click on More to see more information about QuickBooks Pro. Otherwise, click on Next to continue the Interview. The next page tells you that you have finished the Company Info portion of the Interview; click on Next to go on to Preferences.

◄ ◄

Preferences are your choices of different options that affect the way QuickBooks operates. You initially set up preferences during the EasyStep Interview, but you can go back and change your preferences at any time by opening the File menu and choosing Preferences.

◄ ◄

Choosing Your Company Preferences

If you selected a service business as the type of business you are setting up in QuickBooks, the first question in the Preferences tab asks whether your company maintains an inventory. Simple enough.

At this point, your path through the EasyStep Interview may diverge from the one illustrated here, which is for a service business. If you selected a retail business, for example, or another business type earlier in the Interview, you may see different screens in different sequences. Throughout this section, however, you will find all the basic sections, although they may be in different orders.

Click on Yes for yes, No for no. If you click on Yes, the Interview will display a click on screen telling you more about the inventory process and suggesting you use QuickBooks' inventory feature. You will be working through inventory examples in this book just so you know how to do it, so unless you are working with your own business information and you do *not* need the inventory feature, click on Yes. Then click on Next to continue.

Setting Up Sales Tax

Next you are asked about collecting sales tax. If you pay to a single agency, click on the first option. If you pay to more than one agency that collects sales tax, click on the second option. Click on Next to continue.

NOTE How do you know whether you need to choose single or multiple tax rates? If you sell items with different tax amounts, choose multiple. If you sell items at a single tax rate and pay that tax to a single agency, choose single.

You are asked to supply four pieces of information related to sales tax:

1. Enter a name for the sales tax account QuickBooks uses to track the tax. This might be something like **SALESTX**.

2. Type a description of the sales tax to appear on your invoices (for example, **Indiana sales tax**).

3. Enter the sales tax rate you pay (for example, **5.0**).

4. Type the name of the agency to which you pay sales tax (for example, **Indiana Department of Revenue**).

TIP If you are unsure about the tax rate in your area or the agency to which you pay sales tax, contact your account or look in the Yellow Pages under "Government Offices, State" to find the phone number of your state's revenue department.

When you have completed that page, click on Next. The next screen asks you to choose a format for your company's invoice (see Figure 1.4). QuickBooks has already selected an invoice for you based on the type of business you selected earlier in the Interview. You can change this choice now or later and alter the invoice any way you like. In the figure, Service is selected because The Write Company is first and foremost a service business.

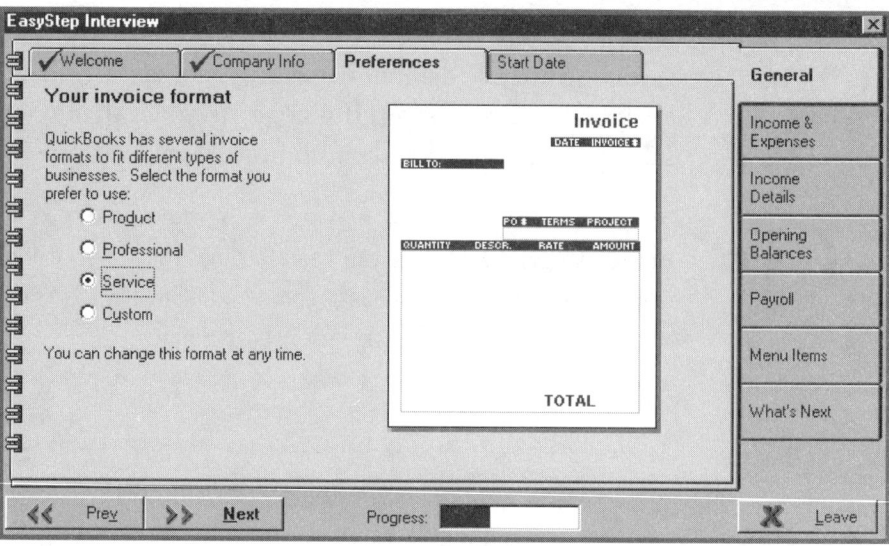

Figure 1.4

QuickBooks selects an invoice type for you based on the type of business you selected earlier in the Interview. You can change the selection if you wish.

The choice you select may be different, depending on the nature of your company. Click on Next to continue.

Getting Started with Payroll and Billing

The next question is a simple one. How many employees are on your payroll? For The Write Company, the number is three. Enter the number you need and click on Next. You are asked whether you want to use QuickBooks' payroll feature. If you plan to automate your payroll accounts using QuickBooks, click on Yes.

NOTE QuickBooks displays a message letting you know which tax table it is using to figure your tax information. You can subscribe to a special online tax table service through Intuit that keeps your tax tables up-to-date. For more about working with tax information, see Sunday evening's session.

Another Preferences screen asks you whether you provide your customers with written or verbal estimates. The Write Company bids on jobs by evaluating costs and submitting a written proposal. If you are following along with this example, click on Yes. Otherwise, click on the answer that fits your business needs. Click on Next to continue.

The next question concerns whether you ever bill when a project is partially completed. For example, The Write Company bills at various stages of a project: when the training is done, when the manuscript is completed and approved, when the layout is complete, and when the final copy is delivered. Although estimates include a total amount from all invoices, several invoices may be submitted during the course of a project. Choose your answer and click on Next to continue.

Setting Up Project Tracking and Expenses

The next screen asks whether you want to track the time spent on each job. The Write Company tracks projects based on the number of hours spent, so Yes is appropriate here. Click on your answer and click on Next. Again, QuickBooks plugs QuickBooks Pro, which is specifically designed to handle estimates and time-tracking tasks. You can click on More Info to see more about Pro and then click on Next to continue. You are then asked about reimbursable expenses. If you bill customers for items you pay for (such as the cost of shipping or travel), click on Yes; otherwise, click on No. Continue by clicking on Next. You then have the choice of tracking the reimbursable income as income; if you do, QuickBooks tracks the reimbursement in an income account. If you don't, the expenses and the reimbursments are kept in an expense account. Neither choice changes the bottom line of your business—these selections affect only the profit-and-loss statement for your company. The Write Company selects No. Make your choice and click on Next to continue.

Deciding on Classes

Do you want to set up classes for your business? That's the next question. Classes are areas you want to track individually within your business. Classes will help The Write Company keep track of the different areas of service they offer: Writing, Training, Consulting, and Sales. Click on Next.

The next question is an important one. How do you want to pay bills in QuickBooks? If you are most comfortable working with the QuickBooks Check Register, you may want to choose Enter the Checks Directly. This is a one-step process that enables you to enter the check and pay the bill at the same time. The other option, Enter the Bills First and Then Enter the Payments Later, has you enter the bills separately and then go through the bill-paying phase. In my own business, I use the first option. The Write Company will do the same. Make your choice and click on Next.

QuickBooks includes a Reminders list that alerts you when things are coming up you need to act on. You determine when you want the Reminders list to appear—at start up, when you request it, or rarely. The Write Company chose When I Ask for It. Make your selection and click on Next. The final question in this tab asks whether you want to work with accrual-based reports or cash-based reports. If you select cash-based, your company records payments when they are actually received; if you select accrual-based, your company includes as income those payments that are billed but still outstanding. Make your choice and click on Next. Now you've finished Preferences and you're ready for the Start Date tab.

Starting with the Start Date

The first screen of the Start Date tab simply explains what the Start Date is about. Click on Next to see a diagram of what information you need and how it relates to the date you start tracking your business data (see Figure 1.5). Make sure that you have all the requested information and click on

WHAT'S IMPORTANT ABOUT THE START DATE?

The start date you enter in QuickBooks is the day you start entering your transactions. This does not mean that today's date is your start date; it's the day you elect to begin entering transactions. For example, you may want to go back to January 1, if that's the beginning of your fiscal year, and enter all transactions that have occurred from that point. Or you may want to begin at the close of the last quarter, or the end of last month.

FRIDAY EVENING Getting Started with QuickBooks 15

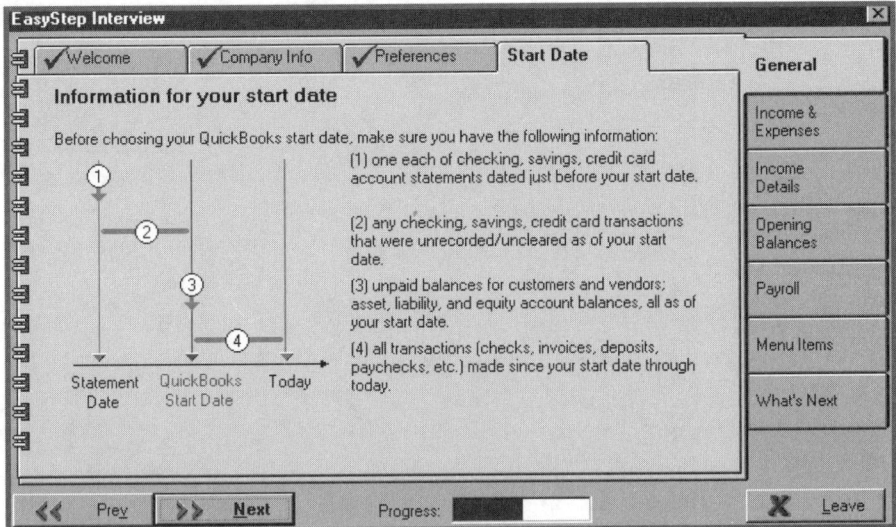

Figure 1.5

QuickBooks shows you the information you need to be able to enter all transactions from your start date to the current date

Next. Then enter your company start date in the box provided. When you're finished, click on Next twice. Congratulations! You have completed the Start Date tab.

If you are starting to use QuickBooks in November and your fiscal year began in January, you don't want to go back and enter all your transactions from January till now (unless you have a lot of time on your hands or you had very few transactions). If you are close to the beginning of a year and entering the data isn't a hardship, go back to the first of the fiscal year; otherwise, choose a logical breaking point, like the end of a quarter or the end of last month. You need to enter all transactions that occurred between your start date and the current date, so make sure you choose a date that is practical for you.

Setting Up Income and Expenses

The Income & Expenses section of the EasyStep Interview asks you questions that help you set up various accounts for tracking your income and your expenses. Click on Next and QuickBooks shows you the income accounts already set up for your business (see Figure 1.6). *Income accounts*

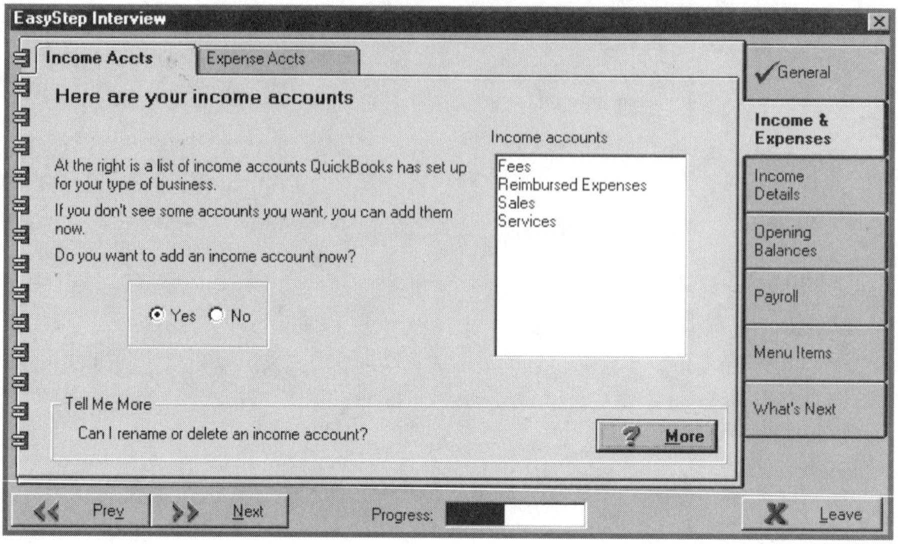

Figure 1.6

Income accounts are already set up by QuickBooks according to the business you created. You can add additional income accounts now or modify the accounts later.

track the ways in which money comes into your business. The income accounts shown in the figure—Fees, Reimbursed Expenses, Sales, and Service—are fine for The Write Company. Click on No and then click on Next. You have finished the Income Accounts section.

Expense accounts track the expenses through which money goes out of your business. Your expenses might include such items as payroll, rent, materials, postage, and more. Within each expense account, you can create *subaccounts* to further break down your expenses. Within the Materials expense account, for example, you might include subaccounts for hardware, software, printing supplies, videotapes, and the like. You can get a more detailed explanation of expenses by clicking on More and then clicking on Next. If you view the detail, click on Next again to continue the Interview. QuickBooks then displays the list of expense accounts it sets up automatically (see Figure 1.7). You can add an expense account by clicking on Yes and then clicking on Next. If you are happy with the accounts shown, click on No and then on Next. This completes the Income & Expenses section; you move on to Income Details.

FRIDAY EVENING Getting Started with QuickBooks

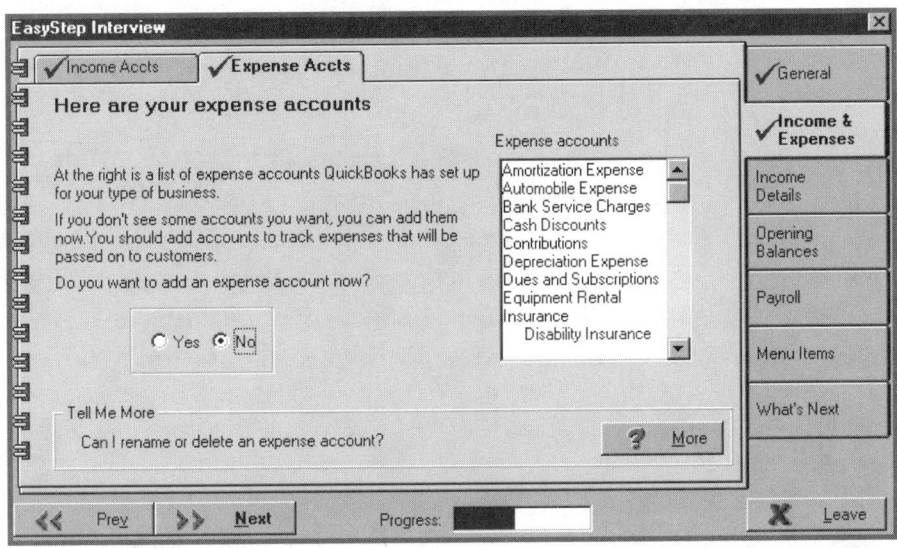

Figure 1.7

Expense accounts track the way money goes out of your business. QuickBooks sets up expense accounts automatically during the Interview process, but you can change them if you wish.

 TIP If you are working with an existing bookkeeping system that has its own categories (such as the ever-popular Dome Book), compare the categories in QuickBooks with the categories you are familiar with. You can easily change the QuickBooks accounts to match the ones you've been using. For information on how to modify, rename, and delete accounts, see "Working with Accounts," later in this session.

Entering Income Details

The Income Details section asks you questions about the income you receive for your products or services. If you are accustomed to traditional accounting terms, you may have seen the term *accounts receivable* applied to this area of bookkeeping. Click on Next. QuickBooks asks whether you receive payment from your customers at the time you sell your product or extend your services. If you choose Always, you don't need to keep track of those customers who haven't paid (because they always pay when services are rendered), so QuickBooks does not set up tracking of this data. If you choose Sometimes or Never, QuickBooks knows you need to keep track of the accounts receivable in your business. The Write Company works on a billing system; they expect payment 30 days after the bill is sent. Never is the option for that company. Choose what works best for your company and click on Next to continue.

The next screen asks whether you want to issue monthly statements that show a particular customer's activity. The Write Company works on a project-by-project basis, so printing monthly statements does not apply here. If your business carries customers from month to month—for example, if you have a data-entry service that always works with the same set of clients—you may want to choose Yes. Make your choice and click on Next.

> **HOW IS A STATEMENT DIFFERENT FROM AN INVOICE?**
>
> A *statement* is simply a report of activity on a particular client's account. An *invoice*, on the other hand, details a specific service or the sale of a particular product and requests an amount due. A statement could list a number of invoices as part of the activity in a given month.

The next screen introduces you to QuickBooks item types. Review the information and click on Next to continue. Because The Write Company is a service business, I want to set up service items, so I click on Yes. Click on Next. The next screen asks you to provide an Item Name, a Sales Description, and a Sales Price for each item (see Figure 1.8). The Write Company uses the service items shown in Table 1.1.

After you enter the name, description, and cost of one item, the next screen asks you to choose an income account to assign to the item (see Figure 1.9). If none of the income accounts seem to fit the income item, you can create a new account by clicking on <Add New> and entering the name of the new account.

FRIDAY EVENING   Getting Started with QuickBooks

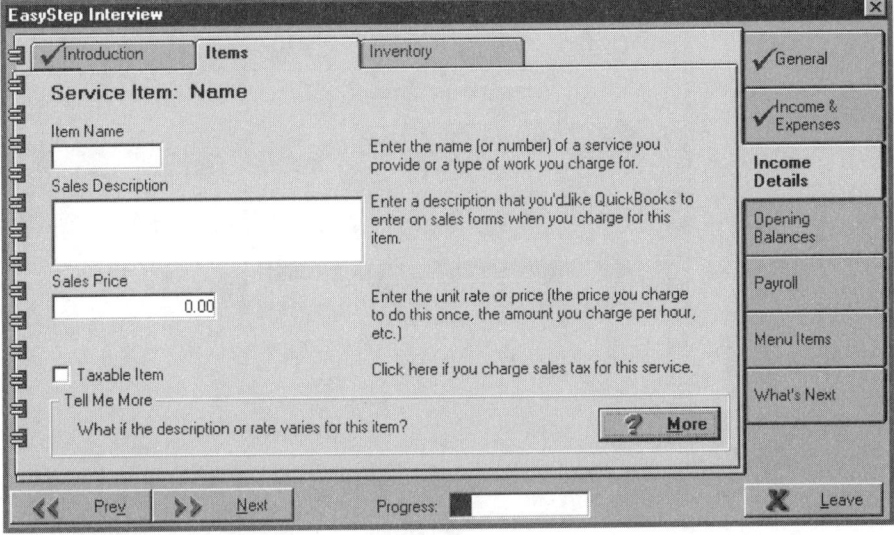

Figure 1.8

The item types help you classify the different types of income you bring in by assigning them names, descriptions, and individual costs.

Table 1.1 Service Items for The Write Company				
Item Name	Writing	Editing	Training	Consulting
Sales Description	Writing services	Editing services	On-site training services	Communications consulting
Sales Price	$35.00	$22.00	$50.00	$100.00
Taxable Item	Manual	None	None	Video

The next screen asks whether you want to set up another income item. Click on Yes if you want to repeat the last two steps and set up other items. If you prefer, you can add other income items later by choosing Items from the Lists menu. If you want to move on, click on No and click on Next. For purposes of illustration, I have set up three of the income items for The Write Company here, and in tomorrow morning's

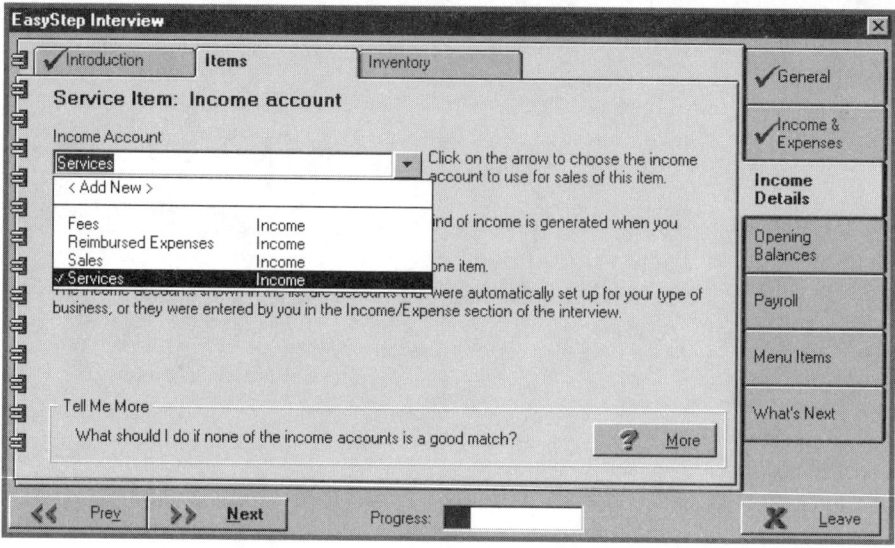

Figure 1.9

After you create an income item, you need to assign it to an income account.

session, in "Adding Income Items On the Fly," I will show you how to add two more as you fill out your company invoice.

The next question asks you about setting up a non-inventory part item. This is a confusing term, but the concept is simple. Do you sell anything you don't buy? If you sell mailing lists, for example, you may generate those yourself and not bring in and stock mailing lists from other companies before you resell them. If that's the case, the booklet of mailing labels would be a non-inventory item. The Write Company sets up the MANUAL and VIDEO income items as inventory items because I need to track the number of books and tapes in stock and the number sold. If you have non-inventory parts, click on Yes and fill in the necessary information on the screen that follows. If you don't have non-inventory parts, click on No and then on Next to continue with the Interview.

Now you get to consider your purchases. When you purchase the item you just set up, how do you want it to be noted on your purchase order? The videotapes I purchase for The Write Company show up on the purchase order as "Blank 60-minute videotapes for training program." Once you enter the description, enter the cost. The tapes cost $0.95 each. Click on Next to continue.

FRIDAY EVENING Getting Started with QuickBooks

In the Inventory Item page (see Figure 1.10), you enter the unit number at which point you want QuickBooks to warn you that you need to reorder. For The Write Company, I've chosen a reorder point of 50. As soon as we enter the sale that drops the videotape inventory to 49, QuickBooks will let me know it's time to reorder the videotapes. The Qty on Hand is, of course, the number of units you have on hand as of your start date. The Total value shows the unit cost multiplied by the quantity you have on hand. When you click on Next, QuickBooks asks whether you'd like to set up additional inventory items. If you click on Yes, you go through the inventory process again; if you click on No, you complete the Income Details section and move on to Opening Balances.

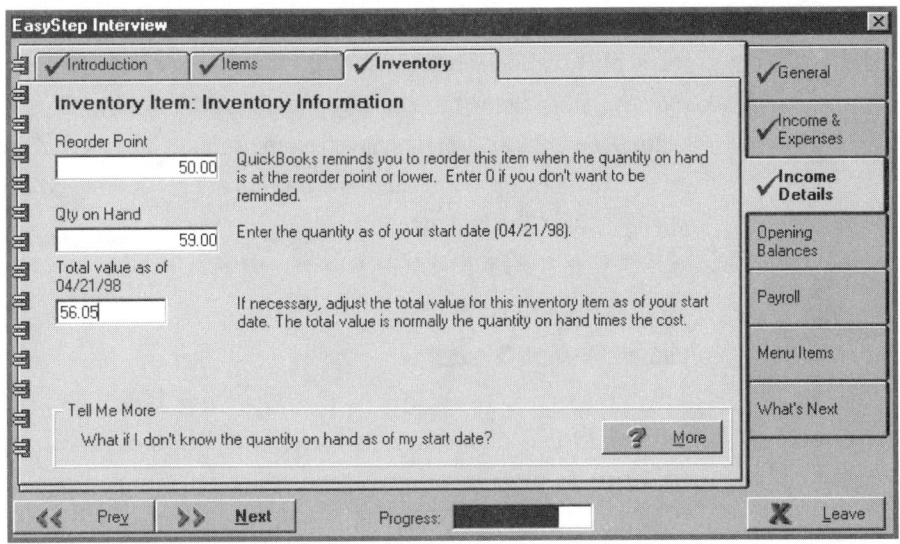

Figure 1.10

When you set up your inventory, you specify the Reorder Point and Qty on Hand. QuickBooks calculates the Total Value.

Entering Opening Balances

The opening balance of your QuickBooks company account helps you get a financial snapshot of your business assets as of your start date. You will find out how much money you have billed but not received, which vendors owe you money, and what the balances of your accounts are.

Before you begin this section, QuickBooks alerts you that you need the following:

- Recent bank statements
- Information on any customers who owe you money
- Information on any vendors who owe you money
- A current balance sheet as of your start date (Have this prepared by your accountant if possible. If you do the balance sheet yourself, determine the values of your assets, liabilities, credit accounts, and any other active accounts.)

TIP What should you do if you don't have everything you need to come up with an opening balance? QuickBooks recommends that you change your start date to a date for which you can gather all the necessary information. Additionally, you may be able to figure the information out by calculating invoices and subtracting received payments from customers and vendors. Last, you can come up with a "best guess" and adjust the amounts later when you have the real amounts.

Who Owes You?

The first major question in the Opening Balances section involves Customers. Do you have any customers who had outstanding balances on their accounts as of your start date? If so, click on Yes; otherwise, click on No. When you click on Next, QuickBooks asks you whether you want to track projects for any of your customers. Click on Yes if you want to have QuickBooks keeps track of the project for you. For The Write Company, I've selected Yes. Click on Next to continue.

In the Adding Customer tab, you have the option of adding the name of a customer who has an outstanding balance as of your start date. Fill in the name (in the form in which you want it to appear on your invoices). If you have more than one job for this customer and want to track the projects individually, click on the Has Multiple Jobs option (see Figure 1.11). This

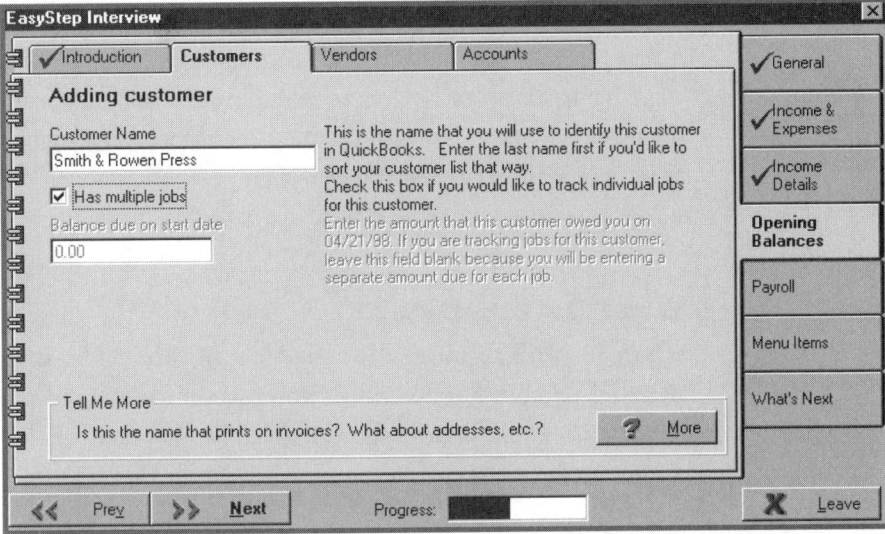

Figure 1.11

When you add a customer, you can choose to keep track of the balance as a lump sum or break the amount according to individual projects.

allows you to keep track of costs per project. For example, The Write Company performs three different tasks for client Smith & Rowen Press: writing instruction manuals, laying out the manuals, and providing quarterly training in corporate communications. Enter the company name, make your selection if necessary, and click on Next.

If you elected to track multiple jobs, you see a page that enables you to add a job to the customer you added. Type a name for the job (for The Write Company, one of the jobs is Contract Writing), enter the balance due amount, and click on Next. The next page gives you the option of adding another job. If you want to add more jobs, click on Yes and click on Next; then repeat the process of adding the job name and the balance. When you are finished, click on No and click on Next to continue. When you complete this process, you have finished the Customers area. Click on Next to move on to Vendors.

A *vendor* is someone you purchase goods or services from. In other words, he will send you a bill for goods or services rendered. Your electric company is a vendor, as is your computer supplier, as is your accountant. The Vendors area enables you to enter the balances you owe each vendor you work with.

What Do You Owe?

Click on Next to move into the Vendors area. The first question asks you whether you have any vendors you owed money as of your start date. If you do, click on Yes. If not, click on No. In any case, click on Next.

Remember that you need to enter the balance you owed your vendors *as of your company's start date*, not according to today's date, even if you've paid against the balance. This helps you get an accurate picture of your company's finances on the start date of your QuickBooks file.

If you click on Yes, the Adding Vendor page is displayed so that you can add the vendor name and balance for each vendor you owe. You'll add only the names and balances now; you can fill in the rest of the vendor information after the Interview is complete. Click on Next after you enter the information, and a page asks whether you'd like to enter more vendors. Click on Yes if you do; otherwise, click on No. Continue entering names and balances for the vendors for whom you show balances as of the start date. When you've entered all the necessary names, click on No and click on Next to complete the Vendors area.

Setting Up Credit Cards

In Opening Balances, you will enter the balances from your balance sheet accounts, which might include such items as credit cards, loans, bank accounts, and more. The first question asks whether you'd like to set up a credit card account. Do this only for business credit card accounts—not those accounts that you use occasionally for business but that are primarily personal accounts. If you click on Yes, you are taken to the Add a Credit Card page, where you can enter the name of the card (such as "Corporate Card" or "CitiCorp Visa"). Enter the name and click on Yes. Next, enter the end date of the last statement you received before your start date. (For example, if your start date is 4/21/98 and you have a credit card statement issued on 4/13/98, use 4/13/98 as the statement ending date.) Enter the statement ending balance and then click on Next. You then are given the option of adding additional cards. If you have more to enter, click on Yes and repeat the steps. When you are finished, click on No and click on Next.

If you currently have a loan or an active line of credit, your answer to the next question will be Yes. Otherwise, click on No. In either case, click on Next to continue. Enter a name for the loan (such as "First National PC Loan"). Enter the statement ending date and the balance. Click on Next. Enter additional accounts if necessary; click on No and Next when you are finished.

Setting Up Loans and Notes

The next page allows you to enter information for tracking loans and payable notes. Click on Yes if you want to track a loan; then click on Next. Enter the name of the liability and the balance; if the liability is going to last more than 12 months, click on Long Term Liability. Click on Next. You can continue adding liabilities by clicking on Yes and Next, or you can click on No to move on through the Interview.

Bank Accounts

The next step enables you to set up your bank accounts. QuickBooks regards savings, checking, and money market accounts as bank accounts. The makers of QuickBooks suggest you set up your petty cash accounts as bank accounts, too, to aid in organizing withdrawals and deposits. Click on Next.

Enter the name of the bank account (for example, "Checking" or "Savings"). Click on Next. Enter the statement ending date and the balance of your account. Use your bank statements to make sure you have the most accurate data. Click on Next. Continue adding bank accounts for all accounts that have open balances; when you're finished, click on No; then click on Next. You move on to asset accounts.

Asset accounts are accounts that track the worth of your business in terms of what you own (furniture, property, equipment, etc.) and income other than earned income that will be coming in (such as money you've loaned another person, or business or investments your company has made). If you'd like to set up an asset account, click on Yes; otherwise, click on No. If you select Yes, you are asked to provide a name and the asset's value. You also need to choose an asset type. You need to choose Fixed, Other Current Asset, or Other Assets. Enter the information for the account and click on Next.

Each of the three types of assets serves a different purpose. A fixed asset is something you own for a year or more. Your personal computer is an example of a fixed asset. Other current assets can be turned into cash quickly. These might include stock certificates your company owns. Other assets are those assets that don't fall into another category; your business's $5,000 loan to a small start-up company you do business with falls into this category.

Equity accounts are next. If you are a homeowner, you probably understand the concept of equity—it's the different between what you have and what you owe. If you purchased a house for $100,000 and now owe $80,000, you have $20,000 in equity built up.

Similarly, you can have equity in your business. Business equity comes primarily from two sources: money you've invested in your business, and the profits your business makes. Click on Next, and QuickBooks shows you the equity accounts it has already established for you. The equity accounts for The Write Company are Capital Stock, Opening Bal Equity, and Retained Earnings. Click on Next. You have completed the Opening Balances section of the Interview. Now, on to Payroll!

Setting Up Payroll

The Payroll section of the Interview is straightforward. QuickBooks needs only the frequency of your pay periods (do you pay weekly, biweekly, monthly, or in another pattern?) and the states for which you withhold payroll taxes. The first page in Payroll (after you click on Next through the opening page) asks you the pay period for your payroll (see Figure 1.12). The Write Company pays on the first and fifteenth of the month.

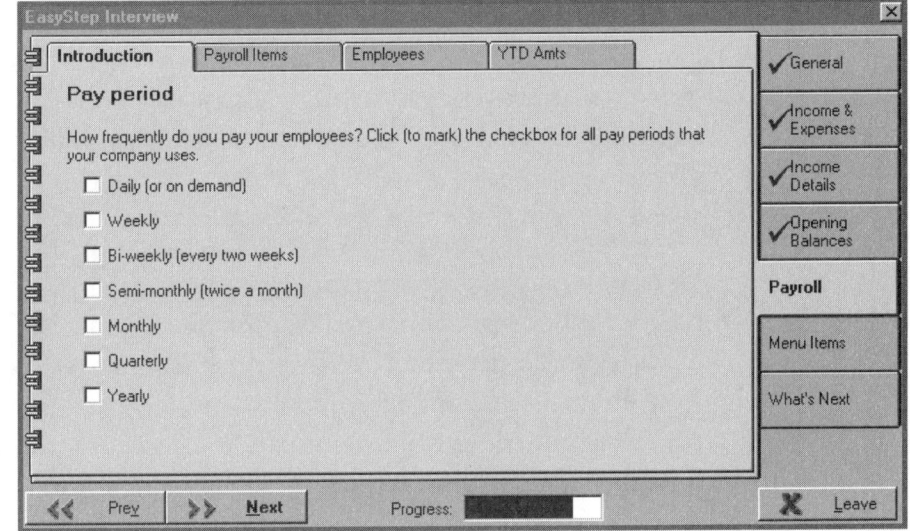

Figure 1.12

Select the frequency with which you pay your employees. You can choose more than one selection if necessary.

The next page enables you to choose the states for which you withhold and pay taxes. Click on the state names in the list that apply. Click on Next. The next screen introduces you to payroll items. These are items QuickBooks deals with related to payroll accounts. The program automatically sets up items for your salaries and both federal and state taxes. Click on Next.

 TIP In order to complete the Payroll section, you need to know the state unemployment rate, the federal unemployment rate, and your state employer tax ID number. Your accountant—and your local, state, and federal tax agencies—will have this information.

In the State Withholding Tax page, enter your employer tax ID for the state shown. If you do not have this information now, you can enter it at a later date. Click on Next. The State Unemployment Tax page asks you to enter your state employer ID as well as the county tax rate. Click on Next. QuickBooks shows you the state accounts that have been set up. Click on Next twice. In the Federal unemployment tax (FUTA) credit page, choose the FUTA rate your business pays (this information needs to come from your accountant).

■ ■

If you are uncertain about your FUTA tax rate and you can't find the rate on your current tax forms, enter the value you think is correct and then edit the rate later if necessary by choosing Lists, Payroll Items, Federal Unemployment Tax, and clicking on Edit. You can then modify the amount as needed.

■ ■

Next, how do you pay your employees (hourly, on salary, by commission)? Check the box that applies and click on Next. You need to choose the type of wages to be tracked. The Write Company pays employees an hourly regular rate plus occasional overtime. Click on Next to continue. The next page lists deductions you may need to track (see Figure 1.13). Click on the ones that apply to your business and click on Next to continue.

■ ■

If you need to set up additional deductions, click on Other Net Deduction in the Payroll Item column. You will have an opportunity to customize the item for your use later.

■ ■

If you have Payroll Additions—that is, items that you will add to your payroll—specify them on the next Interview page. If you want to add a Mileage Reimbursement item, click on that choice. If you want to add additions of your own, click on Other Taxable Addition(s) and click on Next. You are taken to a page that enables you to set up the new addition. Enter the necessary information and click on Next.

FRIDAY EVENING Getting Started with QuickBooks

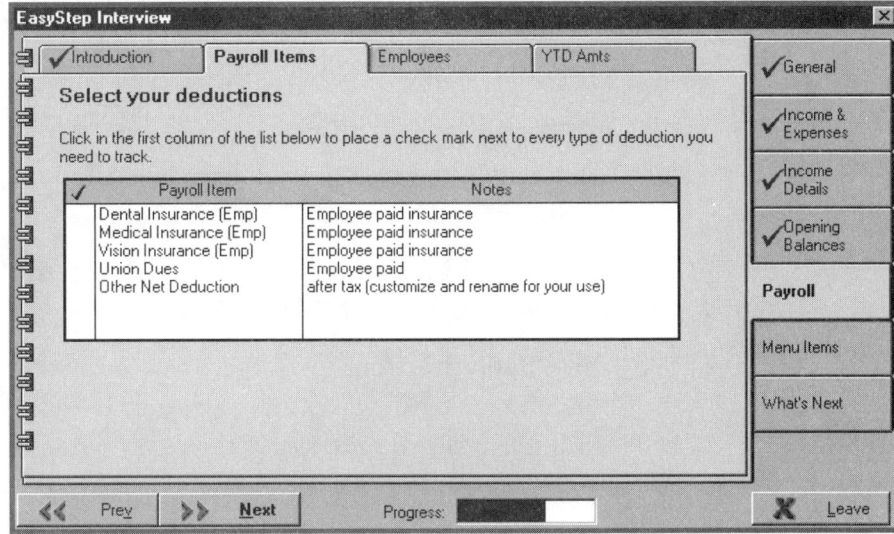

Figure 1.13

You choose payroll deduction from the list QuickBooks provides. You can also add your own deductions as needed.

What does your company contribute to? Choose the contribution in the Payroll Item list. If you want to add an item, click on Other Comp. Contribution. QuickBooks displays a page in which you can set up company contributions. Click on the Set Up button to continue.

Setting Up Additional Payroll Contributions

The Write Company added DayCare Co-Pay to its company contributions because it has an arrangement with a local day-care center to help offset the child care costs for its employees. When you click on Set Up to add a contribution, the screen shown in Figure 1.14 appears. This is a wizard that leads you through the process of setting up a new contribution. Here are the steps involved:

1. Enter a name for the new contribution (such as DayCare Co-Pay).

2. If you will have multiple jobs within that contribution account, leave Track Expenses by Job selected. Click on Next.

3. Enter the organization to which you pay the deduction (in this case, ABC DayCare).

4. Enter the number by which the organization knows your company.

5. Select the liability account to which you want to assign the contribution (if you are unsure, leave Payroll Liabilities selected).

6. Choose an expense account for the contribution (in this case, Payroll Expenses is accurate). Click on Next.

7. Select the tax tracking type if it applies. The Write Company chooses Dependent Care for the ABC DayCare subsidy. Click on Next.

8. QuickBooks lets you know that the contribution is added to employee wages before taxes are taken out. If you want to modify this setup, click on the tax items you want to deselect; then click on Next.

9. Enter the way in which the calculation is shown on the paycheck. It may be an amount you enter directly, a percentage of another amount, or a calculated amount that is a dollar amount multiplied by number of units. Make your choice and click on Next.

10. If the benefit is a standard amount, and if it is assigned a limit, enter these amounts in the Default Tax Rate and Limit page. In The Write Company's example, these items do not apply. Click on Finish.

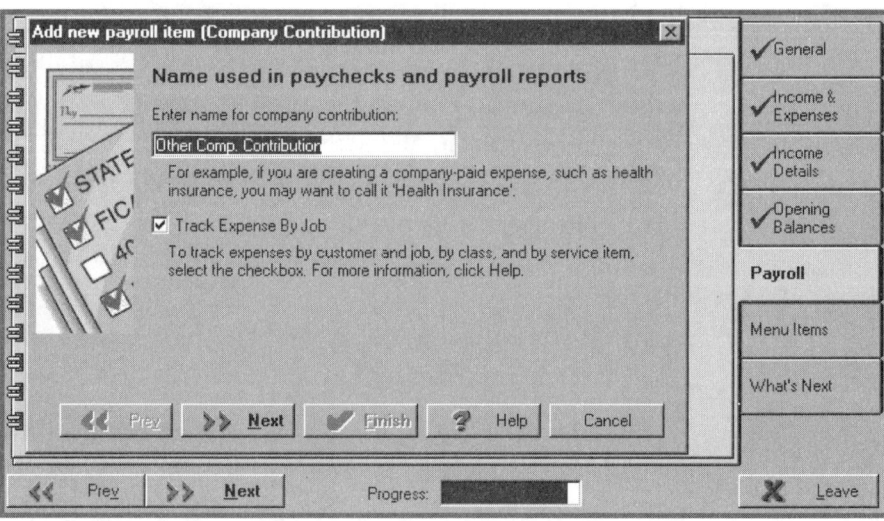

Figure 1.14

A wizard leads you through the process of adding another payroll contribution. Simply answer the questions provided and QuickBooks will help you set up your account.

The contribution is now set up for your business. When you begin entering payroll information, you will be able to track this additional information in the contribution account.

Setting Up Employees

The next step involves setting up your employee records. Click on Next to close the Payroll Items tab and open the Employees tab. QuickBooks will need the following information for each employee:

- Full name
- Address
- Social Security number
- Current wage/salary
- Payroll filing information, such as a W-4
- Information on deductions, contributions, and payroll additions

TIP Where do you get this employee information? Hopefully you have a current file in which you are tracking employee data. If your information is incomplete, you may need to get the data from the employee as soon as possible. As you work through the exercises in this section, be as complete as you can with the data you have. You can go back and fill in the missing pieces later.

The first page in Payroll shows the pay method you selected earlier in the interview. The Write Company selected Hourly Regular Rate and Overtime Hourly Rate 1. If there is one method you use more than another (meaning it applies to all or most of your employees), make sure that item is selected in the left column of the list. Click on Next to continue.

The next page again reviews some information you entered earlier (see Figure 1.15). Here you see the payroll items that apply to all or most employee paychecks. Because all three employees at The Write Company use the DayCare Co-Pay contribution and are covered by medical insurance,

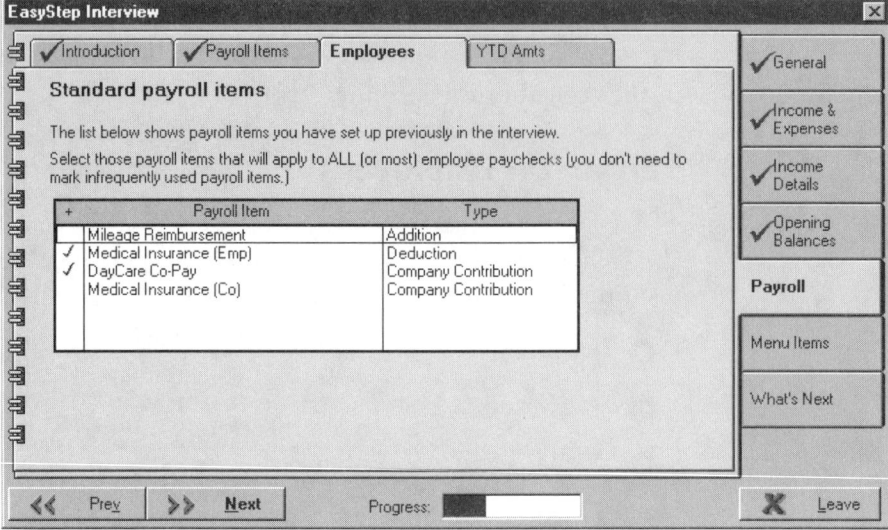

Figure 1.15

As you set up your employee payroll information, QuickBooks displays information you have previously selected for payroll items.

these two items are selected. Make any changes and click on Next.

The next page asks which federal taxes apply to all or most of your employees. Click on the ones that apply. Click on Next to continue. Choose the state in which you file payroll taxes; click on Next.

Do you want QuickBooks to track sick time for your employees? If so, click on Yes. If not, click on No. Click on Next to continue. You then choose how often you give sick time to your employees (at the beginning of the year or every pay period), specify the number of hours you give to each employee, and enter the total number of sick hours an employee can have. Finally, you specify whether to have QuickBooks reset the sick time to zero at the beginning of the year. The information for The Write Company is described in the sidebar.

 **NOTE** QuickBooks does not track sick time based on the number of hours worked but rather on how many hours are given to each employee during a certain period of time (yearly or by the pay period). In other words, an employee cannot "earn" additional sick time by working more than 40 hours in a pay period or accruing a certain number of consecutive work days.

> ### SICK TIME ACCRUAL
> Beginning of year accrual period
>
> Number of hours: 40
>
> Maximum number of hours an employee can have: 40
>
> Reset hours each new year

The next question asks you whether you want to track vacation time. You can track this much the same way you track sick days—by allocating a certain amount for the year or assigning an amount per pay period. If you want to track vacation time, click on Yes; otherwise, click on No. The Write Company elects to track the vacation time. Click on Next to continue.

In the next page, you choose the accrual period, enter the number of hours, and specify the maximum number of hours and choose whether you want the number reset at the beginning of each year. The information for The Write Company is described in the sidebar.

> ### VACATION TIME ACCRUAL
> Beginning of year accrual period
>
> Number of hours: 80
>
> Maximum number of hours an employee can have: 80
>
> Reset hours each new year

Adding Employees

After you click on Next again, you are taken to the Add an Employee page (see Figure 1.16). Follow these steps to add an employee:

1. Click on Add Employee. When the Address Info page appears, enter the necessary information, pressing Tab after each entry. (Note: The Additional Info tab is blank for now.)

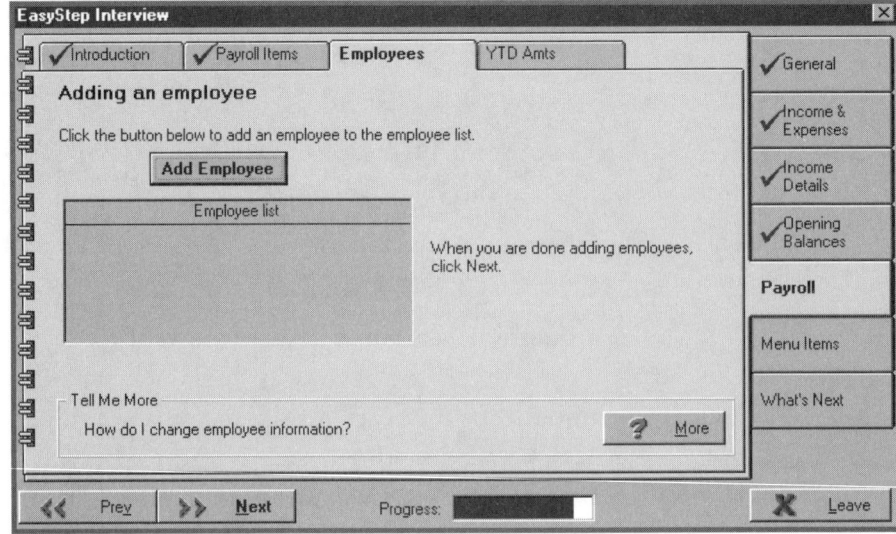

Figure 1.16

The Add an Employee page allows you to add an employee to the list.

2. Click on the Payroll Info tab. Figure 1.17 shows this screen, which contains information you entered during earlier parts of the interview. You can click on the Taxes and Sick/Vacation buttons to check the settings you have selected in those areas of the interview, as well.

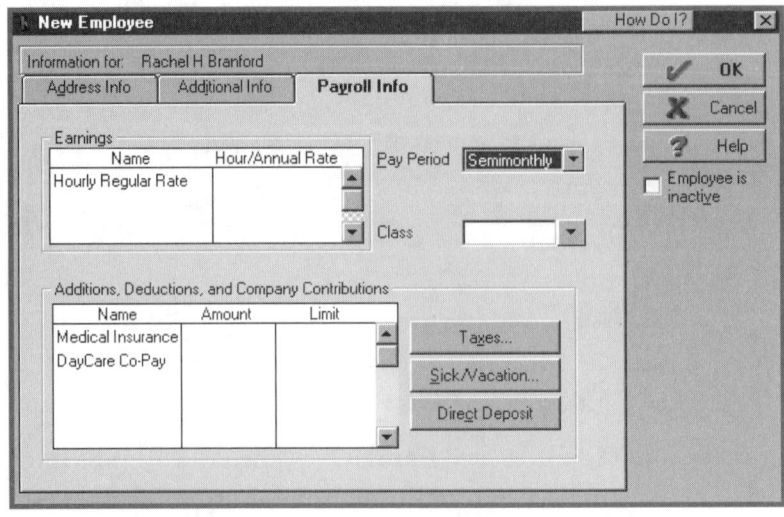

Figure 1.17

The Payroll Info tab shows you the information you entered earlier in the EasyStep Interview.

3. Click on OK. The employee is added to the Employee list, and you can click on Add Employee again to add another employee.

4. Continue adding employees until all your employee data is entered. When you have completed the information, click on Next.

 Direct Deposit is available to you only if you have chosen to use Intuit's Payroll Service. Direct Deposit enables you to deposit paychecks directly into one or two bank accounts your employee specifies.

Setting Up YTD Amounts

The final stop in the Payroll portion of the EasyStep Interview involves setting up your year-to-date amounts. These totals track your payroll and liability accounts, and having this information together will enable you to carry out a number of necessary tasks, including printing W-2 forms. When you click on Next, you are asked to enter the date to be used in the year-to-date summaries; this will probably be your QuickBooks start date. Click on Next. This next page asks you to enter the date that the YTD summaries will affect your bank, liability, and expense accounts. Again, this is likely to be your start date. Click on Next. Finally, enter the date you want to begin your payroll system in QuickBooks. Click on Next.

The next page displays the Employee YTD Summaries page (see Figure 1.18). On this page, you will enter the period totals for salary, hours, and withholding items. Select an employee and click on Enter Summary. The YTD Adjustment page appears (see Figure 1.19). Enter the information from your payroll records for the first quarter; click on Next Period to move to the next period (if your start date precedes the current pay period) and enter the data you need to make the account current. Continue entering the employee data until you have a complete record of payments made to that individual employee. Click on OK when you have entered all the information, and then click on the next employee in the Employee YTD Summaries page and repeat the process. When you are finished, click on Next.

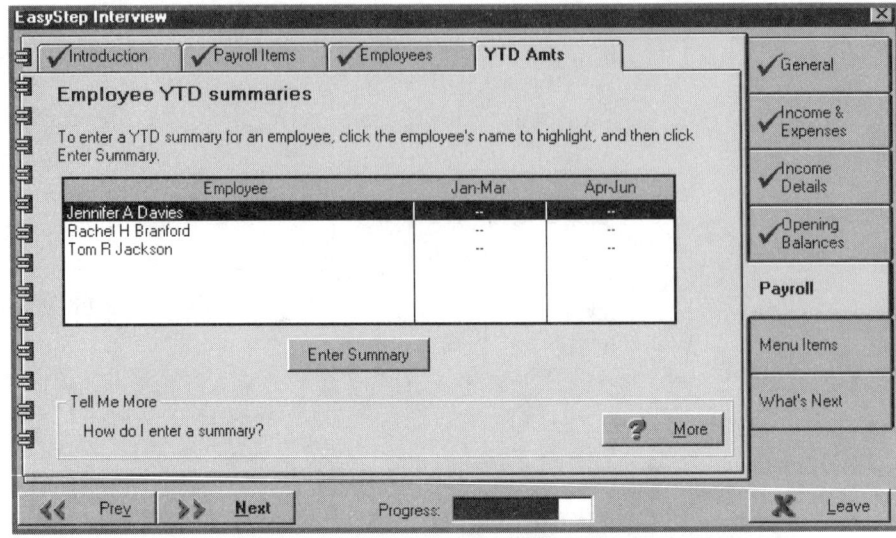

Figure 1.18

The Employee YTD Summaries page helps you record your payroll information for employees.

Figure 1.19

On the YTD Adjustment page, you enter salary, hours worked, and withholding amounts for each individual employee.

Entering Payroll Payments

The next page has to do with summarizing prior liability payments. You will enter the amounts for tax payments you've already made. Click on Create. The Prior Payments page appears, as shown in Figure 1.20. To enter past payments, follow these steps:

FRIDAY EVENING Getting Started with QuickBooks

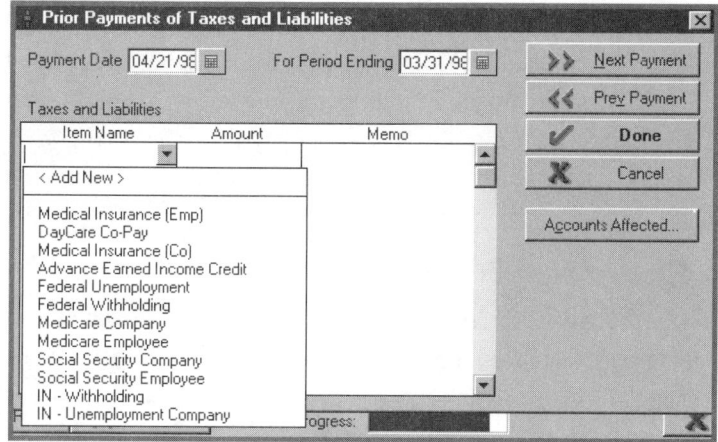

Figure 1.20

In the Prior Payments dialog box, you enter tax and liability payments you made before your start date.

1. Click in the Payment Date box and enter the date you want the payment recorded.

2. Click in the Item Name column. A down arrow appears so that you can click on it to display the Payment list.

3. Click on the name of the item for which you want to enter a prior payment. For example, if you want to enter the amount of medical insurance deducted from each employee's paycheck, select Medical Insurance (Emp).

4. Click in the Amount column and enter the amount for the period.

5. Click in the Memo field and type any notes you need to remind yourself about the transaction.

6. Click on Next Payment to enter that payment and move on to the next.

 TIP By default, QuickBooks chooses the pay period preceding your start date. You can choose another pay period by clicking on the calendar icon beside the For Period Ending box.

CAUTION After you complete the YTD setup, QuickBooks cautions you to make sure that you enter your paychecks through QuickBooks before you write checks from this point on. Otherwise your year-to-date totals and your paychecks will not match.

Choosing Menu Items

The Menu Items segment of the EasyStep Interview enables you to set up lists and activities the way you want them in QuickBooks. Are you getting tired? Don't worry—the next two sections go quickly and then you'll take a break. (I need to get another cup of coffee myself.)

Click on Next twice to get into the Menu Items section. The first question asks you whether you plan to use QuickBooks' To Do list frequently. Click on Yes if you do; otherwise, click on No.

NOTE You might use the To Do feature to remind you when you need to review an employee's performance, start a newly hired employee's insurance plan, call customers, set up lunch with a vendor, or send reports to your accountant.

Click on Next again. This takes you to the Activities menu. Here you are asked whether you want to impose finance charges on those customers whose invoices are overdue. If you do, click on Yes; otherwise, click on No.

If you want QuickBooks to help you budget your business, select Yes in answer to the next question. Budgeting not only helps you gain an accurate picture of where you are financially; it helps you see where you thought you would be and draw comparisons and reports from the related data. Make your choice and click on Next. This completes the Menu Items section.

Finding Out What's Next

The What's Next section gives you ideas of what to do when you complete the EasyStep Interview. First and foremost, QuickBooks suggests that you back up your company data. You also need to enter transactions that have occurred between your start date and today, set up other users (if you are not the only person who will be using QuickBooks in your office), customize forms, set up accounts for independent contractors, and more. Click on Next and review the tasks you still have ahead of you. Finally, click on Leave to finish the Interview.

Congratulations! You have completed the EasyStep Interview! You now have a company set up in QuickBooks, ready to go.

Take a Break

Whew! That first section was pretty labor intensive, wasn't it? Don't despair, though—life with QuickBooks gets easier. The more information you can provide up front, the more information you have to work with and the less you have to enter later. The initial questions are the hardest; everything else is fine-tuning, maintaining, and adding to the data you've already started.

For now, stand up, stretch, walk around a bit and clear your head. Get yourself some juice or another cup of coffee and make sure the kids are sleeping soundly. When you're feeling refreshed, come on back and get familiar with the QuickBooks Navigator.

Touring the QuickBooks Navigator

Even though you've been working with QuickBooks for a while, you may not get a real glimpse of the QuickBooks screen until after you finish the EasyStep Interview. As Figure 1.21 shows, the QuickBooks Navigator first dominates the QuickBooks window, showing you at a glance the various tasks involved in running your business the QuickBooks way. Tabs along the left side of the screen show you how the various tasks are divided. As you click on each tab, you see the different related tasks shown in the diagram in the right side of the window.

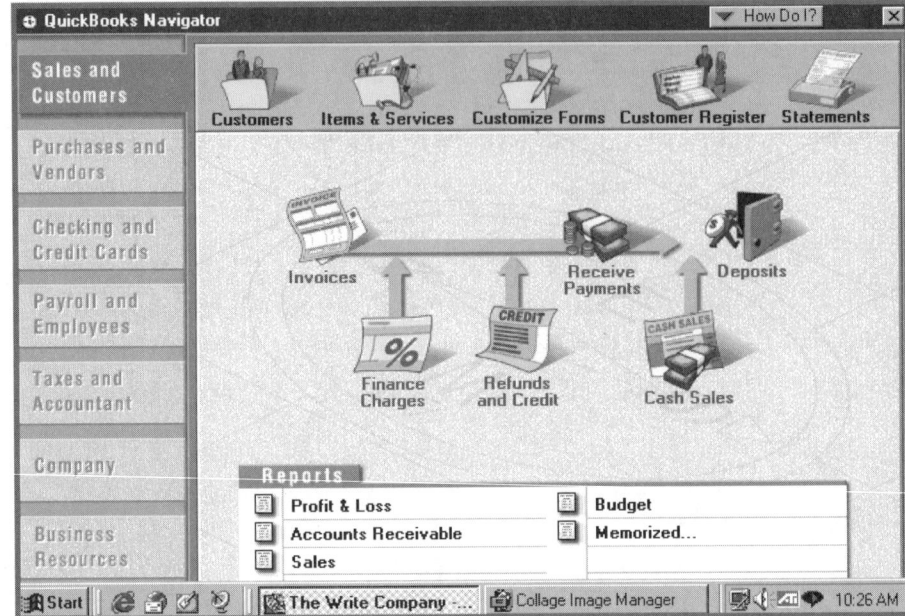

Figure 1.21

The QuickBooks Navigator shows you the various components involved in managing your business with QuickBooks.

The first tab selected is the Sales and Customers tab. As you can see, you track Customers, Items & Services, Customize Forms, Customer Register, and Statements from this tab. The diagram in the center of the Navigator shows you how the process works—from invoices to payments to deposits.

Click on the Purchases and Vendors tab. The Items & Services item remains in the Navigator screen, but everything else changes. An icon for Vendors replaces Customers, and the PO List and Adjust Qty. on Hand icons appear. Likewise, the diagram shows that the process of paying bills goes right from bill to payment, while the process of purchasing using a purchase order goes from order to receipt of goods to receipt of bill to payment. Pretty simple stuff, especially when you see it depicted this way. Notice, too, that the number of reports available has changed to help you create transaction reports.

Now click on Checking and Credit Cards. Only the Check Register icon appears in the icon row at the top of the Navigator. This may be where you spend much of your time—entering checks, transferring money, making deposits, and reconciling your account. Again, the diagram shows the multifaceted process, which all comes together in the balancing, or reconciling, of your accounts. Fewer reports are available for Checking and Credit Cards than those needed in Purchases and Vendors.

Click on the Payroll and Employees tab to see the icons available and the process involved in handling your payroll information. Here you track Employee Information, Payroll Items, Adjustment of Your Liabilities, YTD Amounts, and Tax Table. The flowchart shows that you first create a paycheck, then pay the liabilities (you entered these in the Payroll tab of the EasyStep Interview), and finally produce 941, 940, and W2 forms. The only reports available are Payroll and Memorized reports.

Click on the Taxes and Accountant tab. This looks like a simple one, doesn't it? The icons include Chart of Accounts (an important tool you learn to use later this evening) and Print 1099s, for reporting contractor activities. As you can see, there's really no process to show in the diagram; this tab provides three separate tasks: Accountant's Review, Pay Sales Tax, and Make Journal Entry. A number of reports are available, however, to give you a full battery of reports you can submit to your accountant.

Click on the Company tab. Everything in this tab has to do with the way you set up and keep your business running with QuickBooks. From the Company tab, you can access your Employees file, the Chart of Accounts, Classes, To Do's, and Reminders. Additionally, you can set and change Preferences, Back Up your data, create and work with Budgets, Order Checks and Forms, change your Company Info, create Mail Merge documents, and use the QuickBooks Update Service. Again, a number of reports enable you to print information about your business choices and activities.

Finally, click on the Business Resources tab. No icons appear in the top of the Navigator. In the central area of the screen, however, you see a number of icons that provide you with options for getting help with your business using QuickBooks. You will learn how to explore these resources in a little while.

Exploring the Screen

Return to the Company tab by clicking on it. Now that you've learned what the Navigator has to offer, you can take a closer look at what's on the QuickBooks screen (see Figure 1.22).

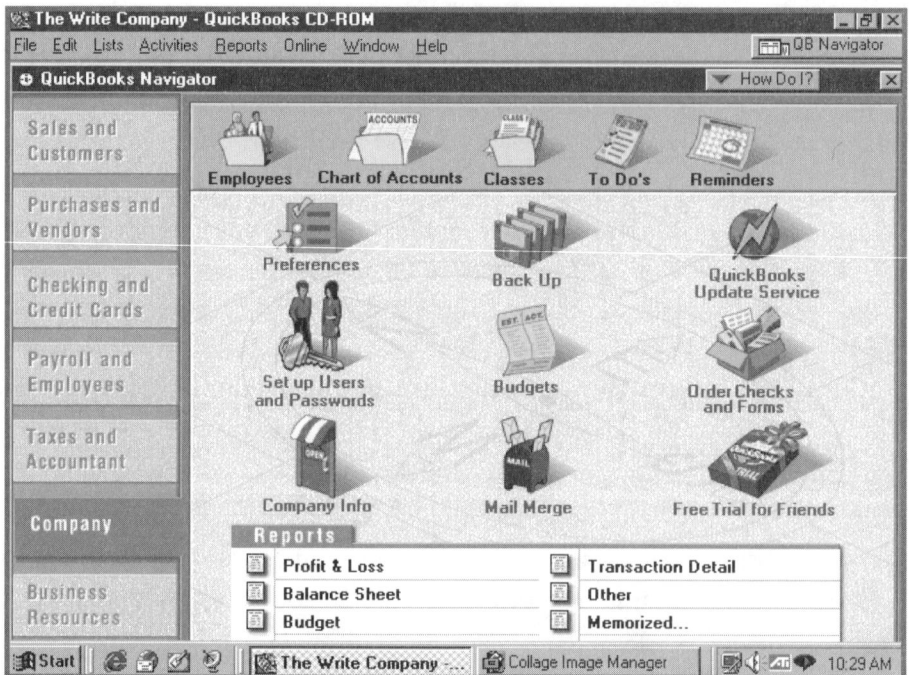

Figure 1.22

The QuickBooks screen helps you get to all the tasks you need easily.

Reviewing the Menu Bar

If you have used Windows before, you are familiar with the menu bar. QuickBooks includes eight different menus, each organized around a particular topic: File, Edit, List, Activities, Reports, Online, Window, and Help. When you need to work with files, you know to look in the File menu. When you want to print Reports, you—no surprise—go to the Reports menu.

Working with Menus

You open the menus either by clicking on them or by pressing Alt and the underlined letter in the menu name (for example, press Alt+F to open the File menu).

Try it now. Point to the Activities menu name and click once. The Activities menu opens, as shown in Figure 1.23. Close the menu by clicking outside the menu area. Now press Alt+A. The menu opens again.

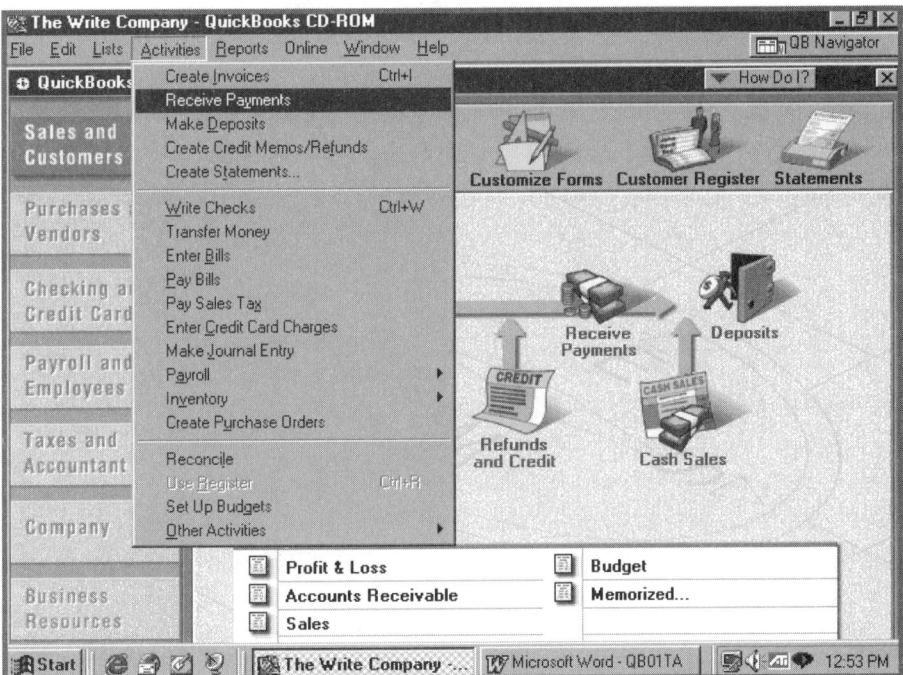

Figure 1.23

You can point and click on a menu name to open it, or you can press and hold the Alt key along with the underlined letter in the menu name.

Checking Out Menu Items

Notice in Figure 1.23 that different options appear differently in the displayed menu. You actually have several ways of selecting items in a menu:

- **Point and click.** The easiest method for choosing an option is to point at it and click on the mouse button.

- **Press a key combination.** For example, take a look at Create Invoices. The Ctrl+I that follows the option name means that you can choose the Create Invoices option without even opening the Activities menu by pressing Ctrl+I.

- **Display a submenu.** A right-pointing triangle to the right of an option means that when you position the pointer over the option, a submenu appears. Try it. Point at the Payroll option and watch the submenu appear (see Figure 1.24). Click outside the menu to close it.

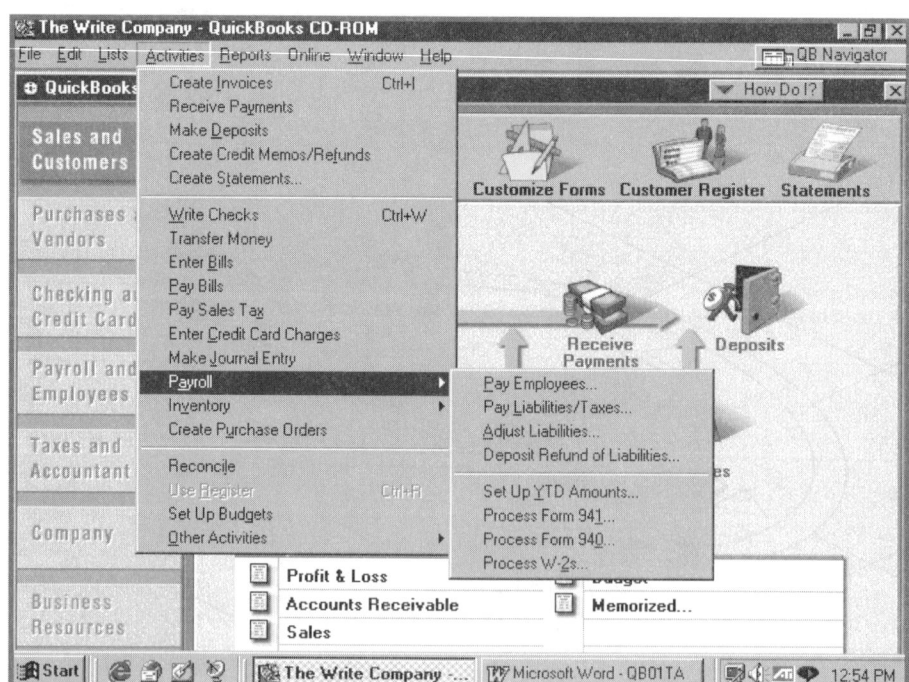

Figure 1.24

The right-pointing triangle beside an option means a submenu appears when you point to the option.

Using the Navigator

The Navigator is a great way to move around in QuickBooks. Because it's all displayed for you on the screen, you never have to look far to discover what to do next. You move through the Navigator using your mouse—

simply point and click on the tab you want to use, position the mouse pointer over the item you want to select (notice that the item "lights" when you point to it), and click on the mouse button once.

Choosing an Icon

Choosing an icon is the same as selecting it. Just move the mouse pointer to the item you want to choose and click on the mouse button once. This selects the icon, and a dialog box, list, or wizard displays.

▲ ▲

A *wizard* is Microsoft-speak for an automated process that helps you create or configure something by asking you a series of questions. When you click on YTD Amounts (displayed in the icon bar when the Payroll and Employees tab is selected), a wizard begins, helping you create year-to-date adjustments for your business accounts.

▲ ▲

Try your hand at this:

1. Make sure the Company tab is selected. (If it's not, click on it.)

2. Move the pointer to the Preferences icon. The pointer itself changes from an arrow to a pointing hand. When the pointer is positioned over Preferences, the icon "lightens" slightly, showing that the icon is targeted.

3. Click on the mouse button. This action opens the Preferences dialog box, as shown in Figure 1.25.

Working with Dialog Boxes

Most programs today include dialog boxes of one sort or another, and QuickBooks is no exception. You will find, however, that QuickBooks does include some unique features in its dialog boxes and also uses list boxes to help you organize and keep track of different kinds of accounts. Do a quick exercise to get used to the different controls in the QuickBooks dialog boxes:

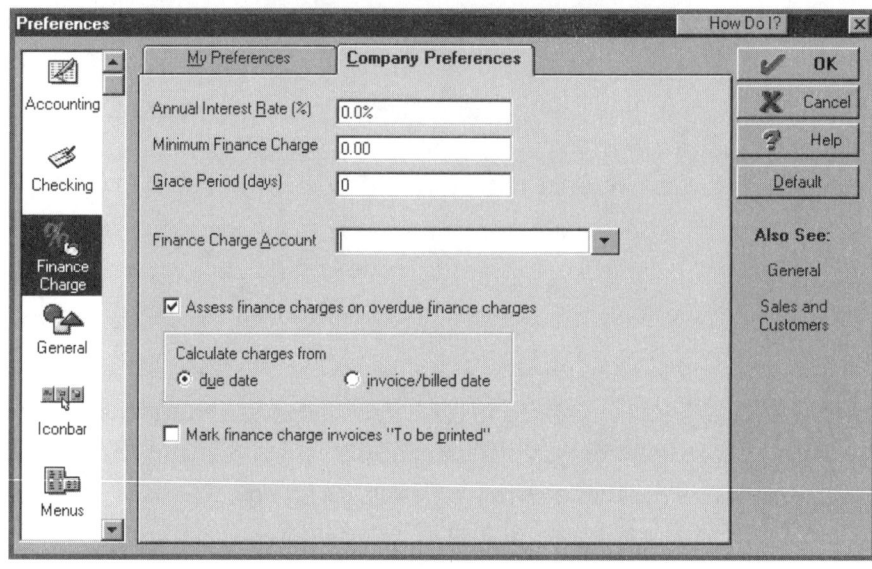

Figure 1.25

In the Preferences dialog box, you choose the option you want to set preferences for and make your selections from the displayed items.

1. Click on the Finance Charge icon at the left side of the Preferences dialog box.

2. Click on the Company Preferences tab. The page displays a number of different controls (see Figure 1.26).

3. The Annual Interest Rate text box is highlighted. Type **9.9**. The value replaces the highlighted amount.

4. Press Tab. The value in the Minimum Finance Charge box highlights. Type **3.00**.

5. Click on the down-arrow to the right of the Finance Charge Amount text box. A drop-down list appears (see Figure 1.27). Click on Fees. The list closes.

6. Click on the check box to the left of Assess Finance Charges on Overdue Finance Charges. The check mark disappears, which means you have deselected the option. (To reselect it, click on the check box again.)

FRIDAY EVENING Getting Started with QuickBooks

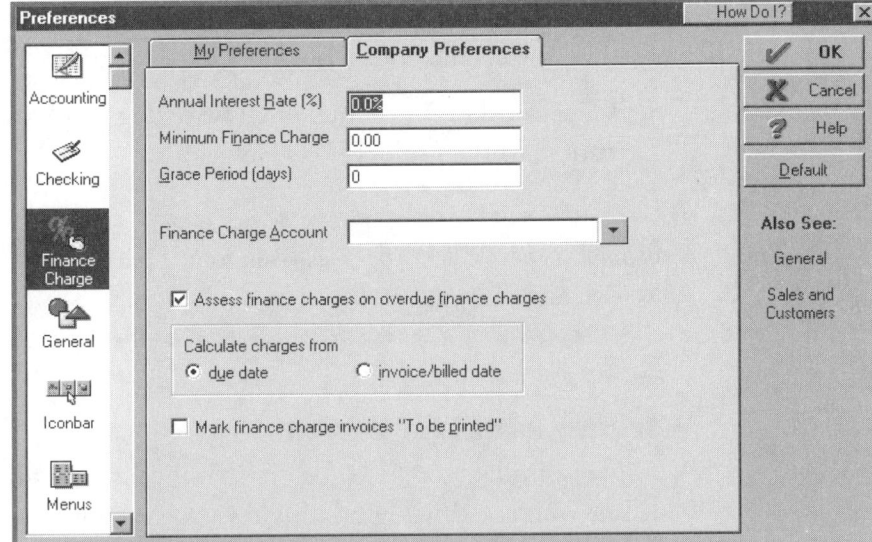

Figure 1.26

The Company Preferences tab of the Finance Charge dialog box gives you a number of controls to work with.

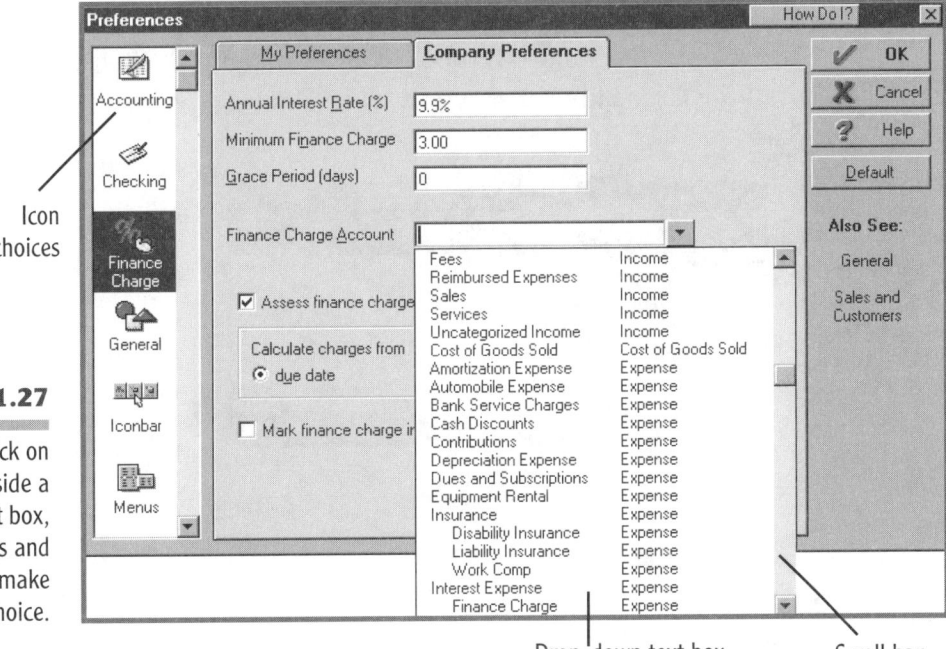

Icon choices

Figure 1.27

When you click on the arrow beside a drop-down text box, a list appears and you can make your choice.

Drop-down text box   Scroll bar

7. In the Calculate Charges From area, click on Invoice/Billed Date. This selects the option button and deselects the Due Date selection.

8. Click on the Cancel button. The dialog box closes and you are returned to the QuickBooks Navigator.

▶▶▶▶▶▶▶▶▶▶▶▶▶▶▶▶▶▶▶▶▶▶▶▶▶▶▶▶

A *control* is a specific item you select—an icon, a tab, an option button, a command button—to cause a specific action.

▶▶▶▶▶▶▶▶▶▶▶▶▶▶▶▶▶▶▶▶▶▶▶▶▶▶▶▶

Working with List Boxes

A *list box* is similar to a dialog box in that it calls for additional action from you. But whereas a dialog box invites you to choose commands or select options related to a particular task, a list box displays a list of your choices for a certain QuickBooks item. You use list boxes to work with the items and accounts you have set up and to add to and modify your settings. For example, the Vendor List box, shown in Figure 1.28, lists the vendors The Write Company has set up in QuickBooks.

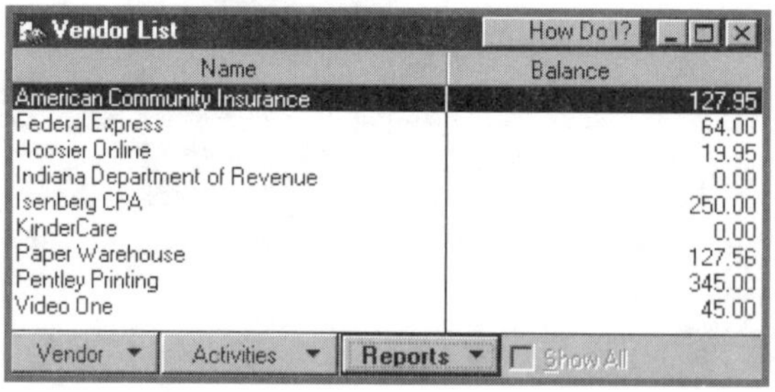

Figure 1.28

When you click on Vendor in the Purchases and Vendors tab of the Navigator, the Vendor list appears. You use a list box

The three buttons at the bottom of the list box enable you to add to or change the information you have entered in the list. These buttons are described in Table 1.2.

TABLE 1.2	BUTTONS IN THE VENDOR LIST BOX
Button	Description
Vendor	Displays a submenu of choices that you use to add, edit, or delete vendors in the list. You can also choose a particular vendor, search for a vendor, make a vendor inactive, or print a list of vendors or the related 1099s.
Activities	Gives you the options for writing checks to the vendors, entering or paying bills, creating purchase orders, checking in items, and more.
Report	Enables you to create a report for the currently selected vendor. You can also print a phone list or a contact list.

The process of using a list box is simple. Follow these steps to display, work with, and close a list box:

1. With the QuickBooks Navigator displayed on the screen, click on Payroll and Employees.

2. Click on the Employees icon. The Employee List box opens (see Figure 1.29).

3. Highlight an employee and click on the Reports button.

4. Click on Phone List. QuickBooks quickly generates an onscreen report of the phone numbers you entered in your employee account (see Figure 1.30). When you are ready to close a list box, simply click on the Close button in the upper right corner of the box.

Figure 1.29

A list box looks a little different from a dialog box. Use the command buttons in the bottom portion of the box to make changes in the list information.

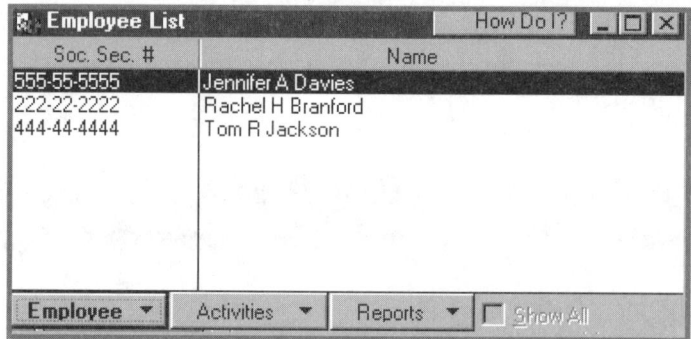

Figure 1.30

The Phone list includes numbers for those you've listed in your employee account.

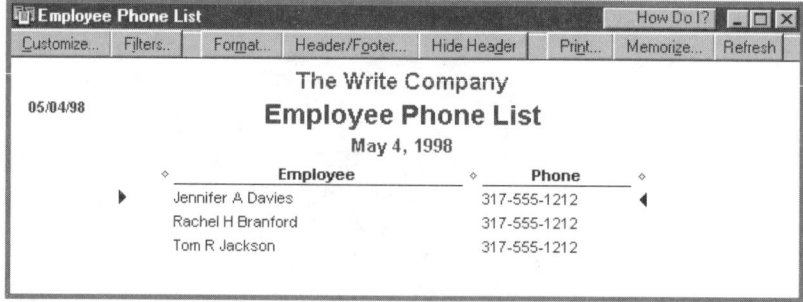

Closing and Reopening the Navigator

Although the Navigator makes it easy to move among the different areas of QuickBooks, you don't have to work with the Navigator during your entire QuickBooks work session. You might want to use the Navigator to move quickly to a particular area (such as the Vendor list in the Purchases and Vendors category) and then close the Navigator once you've displayed the item you want.

To close the Navigator, simply click on the Close button. A message appears asking whether you want to close the Navigator and telling you that you can redisplay the Navigator by clicking on the QB Navigator button in the upper right corner.

Getting Help

QuickBooks knows you may need a little help now and then. In fact, when it comes to business information, most of us need more than a *little* help.

We need mentors. We need accountants. We need people who have been there before, in the industry we are part of, to answer questions and help fill in the gaps in our knowledge. QuickBooks seeks to fill in the knowledge you need by offering a variety of help services. By using the options in the Help menu and the features in the Business Resources tab of the QuickBooks Navigator, you have access to all kinds of step-by-step help as well as online resources that connect you directly to people who can answer questions specific to your business situation.

Checking Out the Help Index

The Help Index is a search-it-yourself help utility that enables you to enter a keyword (or words) you want to find out more about and have QuickBooks bring up the pertinent information. Follow these steps to use the Help Index:

1. Open the Help menu and choose Help Index. The Help Topics dialog box appears, with the Index tab displayed (see Figure 1.31).

2. Select the help topic by typing the word (such as **interest**) or by scrolling down the list until you see the word you want.

3. Click on Display to show the information.

> **TIP** Once you display help information, you can copy, annotate, or print the information. Click on the Options button in the Help window button bar to see your available choices.

How Do I? and Qcards

On most pages and in most dialog boxes, QuickBooks contains an unassuming little button in the top right corner of the windows (to the left of the Minimize, Maximize, and Close buttons) that says, simply, "How Do I?" When you want to know the process for oft-performed QuickBooks tasks (such as "Creating Credit Memos" or "Handling Returns and Refunds"), you can click on the How Do I? button and choose the context-sensitive topic you want from the submenu that appears (see Figure 1.32). After you

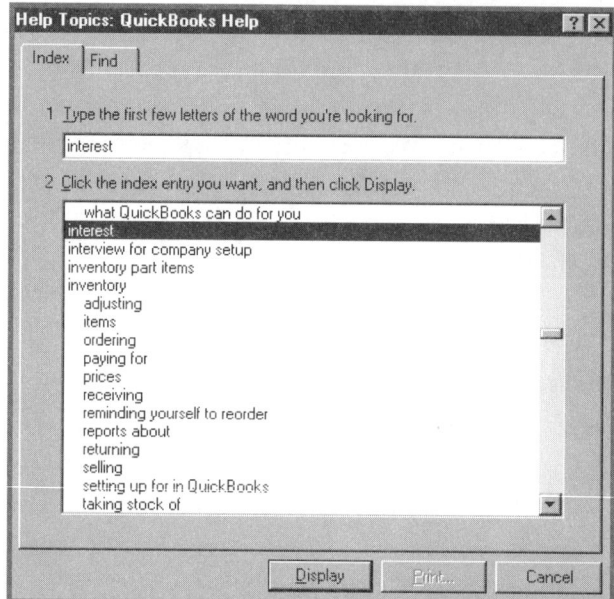

Figure 1.31

The Index tab of the Help Topics dialog box enables you to enter a keyword and search for the topic you want help with.

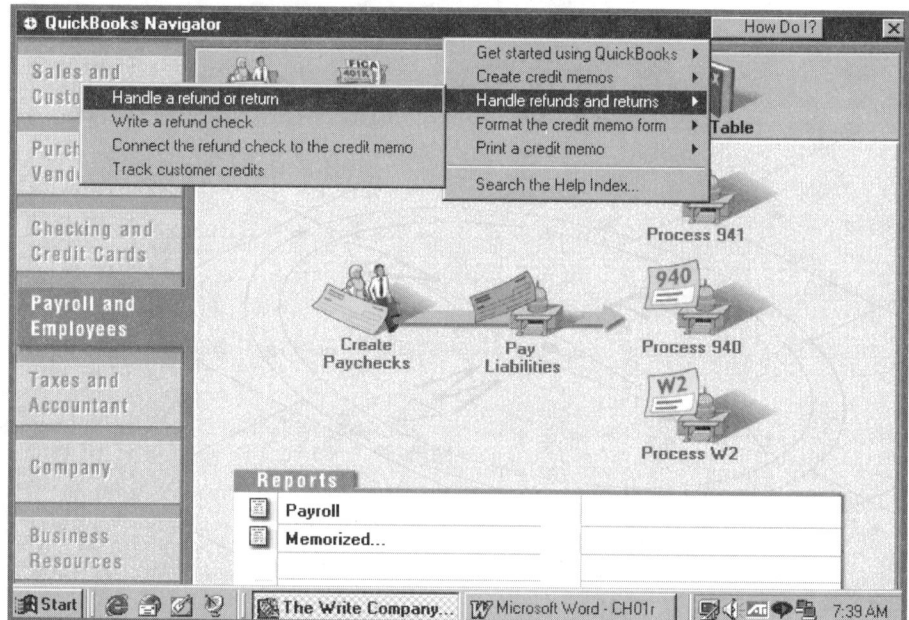

Figure 1.32

When you click on the How Do I? button, you get step-by-step help on specific tasks.

read the help, you can either leave it on the desktop while you work or put it away by clicking on the Close button.

QuickBooks also includes *Qcards*—helpful little yellow notes—to give you a general overview of tasks as you work through your QuickBooks procedures. When you first begin working with QuickBooks, the Qcards feature is turned off. You can turn on the Qcards feature by following these steps:

1. Display the QuickBooks Navigator.
2. Click on the Company tab.
3. Click on Preferences.
4. Click on the General icon.
5. On the My Preferences tab, the first option, Hide Qcards for All Windows, is selected. Click in the check box to enable the Qcards feature.
6. Click on OK.

Once you enable the Qcards feature, you can turn the feature on and off easily. To tell QuickBooks you want to see Qcards as you work, open the Help menu and choose Hide/Show Qcards. Or you can use the quick key, Ctrl+F1, to turn Qcards on and off. When you are working through a procedure that has Qcard help available, the Qcard appears in a small yellow box beside the item you are using (see Figure 1.33). To remove the Qcard after you've read it, click on the small Close button in the upper left corner of the Qcard.

How QuickBooks Can Help in Your Industry

QuickBooks knows that each business is a little different. And what you need in your business today is slightly different from what you will need tomorrow, as you learn new things and your business data needs change. Because so much of working with business data involves industry-specific tasks—a retail business has to track sales tax, for example, while a service business does not—QuickBooks includes an industry-specific help component that can help you learn what you need to know about the type of business you have.

You can find out what QuickBooks knows about your industry in one of two ways:

- You can open the Help menu and choose QuickBooks and your industry.

- You can click on the Business Resources tab (see Figure 1.34) and click on the QuickBooks and Your Industry icon.

A help window appears with a listing of various industries and links to more information related to each. If you don't see your industry listed, or if you want to provide QuickBooks with more information about what you do and the type of data needs you have, you can click on the link that says "Click here to give us feedback about this industry-specific documentation" and teach QuickBooks more about your business.

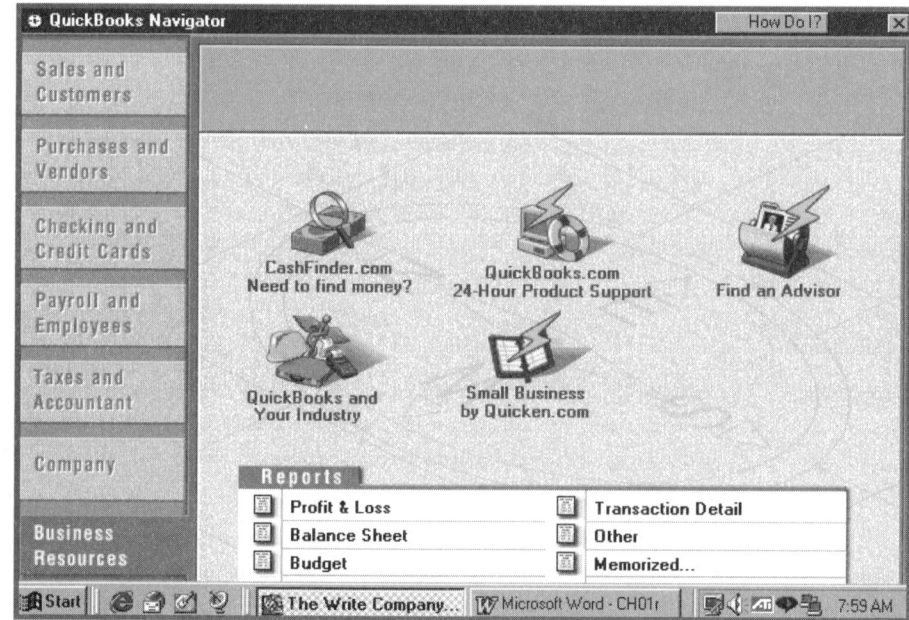

Figure 1.34

The Business Resources tab of the QuickBooks Navigator displays links to all kinds of help—online and otherwise.

FRIDAY EVENING   Getting Started with QuickBooks   55

> **INDUSTRY FEEDBACK**
>
> QuickBooks wants to hear from you. The contact information for sending in industry-specific info is as follows:
>
> Intuit
>
> Industry Feedback
>
> QuickBooks Documentation Group
>
> P. O. Box 7850
>
> Mountain View, CA 94039-7850
>
> Fax: 800-790-4625

Good Advisors Are Worth Their Weight in Gold

Another help feature QuickBooks offers is the expertise of people who have been there and done that. Who can help you more with your business questions than someone who has blazed the trail ahead of you? QuickBooks has built a feature into the program that enables you to find a business advisor online to help you with questions from startup to backup to business plans.

You can start the process of finding an advisor in one of two ways:

- By opening the Help menu and choosing Locate an Advisor in Your Area

- By clicking on the Business Resources tab and choosing Locate an Advisor

Try this now to find an advisor close to your area. Follow these steps:

1. Click on the Business Resources tab.

2. Click on the Find an Advisor icon. QuickBooks displays a message that the program needs to launch your Web browser. Click on Yes to continue. The first time you go online, this launches the Internet Connection Setup Wizard. In subsequent online sessions,

QuickBooks will display the Connect To dialog box and begin making the connection if you are not already online.

3. The Intuit Web page appears, as shown in Figure 1.35. Scroll down and enter the city, state, and ZIP code for your area. Click on Search to begin.

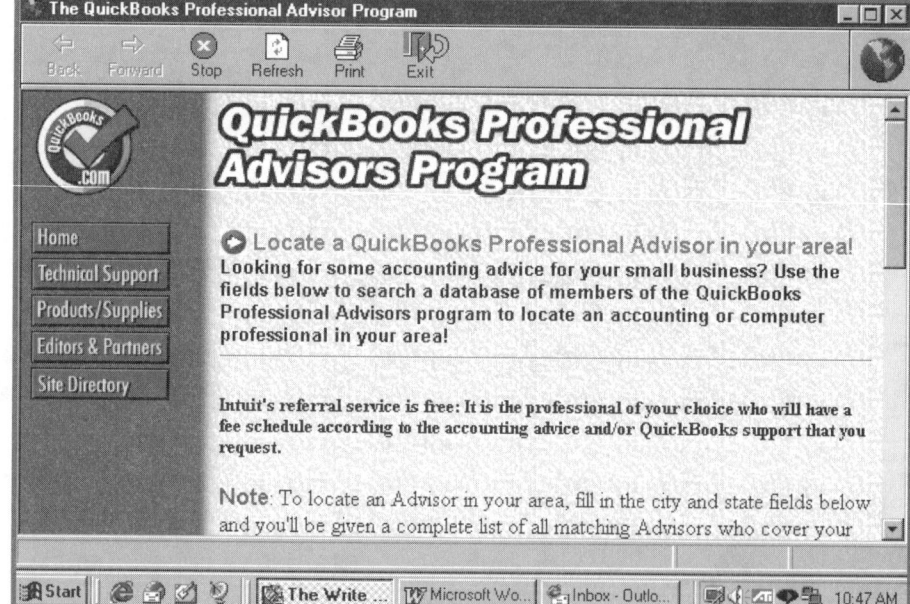

Figure 1.35

The Intuit Advisor Web page helps you find the advisor you need to help with your unique business requirements.

THE INTERNET CONNECTION SETUP WIZARD

The first time you use one of QuickBooks' online resources, the program will automatically take you through the Internet Connection Setup Wizard. This Wizard asks you a series of questions about how your computer is set up to use the Internet. Answer each question and click on Next. You need to use the Setup Wizard only once; the next time you use the online help feature, QuickBooks will have access to the information and will dial up and launch the browser without further ado.

Online Help

Having an advisor is a good thing, but it's not going to solve all your problems. For those times when the form won't print right, or your system hangs, or you get errors you don't understand, you need a tried-and-true technical support person. QuickBooks offers tech support online in addition to all its other help features.

To get to QuickBooks tech support, follow these steps:

1. Click on the Business Resources tab in the QuickBooks Navigator.

2. Click on QuickBooks.com 24-Hour Support. You are taken to the QuickBooks Web site.

3. Click on the Technical Support button at the left side of the screen. This takes you to another page where you can review the FAQ (frequently asked questions about QuickBooks) or find out about the various technical support plans QuickBooks offers.

4. When you're finished with the Web site, click on the Close button to exit and return to QuickBooks.

QuickBooks also provides an active Web site with a wide range of information for small businesses. To access the online resource, go to the Business Resources tab and click on Small Business by Quicken.com. Figure 1.36 shows the wealth of online information available on the Small Business page.

Take a Break

Now that you've been through the various help components and know your way around the QuickBooks screen, it's time to take another break. Stretch your legs, get a fresh cup of coffee (better make it decaf—it's getting late!), and when you're ready, come back for the final section this evening, to cover the last few details you need to consider before you wind things down for the night.

Figure 1.36

In addition to 24-hour tech support, you can access the Small Business Web page to get all kinds of up-to-date information related to your business.

Backing Up Your Data

Each time you exit QuickBooks, the program will give you the option of backing up your data. This is a good idea. When you see the message, simply click on Yes to have QuickBooks copy your data file to a file you specify.

If you would rather *not* back up your data each time you exit QuickBooks, you can do it manually by following these steps:

1. Open the company file you want to back up (in this case, The Write Company file).

2. Click on File, Back Up. The Back Up Company To dialog box appears, as Figure 1.37 shows.

3. Leave the file name as entered or type a new name for the file.

4. Click on Save. QuickBooks backs up the data by saving it to the file you specified.

NOTE You can also back up your data by displaying the Company tab in the QuickBooks Navigator and clicking on the Backup icon.

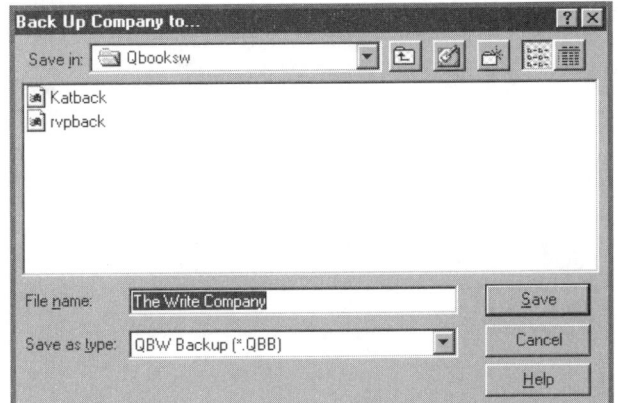

Figure 1.37

Remember to protect your business data—back up regularly.

TIP It's a good idea to save your backup files on something *other than* your computer's hard drive. For example, you might save the files to a removable drive such as a Zip disk or a floppy disk. That way, if your hard drive ever crashes, you still have access to your business data.

Understanding the Chart of Accounts

As you begin to work with QuickBooks, you soon realize that the Chart of Accounts is an important part of tracking your business data. The Chart of Accounts shows you all the accounts you have set up in your business, according to the type of account you've set up (see Figure 1.38).

Taking a Look at the Chart of Accounts

You display the Chart of Accounts by clicking on the Company tab in the QuickBooks Navigator and clicking on the Chart of Accounts icon. The list box shown in Figure 1.38 appears.

The first column shows the name you specified for the account (you set up these accounts during the EasyStep Interview, earlier this evening). The second column lists the type of account. QuickBooks is set up to work

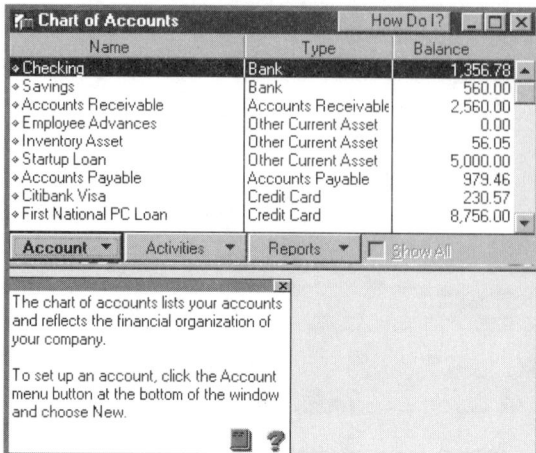

Figure 1.38

The Chart of Accounts lists all the accounts you have set up for your business.

with two different types of accounts: *balance sheet accounts* and *income and expense accounts*. The income and expense accounts track the money that comes into and flows out of your business. The balance sheet accounts allow you to categorize your various expenditures so that you can easily see where the money goes. You can have up to nine different types of balance sheet accounts: bank accounts, accounts receivable, other current asset, fixed asset, other asset, accounts payable, credit card, current liability, and long-term liability.

Along the bottom of the Chart of Accounts, you see three buttons: Account, Activities, Reports. When you click on a button, a submenu appears. The commands in the Account menu enable you to create new accounts, edit existing accounts, and make selected accounts inactive. The Activities menu gives you the commands you need to do such things as write checks, make deposits, reconcile your account, transfer money, and use your check register. Finally the Reports menu helps you produce reports using the various accounts you have set up.

Working with Accounts

This section gives you an overview of the procedures involved in working with your business accounts. Throughout this book you will be creating and working with accounts, so you will get more practice, account-wise, in other examples you follow this weekend.

Renaming an Account

When you set up your accounts during the EasyStep Interview, the whole idea of accounts was new and you may now be wishing you had named the accounts differently. Changing account names is a simple thing. Just follow these steps:

1. Display the Chart of Accounts.
2. Click on the account you want to change.
3. Click on Account, and then select Edit. The Edit Account dialog box appears (see Figure 1.39).
4. Highlight the text in the Name field.
5. Type the new name for the account and click on OK.

Figure 1.39

You can easily rename an account by changing the Name entry in the Edit Account dialog box. You can make other modifications to the account in this dialog box as well.

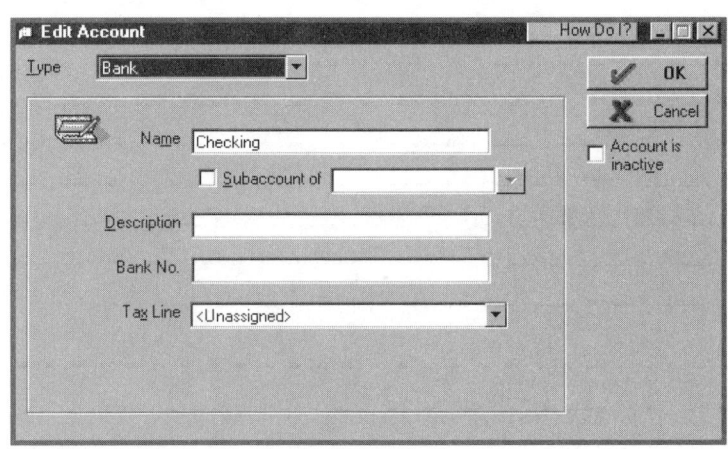

Modifying an Account

You use the same dialog box—Edit Account—to make other modifications to the account. What kinds of changes can you make?

- You can change the type of the account.

- You can make the account a subaccount of another account. For example, you might want to create a *Car insurance* expense account within the *Vehicles* account.

- You can enter a description for the account.

- You can add a number to be used in identifying the account.

- You can choose the tax category for the account by clicking on the down arrow to the right of the Tax Line field and selecting the category you want from the displayed list.

- You can elect to make the account inactive by clicking on the Account is Inactive check box.

Make any necessary modifications and click on OK. The changes are made to the account as you specified.

TIP How do you know which type of account to use? QuickBooks gives you an overview of the different account types when you choose How Do I? and select Choose the Account Type.

Deleting an Account or Making It Inactive

If you have set up but not used an account, you can delete it by highlighting the account, clicking on the Account button, and clicking on Delete. If you *have* used the account, QuickBooks tells you that the account has been used or has data assigned to it and cannot be deleted. If you want to remove an account from use and you have used it in the past, you can simply make it inactive. To do this, display the Chart of Accounts, click on Account, and then click on Make Inactive.

Making an Inactive Account Active

You can later make an inactive account active by selecting the account in the Chart of Accounts, clicking on the Account button, and choosing Show

All Accounts. This displays all accounts, even the inactive ones. Any inactive accounts show a small icon to the left of the account name (see Figure 1.40). Finally, highlight the inactive account, click on Account, and then click on Make Active.

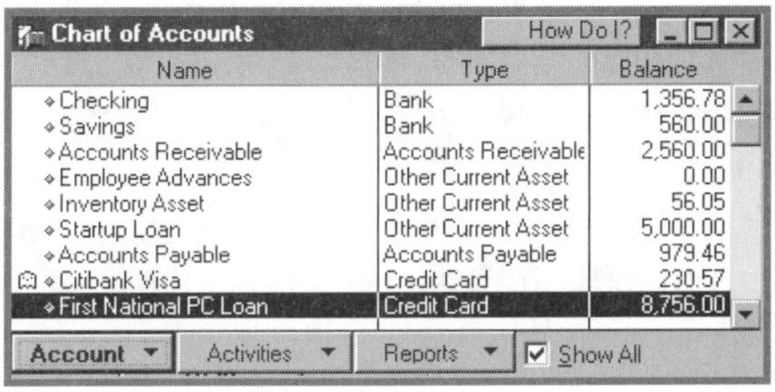

Figure 1.40

Inactive accounts show small icons to the left of the account name.

Adding an Account as You Go

QuickBooks doesn't hold you to a strict process of entering accounts and then using them. You can create accounts on the fly as you enter information in your business checkbook. This is both a good thing and a challenge, however. Because you can create accounts so easily, it is simple to create accounts you won't use or create a duplicate account you simply worded a little differently. For example, you might create an expense account called *Delivery* and then, the next time you type the account in the register, call it *Deliveries*. Having both these accounts set up to record the same data may not cause huge problems, but it can get messy for record keeping and cause your data to be less organized than it might otherwise be.

In just a little while, you will learn how to display and work with the Check Register and add accounts on the fly. Remember, however, that you should first check the Account list or Chart of Accounts to determine whether the account already exists or you have created something similar.

Lots of Lists

Now you know about the Chart of Accounts, an important piece of the QuickBooks puzzle. Another item QuickBooks relies on heavily is the list. QuickBooks *loves* lists. Lists help you organize business data, customers, vendors, tasks, and more. You get to the commands you need to work with these lists by opening the Lists menu (see Figure 1.41).

Earlier in this session, you learned about list boxes. These are the boxes QuickBooks uses to display list information. What you may not realize is how many different lists your business will use. When you did the EasyStep Interview, QuickBooks gathered the information it needed to create a number of essential lists:

- Items
- Payroll Items

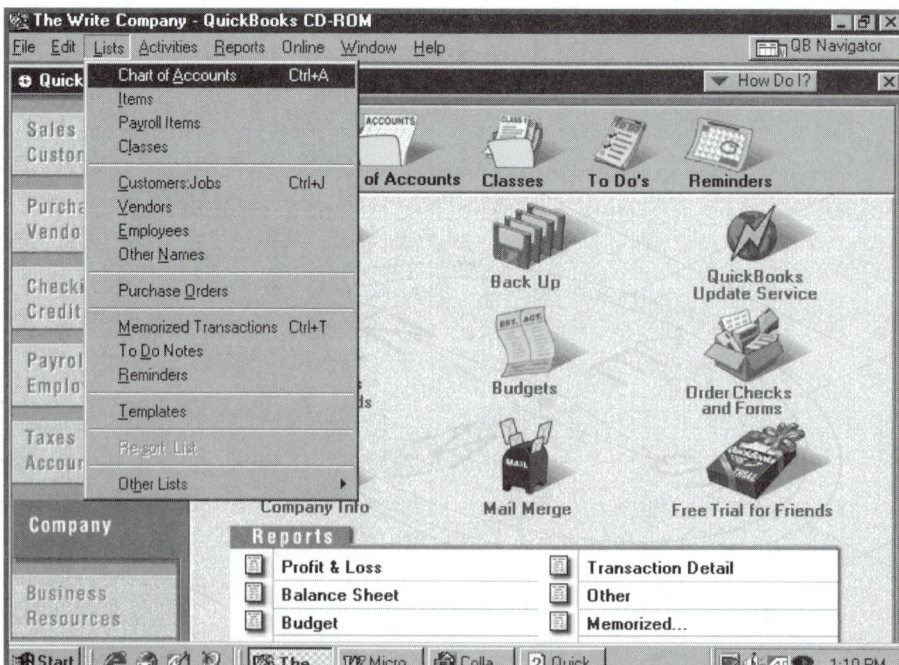

Figure 1.41

The Lists menu contains everything you need to display and work with the various lists your business needs.

- Classes
- Customers: Jobs
- Vendors
- Employees

> **TIP** The lists shown in your Lists menu may be different from the ones shown in this list because QuickBooks customizes the Lists menu to fit the needs of your business. The Write Company is a service business, so the lists selected are unique to that type of business. When you respond to the questions in the EasyStep Interview, QuickBooks places some items in the main part of the Lists menu; other lists the program does not anticipate your business using are placed in the Other Lists item at the bottom of the menu.

To display a list, simply choose the one you want from the Lists menu. Figure 1.42 shows the Vendor list. On the left side of the box you see the vendors' names; on the right side you see the outstanding balances of the vendors' accounts. At the bottom of the Vendor List box, you see three buttons: Vendor, Activities, and Reports. The Vendor button opens a submenu that contains commands you use to create new vendor accounts, edit existing accounts, make the account active or inactive, print 1099s, and more. The Activities button, identical to its function in the Chart of Accounts, enables you to write checks, pay bills, and more. The Reports button, also similar to the button of the same name in the Chart of Accounts, allows you to create reports based on the data in the displayed list.

> **NOTE** The examples in this book contain various types of lists. I include this section here just to give you a general introduction to lists so that you understand their form and function in QuickBooks.

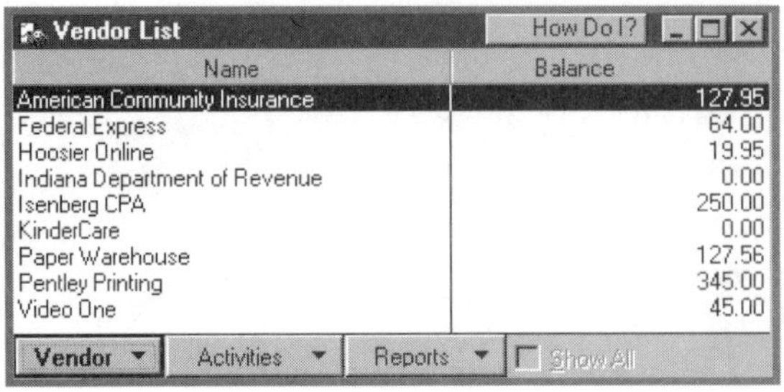

Figure 1.42

The Vendor List box shows one example of a list you use to track business information in QuickBooks.

Setting Up Your Checkbook

As part of the EasyStep Interview, you entered the current balance on your business checking account, so QuickBooks knows how to start tracking your checking activity. Part of getting set up in QuickBooks involves entering past transactions, however, and you will do that using your checkbook and any checks you have paid between your start date and today.

For this part of the work session, you will need these things:

- Your check register
- Your most current bank statement
- ATM receipts
- Your cancelled checks

Displaying the Register

Take a look at the QuickBooks Check Register. Follow these steps:

1. Click on the Checking and Credit Cards tab of the QuickBooks Navigator (see Figure 1.43).

2. Click on the Check Register icon. If you set up more than one account in the EasyStep Interview, a small pop-up dialog box asks you to choose the name of the account you want to view. Click on Checking. The Register appears, as shown in Figure 1.44.

FRIDAY EVENING   **Getting Started with QuickBooks**   **67**

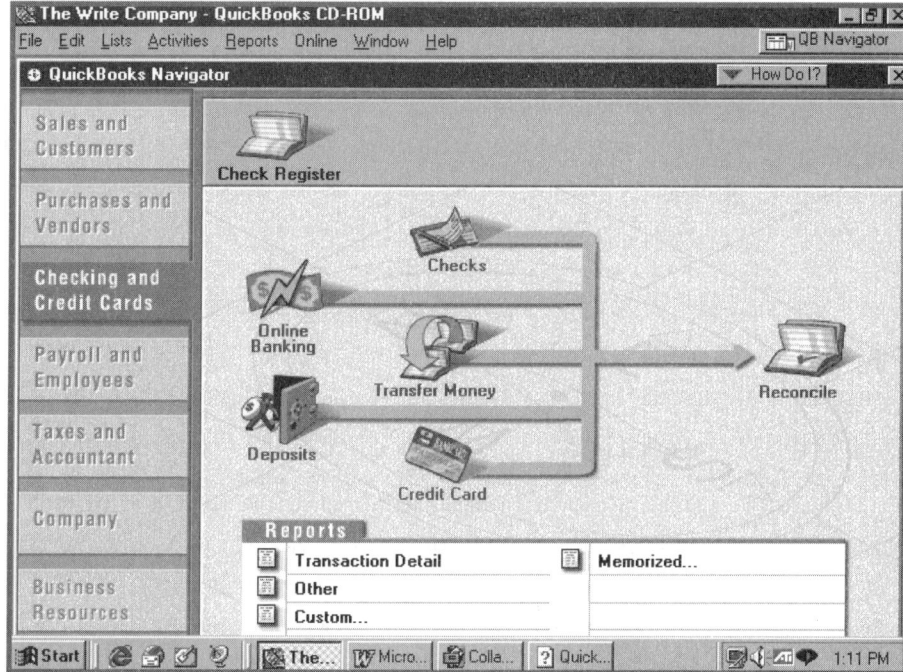

Figure 1.43

You can display the Check Register by clicking on the icon in the Checking and Credit Cards tab.

 TIP   You can also access the Check Register from the Chart of Accounts by clicking on Activities and choosing Use Register or by pressing the quick key Ctrl+R.

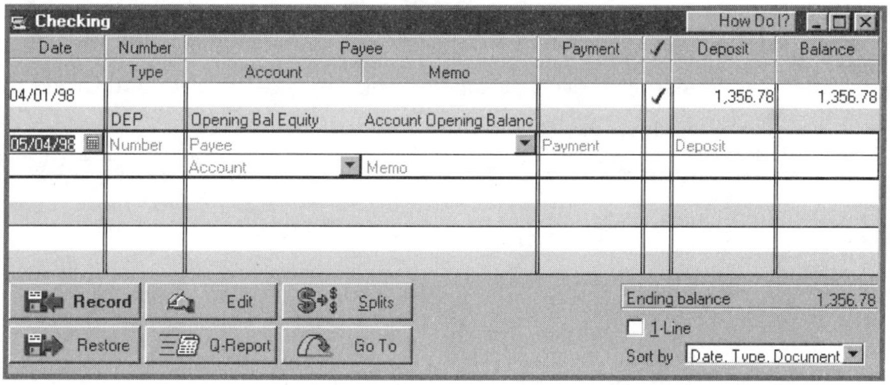

Figure 1.44

The Check Register looks similar to your traditional register—you can use the Register to enter transactions.

If you have ever written a check or balanced a checkbook, the Check Register will be familiar to you. QuickBooks shows a balance entered—you supplied this during the EasyStep Interview. The Check Register calls for all the traditional information—date, check number, payee, amount, and balance. There's even a spot for a check mark once you've reconciled the account and can show that the check has cleared.

You can enter checks directly in the Check Register, or you can use the check display (which you'll learn about in the session tomorrow afternoon). For now, you will enter a check to record a past transaction in the Check Register.

Entering a Check

Tonight, you'll enter cleared checks that record past transactions. Tomorrow when you begin working with the Check Register again, you will be dealing with checks you are currently paying, which is a slightly different procedure. Before your QuickBooks data will be complete, you need to enter any past transactions that have occurred between the date you selected as your start date and today.

So get those checks now, and begin entering them. Follow this process to enter each check:

1. Click in the Date field, if the date is not already highlighted. Type the date of the check. Press Tab. The cursor moves to the next field.

TIP You can enter the date without any punctuation at all—QuickBooks will add the slashes for you. This means you can type **052398** and QuickBooks will turn the date into 05/23/98.

2. Type the check number. Press Tab.
3. In the Payee area, type the name of the person or vendor to whom you wrote the check. (In The Write Company example, I entered

FRIDAY EVENING Getting Started with QuickBooks

Federal Express.) If the company you enter is on your Vendor list, the name will appear automatically as you begin to type. You can press Tab to accept the name and move on to the next field, or you can continue typing the correct name. If you prefer, you can click on the down arrow to display a list of vendors (see Figure 1.45). To choose a payee from the list, click on the one you want. When you are finished, press Tab.

4. In the Payment box, enter the amount of the check. Press Tab.

5. In the Account box, click on the down arrow. You see a list of accounts to which you can assign the transaction. For The Write Company's example, the account is Postage and Delivery. Click on the account that best fits the transaction and press Tab.

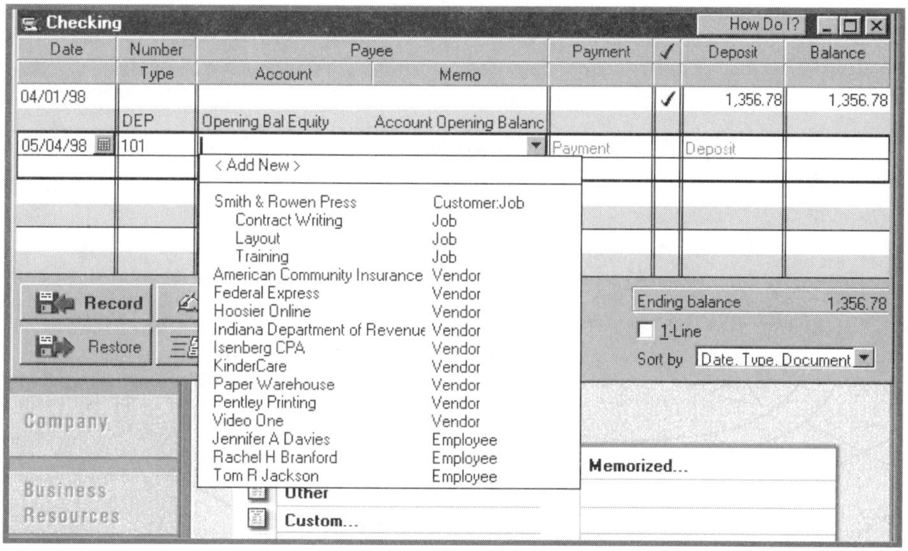

Figure 1.45

You can select a payee from the list or type the name in as you go.

6. In the Memo field, enter any information you want to help you recall the transaction.

7. Click on Tab to move to the next entry.

You can also press Ctrl+End to move to a new transaction quickly.

You will learn a variety of other tasks involving checks and check writing in the session tomorrow afternoon, in "Writing the Check: Paying for Goods and Services."

Entering Past Transactions

Now that you have entered a check, you know the basic process. Continue entering cancelled checks using the preceding steps 1 through 7. When you have entered all transactions from your start date till today, you are ready to move ahead into using QuickBooks to automate your business practices and plans.

As you work, QuickBooks remembers to save the file for you. Periodically QuickBooks will save the file out to your backup file so that the most current picture of your data is always on record.

Closing the Register

When you are finished entering the past transactions, you can close the Register and go about your other tasks. Simply click on the Close button in the upper right corner of the Check Register.

Exiting QuickBooks

By finishing up the Register, you've come to the end of your whirlwind QuickBooks tour. Time to power-down QuickBooks for the night. Simply open the File menu and choose Exit or press the quick key Alt+F4. QuickBooks displays a little status window showing you that it is checking data integrity. When it's finished, QuickBooks closes and the Windows desktop is displayed.

What's Next?

Congratulations! You've made it through the first QuickBooks work session. If you're tired, don't worry—other segments won't be quite as grueling as this one. Because of the amount of data QuickBooks needs in order to set up your company properly, the first step is the longest—getting all your information into QuickBooks to start with. The rest of the tasks will be interesting and challenging, but not nearly as labor-intensive.

So get some sleep—you've earned it! And come back tomorrow morning refreshed and ready to dive into the following tasks:

- Organizing your customer information
- Creating invoices
- Figuring finance charges
- Printing mailing labels and invoices
- Recording payments
- Working with credit memos
- Recording cash sales
- Making deposits

See you in the morning!

SATURDAY MORNING

Tracking and Recording Sales

- ✪ Creating Invoices
- ✪ Figuring Finance Charges
- ✪ Making Deposits
- ✪ Using Credit Memos
- ✪ Checking the Customer Register

Good morning! I hope you slept well, even if you had visions of check registers dancing in your head. This morning you will start out with important tasks that enable you to get a major portion of your business data organized.

Different business pundits will claim different parts of business operations are of supreme importance, but there aren't too many facets of your business more important than tracking and recording sales. Yes, the quality of your product or service is important. And yes, the way you treat your customers, your employees, and your vendors is a prime factor in the success of your business. But assuming that you have a good idea or product and you know how to practice good customer relations, one of the tasks at the top of your must-do-well list is handling the sales once they start pouring in.

When a customer becomes a customer, how do you record that information? Are your invoices professional? How do you record the sales when you receive them? What happens when and if a customer wants a refund? You learn to handle these issues and more this morning. Specifically, this session covers how to:

- Set up your customer information
- Create invoices and figure finance charges
- Print your invoices

- Record payments, enter cash sales, and make deposits
- Use credit memos
- Check the customer register

So grab yourself another cup of coffee or some juice and settle in for a fast-paced morning session. Sure, it means giving up the Bugs Bunny & Road Runner hour, but your business will be in a lot better shape by noon. (Besides, they're all reruns, anyway.)

Setting Up Customer Information

It's possible to keep customer information in your head, assuming that you don't have too many customers. In fact, that pretty much decides the fact that you *won't* have too many customers—how many facts can you store up there without a mistake at some point? Willy Loman might have felt it important to rely on relationships to make sales, but most of us who are running our own businesses know that it's a warm heart, a cool head, and a good computer that continue to make the sales.

Each time you sell something—whether it's a service or a product—you get a volume of important information in return. You get basic facts, like the customer name, address, and phone. You get financial information—how much did they spend?—and you get a check or cash (hopefully). But you also get data that helps you know the customer better and anticipate his needs and wants down the road, an ability that in turn helps you offer a better product or service and guarantee more sales. You discover the customer's *likes* (he chose this product over that one) as well as his *spending habits* (he was interested in buying a case of videotapes because he saved 20 percent).

Starting Out with Customer Info

Before you begin working with the Customer list in QuickBooks, make sure you have your current customer information. How do you track customer info now? If it's on three-by-five cards, go ahead and get them. Is it in a printed database? On a Rolodex? However you track your customer data, get the information now so that you can enter some of your customers in this morning's QuickBooks session.

1. Click on the Sales and Customers tab in the QuickBooks Navigator.

2. Click on the Customers icon. The Customer: Job list appears, as Figure 2.1 shows. In the left side of the list, you see the names of Customers you have previously entered (you may have done this during the EasyStep Interview). The center column shows you any current balance the customer owes you. The rightmost column displays any notes you may have entered about the customer.

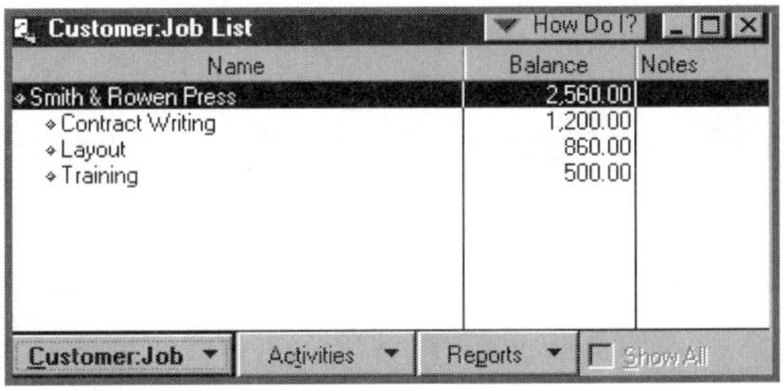

Figure 2.1

The Customer: Job list shows you current information about your clients.

Adding Customers

If your business is growing, which it hopefully is, you will be continually adding new customers to your QuickBooks Customers list. You can add customers easily from the Customers list box by following these steps:

1. Click on the Customer: Job button. When the submenu appears, click on New. The New Customer dialog box appears, as Figure 2.2 shows. This dialog box gives you the opportunity to enter a great deal of information about your customer.

2. The cursor is positioned in the Customer text box. Type the name of the customer and press Tab.

3. Enter the company name and other contact information, pressing Tab after completing each field.

4. In the Bill To box, type the address to which the invoice should be sent. If the customer wants the merchandise shipped to the billing address, click on Copy to copy the billing address to the shipping area.

5. When you've completed the Address Info tab, click on Additional Info.

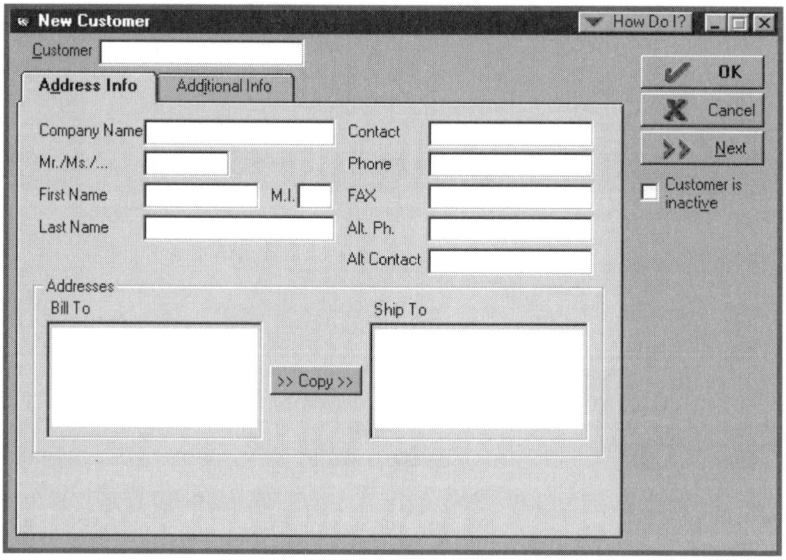

Figure 2.2

You enter customer information in the Address Info tab of the New Customer dialog box.

Entering Custom Information

Every business has different data needs. In a furniture business, you might need to track whether your customer is a walk-in customer or a delivery customer. If you are a real estate agent, you might want to enter information about the price range in which the customer is interested (you could create a special type to track that information). There are as many ways to organize data as there are data types to organize. And the Additional Info tab gives you the means to create and organize the special data needs you have in your own business.

To get to the Additional Info tab, click on the tab name when the New Customer dialog box is displayed (see Figure 2.3). You then enter the information as needed in any of the boxes that apply. Table 2.1 gives you an overview of what the different items on this tab are for and how you might use them.

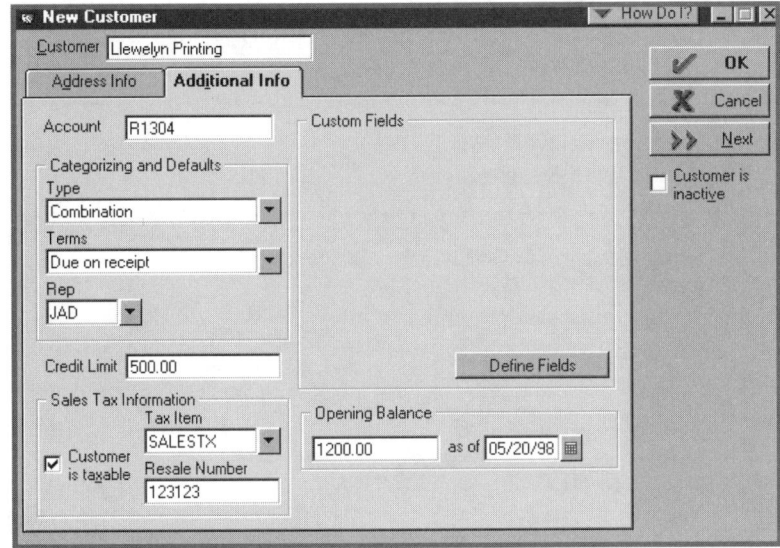

Figure 2.3

The Additional Info tab enables you to track information related to your particular business.

To fill in the fields in the Additional Info tab, you simply click in the field you want to enter information for and type the data. Some fields, such as Type, Terms, and Tax Item, present you with submenus when you click on the down-arrow to the right of the field. Others—such as Credit Limit, Resale Number, and Opening Balance—require that you type the information in the blank provided.

Table 2.1 Choices on the Additional Info Tab

Item	Description	Example
Account	Allows you to track the customer using your business numbering system.	R1304
Type	Enables you to create different types of customers. You might organize customers by sales level or something else that fits your business needs. The Write Company organizes type by product or service offered.	Customer types include Writing, Training, Sales, and Combination. (Several of The Write Company's clients use two or more services.)
Terms	Lets you select the payment terms you have arranged with this customer.	Due on receipt
Rep	Tracks the employee responsible for working with this customer.	JAD (employee initials)
Credit Limit	Records the spending limit you determine for the customer. If an invoice amount exceeds the credit limit, QuickBooks warns you.	500
Tax Item	Provides you with choices to handle in-state or out-of-state tax considerations.	SALESTX (*Note*: The name that appears is determined by the text you entered for the name of the sales tax account in the EasyStep Interview.)
Customer Is Taxable	Allows you to specify whether the customer is charged tax	Customer Is Taxable (checked)
Resale Number	Customers who resell items they purchase ordinarily are not charged sales tax; enter their resale number here.	123123

(continued)

SATURDAY MORNING Tracking and Recording Sales

TABLE 2.1 CHOICES ON THE ADDITIONAL INFO TAB (CONTINUED)

Item	Description	Example
Define Fields	Gives you the ability to create new fields to track customer data. The Write Company records information about the number of employees on site for each customer and the dates and locations of each training seminar.	No. of Employees
Opening Balance	Lets you enter the outstanding balance owed by your customer as of the start date.	1200.00

When you are finished entering the information, you can click on OK to return to the Customer: Job list. If you want to enter information for more customers, click on Next to continue to a new screen in the New Customer dialog box.

Defining Custom Fields

In the Additional Info tab of the New Customer dialog box, you have the option of adding fields to store specialized information about your client. Here are a few ideas of the types of fields you might want to create:

For The Write Company:

> Number of employees:
>
> Training proposal?
>
> Training 1:
>
> Training 2:
>
> Comments:

 **NOTE** QuickBooks' Notepad feature enables you to attach notes to a customer file, so if you add a Comments field, be sure to use it to store data you want printed on invoices and reports. Record more private information using the Notepad feature.

For Carole's Custom Interiors, an interior design firm:

> Décor type:
>
> Client since:
>
> Referred by:
>
> Show home?

For Asset Accounting Services:

> Individual or business:
>
> Fiscal year:
>
> Qtrly reports?
>
> Next appointment:

For Reynolds Realty:

> Target date:
>
> Purchasing or selling?
>
> Property Location:
>
> Referred by:

To define custom fields, follow these steps:

1. Click on the Define Fields button in the Additional Info tab. The Define Fields dialog box appears, as Figure 2.4 shows. As you can see, you have the option to display the fields when you are working with jobs, vendors, or employees.

2. Type the name for the field. You can use spaces in the name but limit the name to 20 characters or less.

3. Click on the check box beside the item with which you want the fields to be used. You can choose one, two, or all three items.

4. Click on OK. A message appears letting you know that you can use these custom fields in other transactions as well if you turn them on when you are working with your custom templates.

5. When you are finished working with the New Customer dialog box, click on OK to return to the Customer: Job list box.

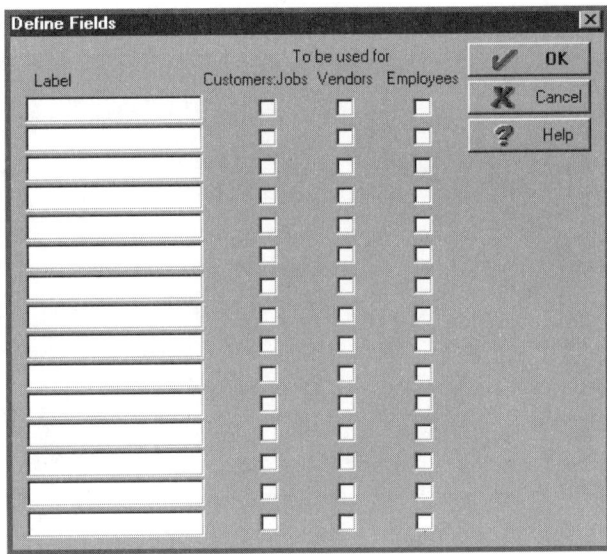

Figure 2.4

You can choose to make the custom fields available when you are working with jobs, vendors, and employees.

Adding Jobs

Depending on the nature of your business, you may need to add other jobs for each customer. The Write Company not only offers writing services, but also does communications training and sells a product—the videotape training series. This means I need several jobs to track the various ways The Write Company brings in sales.

You add jobs by following these steps:

1. In the Sales and Customers tab, click on Customers.

2. Click on the Customer: Job button. From the submenu, choose Add Job. The New Job dialog box appears, as shown in Figure 2.5.

3. If you have entered customer information in the New Customer dialog box (using the process explained in the last section), you will see some information for the currently selected customer displayed in the dialog box. If you are just beginning to enter information, the text boxes will be blank. Click on the Customer down arrow. A list of your current customers will appear; choose the customer you want or type the name of a new customer.

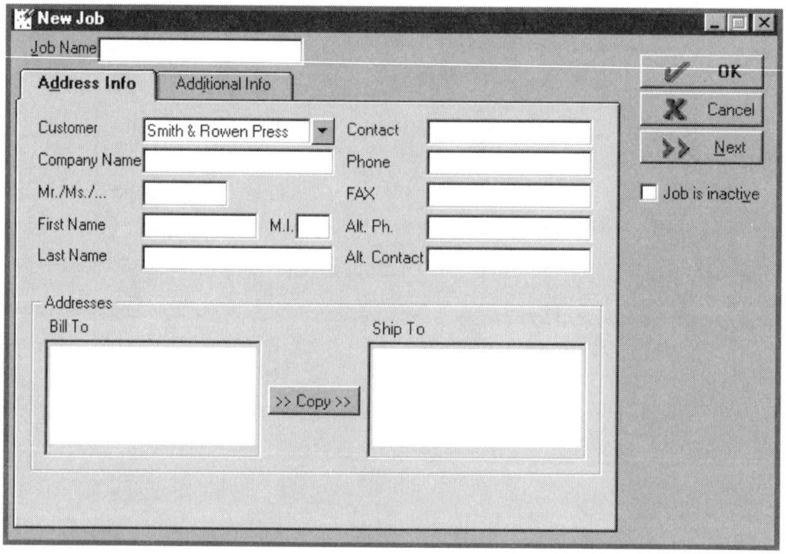

Figure 2.5

When you want to add a new job for a particular customer, click on Customer: Job and choose Add Job to display the New Job dialog box.

TIP You can add customers on the fly by typing a new customer name in the Customer field and then pressing Tab. QuickBooks displays a pop-up dialog box letting you know that the customer you entered is not on the current Customer: Job list. Click on Quick Add to add the customer to the list.

4. Enter the necessary information to further define the jobs you offer in your business. Table 2.2 suggests a few ways different companies might divide jobs to make them easier to categorize and track.

5. If you have more information to enter, click on Additional Info. Notice that the fields you created in the Additional Info page of the New Customer dialog box have been added to this page, as well.

6. When you have finished adding the new job, click on Next if you want to add another one, or click on OK to return to the Customer: Job list box.

Table 2.2 Choices

Company	Client	Possible Jobs
The Write Company	Pronto Press, a small publishing house	Writing Training, sales (of videotape)
Carole's Custom Interiors	Ann Reimer, homeowner	Consulting, design, purchasing
Asset Accounting Services	Taco Bill's Restaurant	Bookkeeping, payroll, tax preparation, audit assistance
Reynolds Realty	Cummins Engine	Relocation package, area research, move management, property management

TIP Throughout this chapter, I begin and end the tasks at the QuickBooks Navigator. You don't have to use the Navigator for all these tasks, although personally I think it's the easiest way. If you want to use the menus instead, you can click on Lists and choose Customer: Job. Then click on Add Job to display the dialog box.

Editing Customer Information

Things may change once you get the information entered. Contact people come and go. Addresses change. Luckily, you can easily edit the customer information you've entered. Edit one of the added records:

1. Back at the Navigator, click on the Sales and Customers tab.

2. Click on Customers. When the Customer list appears, click on Customer: Job.

3. From the submenu, click on Edit. The Edit Customer dialog box appears. (This looks just like the New Customer dialog box except that data appears in the fields. If you need to see a picture of the dialog box, check out Figure 2.2.)

4. Change the information you want to edit. This could be anything from a misspelling to an incorrect amount to an erroneous option choice. Simply click in the box and type the correct info.

5. When your changes are complete, click on OK. You are returned to the Customer: Job list box.

Adding Customer Notes

A very cool feature is available to you while you are editing your customer information: Notes. If you're an information hound, as I am, you like to write down everything you learn about a particular topic, client, or job. The Notes feature enables you to record information about phone calls, client visits, future plans and proposals, and so on. You simply type the information, and QuickBooks stores it right along with the other customer data you have entered. Clean and simple—and organized, too. Here's how you use the Notes feature:

1. Display the Edit Customer dialog box by choosing Customer: Job from the Customer list box and selecting Edit.

2. Beneath the Cancel button you see the Notes button. Click on the button to display the Notepad for the current customer (see Figure 2.6).

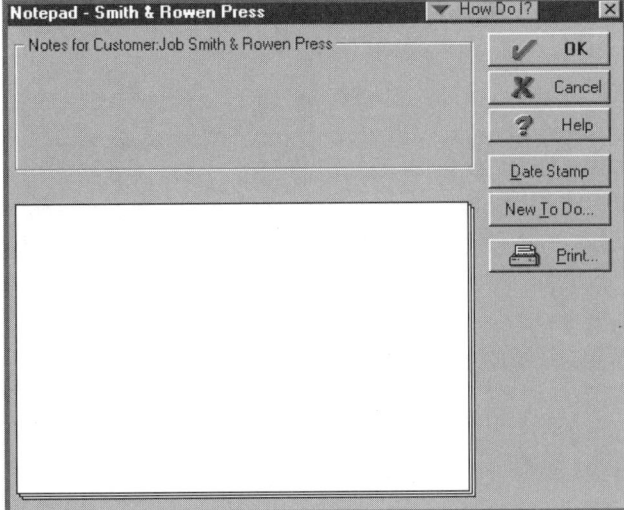

Figure 2.6

When you edit customer information, you have the option of adding notes about your changes or other pertinent items.

Adding To Do's to the To Do List

Yet another new button becomes available in the Notepad dialog box; New To Do. You've heard of the QuickBooks To Do list feature—you can click on this button to display the list so you can add more action items to it.

Click on New To Do. The New To Do dialog box appears, as Figure 2.7 shows. Type the item in the text box; then click on the calendar icon beside Remind Me On to enter a date you want to be reminded of the task. QuickBooks will remind you of the To Do you entered each time you start the program after the date you specified until you complete the item and click on the Done check box.

Making Customers Inactive

From time to time, you may want to make customers inactive. Suppose that your business is Armstrong Heating & Cooling, and you send out invoices on a monthly basis. When you have a client who has not ordered any service within a six-month time frame, you may want to make the client inactive and thereby remove that client from the invoice list.

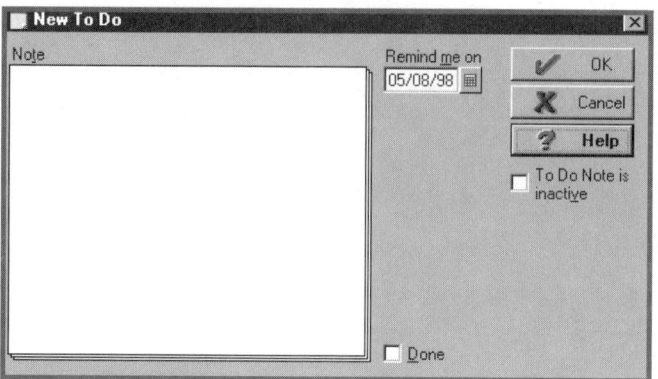

Figure 2.7

To Do items remind you of tasks you need to carry out on particular days. QuickBooks will remind you automatically.

To make a customer inactive, you can do one of two things:

1. Click on the Customers icon in the Sales and Customers tab.
2. When the Customer: Job list is displayed, click on the name of the customer you want to make inactive.
3. Click on the Customer: Job button; the submenu appears.
4. Click on Make Inactive.

If you prefer, you can make the customer inactive using this process:

1. Display the Customer: Job list box.
2. Press Ctrl+E. The Edit Customer dialog box appears.
3. Click on the Customer Is Inactive check box beneath the command buttons.

When customers are inactive, the name of the customer disappears from the Customer: Job list box. You can make customers active again by displaying the Customer: Job list box, clicking on Customer: Job, and choosing Show All Customers. The returned customer name appears with a small hand icon to the left of the customer name (see Figure 2.8).

To make the customer active again, simply click on the customer name, click on Customer: Job, and choose Make Active. The hand icon is removed, and you can work with the customer information as normal.

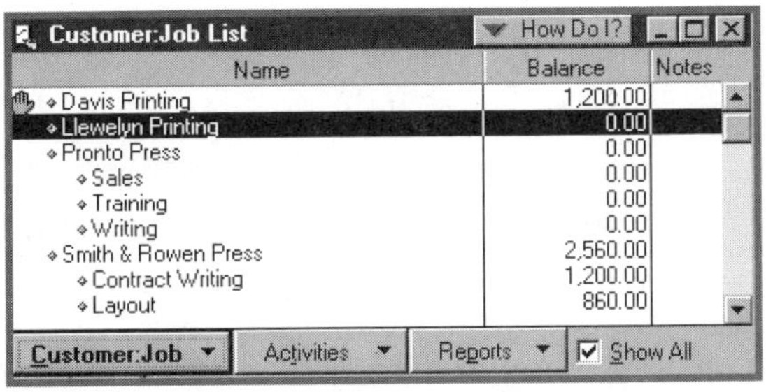

Figure 2.8

When you display an inactive customer, QuickBooks marks the customer name with a hand icon.

Deleting Customer Jobs

As you continue to work with customer data, there will no doubt be those customers you want to delete from the system. You may have entered the data incorrectly; or a client that has been inactive for a while has moved from the area and you no longer need to record his information in the system. Deleting the information is a simple four-step process:

1. Display the Customer: Job list box.
2. Click on the line with the customer information you want to delete.
3. Press Ctrl+D. A prompt appears asking you to confirm that you do want to delete the job.
4. Click on OK to delete the item.

TIP If you delete a customer job and then realize you've made a mistake and deleted the wrong thing, don't panic—you can Undo the deletion by pressing Ctrl+Z if you catch it before you do anything else.

Printing a Customer List

Another feature that comes in handy is available in the Customer: Job pop-up menu. You can print a customer list that details the customer information, jobs, and balances of your current customers. To print a customer list, follow these steps:

1. Display the Customer: Job list box.

2. Click on the Customer: Job button. When the submenu appears, click on Print List or press Ctrl+P. A message appears telling you that you might want to instead print a report that lists the information you need. The Print Lists dialog box appears, as Figure 2.9 shows.

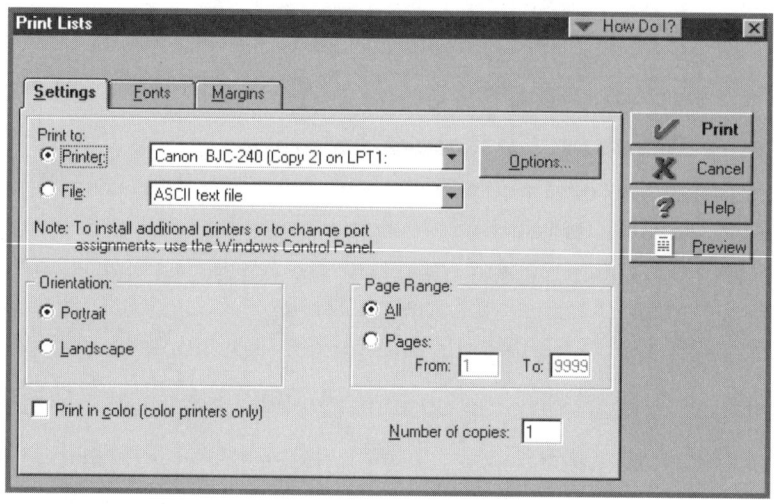

Figure 2.9

The Print Lists dialog box enables you to choose print settings, select fonts, and control the margins of your printout. You can also click on Preview to see how the page will look before you print it.

TIP It's always a good idea to preview a printout before you click on that final Print button and begin printing. This can help you avoid those out-of-alignment columns, data divided in the wrong place, or headings out of proportion to the rest of the page. For more about working with printouts and reports in preview mode, see tomorrow morning's session, "Tracking Results: Reporting Your Financial Data."

Creating Invoices

Now that you know who your customers are and you've got a system in place to record important data about them, you need to add another big piece of the puzzle: billing. How do you let customers know how much they owe you or remind them of their balances on their accounts? Invoices are printed documents that communicate the following things to the customer:

- How much they owe
- What the terms of your agreement are
- What services or products they purchased from you
- When you expect payment
- Where to send the payment and how to contact you with questions

---

TEN FEATURES OF AN EFFECTIVE INVOICE

1. Your contact information is clear and inviting.
2. Customers can easily see what they are paying for.
3. The due date stands out and lets customers know when you expect payment.
4. The page is organized and uncluttered.
5. The document makes it easy for customers to respond. You might include a tear-off portion they send in with their payments or package an envelope in with the invoice.
6. Your company logo stands out and gives additional impact to the customer's identification of your business.
7. You include room for comment lines to explain additional amounts, charges, and miscellaneous costs.
8. Your contact number includes a phone number so that clients can contact you with questions.
9. You include a thank-you note or customized message.
10. The printout is easy to read and printed on a new ribbon or toner.

When you are ready to create your first invoice, follow these steps:

1. Open the Activities menu.
2. Choose Create Invoices (or press Ctrl+I). The Create Invoices dialog box appears, as Figure 2.10 shows.

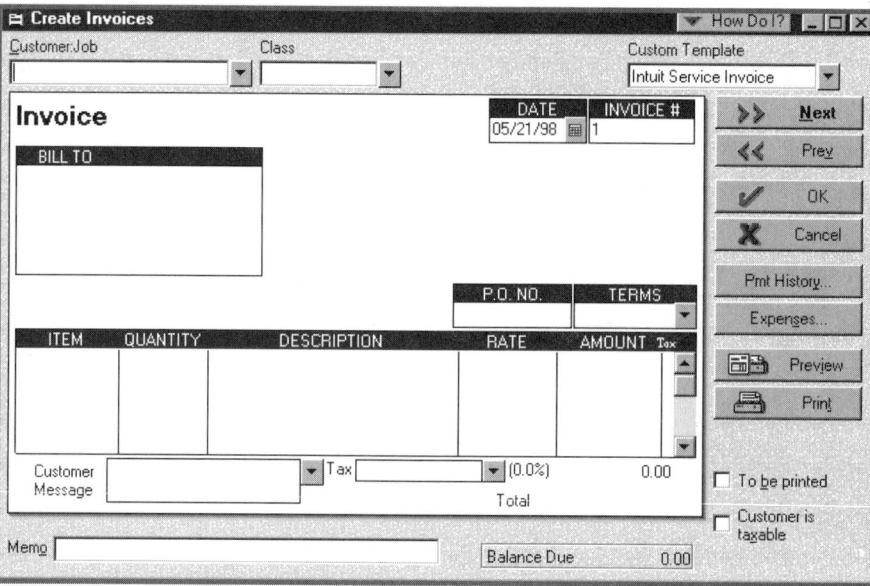

Figure 2.10

Using the Create Invoices dialog box, you choose the Customer: Job and enter the information necessary to bill your customers.

3. Click on the down arrow to the right of Customer: Job and select the customer for which you are creating the invoice. Press Tab.

4. If you want to create a class or use a classification you've already created, enter it in the Class box. Press Tab.

5. Choose the template you want to use for the invoice. Intuit Service Invoice is selected by default if you set up your company as a service business during the EasyStep Interview.

CHECKING OUT INTUIT INVOICE TEMPLATES

Intuit includes three different invoice templates you can use to create your own invoices:

- The Intuit Product Invoice includes the greatest number of information items, with spaces for shipping information, quantity, sales tax, and more.

- The Intuit Professional Invoice is a simple invoice that includes only ITEM, DESCRIPTION, QTY, RATE, and Amount tax.

- The Intuit Service Invoice is similar to the Professional Invoice, except that it includes a place for the PO (purchase order) number.

SATURDAY MORNING Tracking and Recording Sales

TIP If you have information you want to include with the customer file but not print on the invoice, click in the Memo field and type the notation. The information will print on any customer statements and accounts receivable information, however.

6. Enter the rest of the information on the invoice as needed. Figure 2.11 shows an invoice The Write Company prepared for Llewelyn Printing.

7. To enter information for the next invoice, click on the Next button. If you are finished with the invoice, click on Preview to see how the invoice will look when printed.

8. Click on Print, and the invoice is sent to the printer.

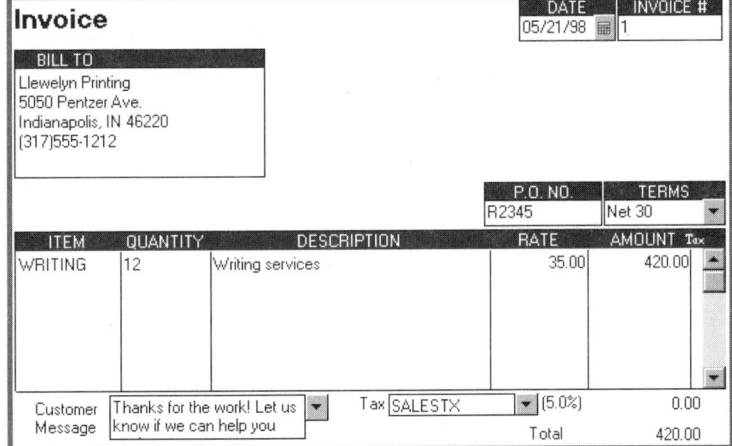

Figure 2.11

The Write Company uses the Intuit Service Invoice to bill for writing and training services.

TIP If you are creating several invoices and want to print them all at once, click on the To Be Printed check box to save the invoice for printing later.

NOTE If you have expenses you need to be reimbursed for and want to include that information on the invoice, click on the Expenses button in the Create Invoices dialog box. A pop-up window appears, allowing you to enter the expenses and choose how you want the items listed on the invoice. Examples of reimbursable expenses might be travel expenses, postage, and supply purchases.

Figuring Finance Charges

The next step in the process of billing customers is figuring in finance charges. This may not apply to your business, so you can skip ahead to the next session (or get yourself a chocolate chip cookie and a fresh cup of coffee) if finance charges are not something you need to be concerned about.

TIP When do finance charges matter? Different businesses have different finance charge arrangements, but basically finances charges are used when a relatively large balance is carried from month to month on a customer's account.

How QuickBooks Figures Finance Charges

When you set up QuickBooks to figure finance charges for you, the program uses the following formula to determine the amount:

```
# days past due x amount due x interest rate / 365
```

This means that if Davis Printing is 60 days past due on an amount of $250 and you charge an interest rate of 12 percent, the formula looks like this:

```
60 x 250 x .12 / 365
```

SATURDAY MORNING Tracking and Recording Sales

Setting Up Finance Charges

To set up the finance charge component of QuickBooks, follow these steps:

1. Display the QuickBooks Navigator and make sure the Sales and Customers tab is selected.

2. In the graphic displayed in the Navigator window, click on Finance Charges. A pop-up box asks whether you want to set up finance charges now. Click on Yes.

3. QuickBooks displays the Preferences dialog box with the Finance Charges item selected (see Figure 2.12). Enter the Annual Interest Rate, the Minimum Finance Charge, the Grace Period, and the other finance charge–related settings in the displayed dialog box.

4. Do you want to add finance charges to the finance charges if payment is overdue? If so, click on the check box that enables you to assess finance charges on overdue finance charges.

Figure 2.12

You can set up the finance charge information by entering the interest rate, minimum charge, grace period, and date when you want to calculate the charges.

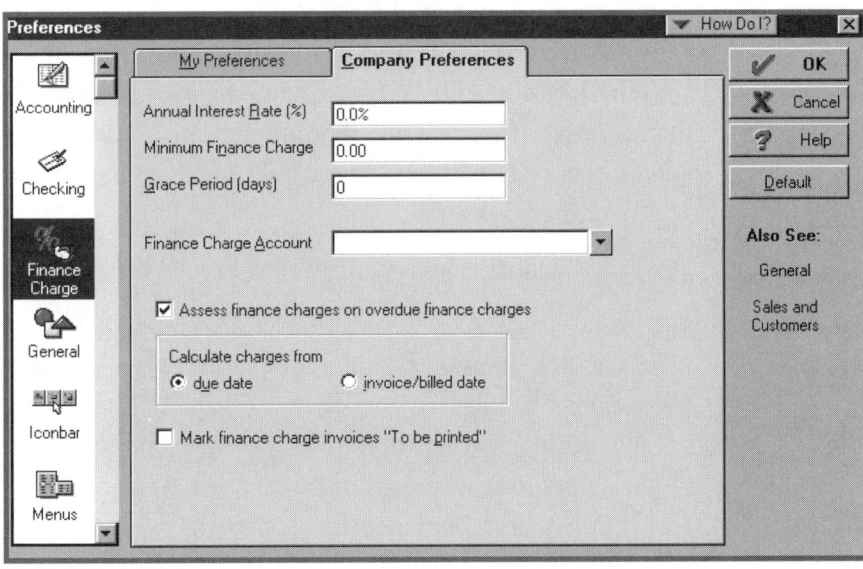

CAUTION Adding finance charges on top of finance charges is not a legal practice in all states. Check with your accountant or legal advisor to find out the laws about finance charges in your area.

5. You also need to choose from which point you want to begin calculating the interest. You can elect to do the calculations from the invoice due date or from the billing date.

6. Again, if you want the invoice to be saved to a queue for later printing, click on the check box for Mark Finance Charge Invoices "To Be Printed."

7. Click on OK when you have finished entering the finance charge information. Now you are ready to apply finance charges to those customer accounts with outstanding balances.

Assessing Finance Charges

Once you set up QuickBooks to handle the finance charges for you, you simply need to create and send invoices as usual and record the payments when they come in (you learn to do that after the break). QuickBooks takes care of figuring out that a payment is late and attaching the finance charge as needed. Here's how to tell QuickBooks to assess the finance charges on overdue accounts:

1. When the Customer: Job list box is displayed, click on the Activities button. The submenu appears.

2. Click on Assess Finance Charges. The Assess Finance Charges dialog box appears, as shown in Figure 2.13. The names of the delinquent accounts are displayed in the Customer column, and the amount of the finance charge, as of the current date, is calculated and applied to the total balance.

SATURDAY MORNING Tracking and Recording Sales

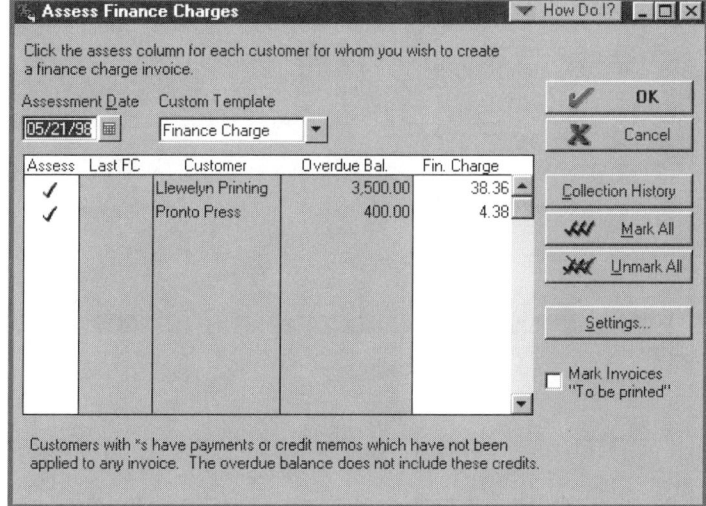

Figure 2.13

The Assess Finance Charges dialog box shows you the customers that have past due amounts in their accounts.

3. If you want to print a finance charge invoice for the clients, make sure that the customer line is selected in the Assess column.

4. Click on OK. You are returned to the Customer: Job list box, and when you print invoices, the finance charge invoice for the overdue customer accounts will print as well. Figure 2.14 shows an example of a finance charge invoice that is prepared for printing along with the regular customer invoice.

Printing Mailing Labels and Invoices

Ready to print? If you've been selecting the To Be Printed check box as you create your invoices, you may have a whole slew of pages to be printed. The customer addresses are pasted into the invoices automatically. (QuickBooks retrieves them from the customer information you filled out in the New Customer dialog box.) What if you want to print mailing labels or the envelopes to hold the invoices you are going to mail? In this section, you learn to use QuickBooks' mail merge feature so that you can finish off those invoices and get them in the mail today.

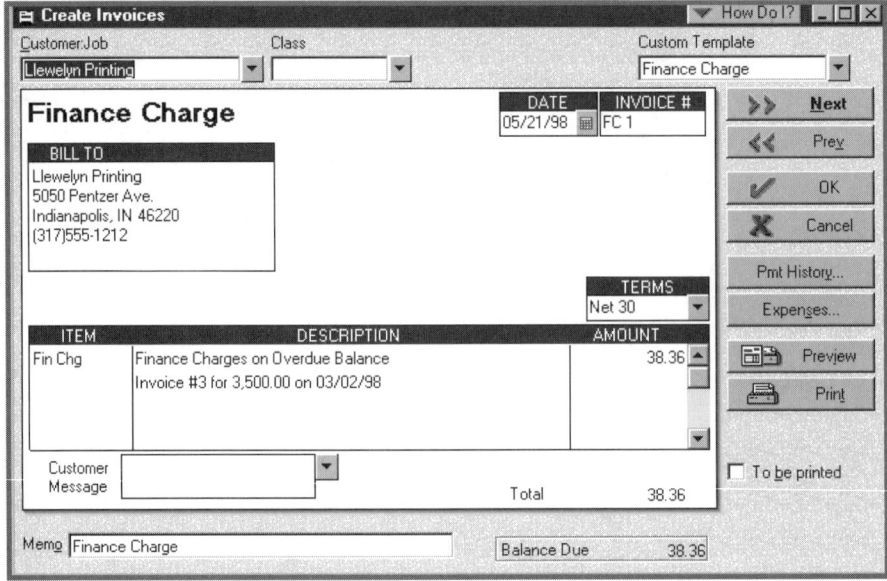

Figure 2.14

QuickBooks prepares a finance charge invoice to bill the customer for the finance charges on the past due amount.

Creating Mailing Labels

QuickBooks makes it easy for you to print mailing labels to go along with your invoices. You need to print them first, however—before you print the invoices themselves. This way, QuickBooks prints one mailing label for each customer instead of printing multiple mailing labels for those customers who have more than one invoice.

To print mailing labels to go along with the invoices, follow these steps:

1. Open the File menu and choose Print Forms. A pop-up menu appears, as Figure 2.15 shows.

2. Choose Print Mailing Labels. The Select Mailing Labels to Print dialog box appears, as Figure 2.16 shows.

3. Choose the group for which you want to print the mailing labels. You can choose all names or specify a customer or vendor type. For example, if The Write Company were sending out a special notice advertising a sale for customers who use their writing services, they could print labels for only that customer type by clicking on the Customer Type option and choosing WRITING from the drop-down list.

Figure 2.15

QuickBooks gives you a whole smorgasbord of forms to print when you select Print Forms from the File menu.

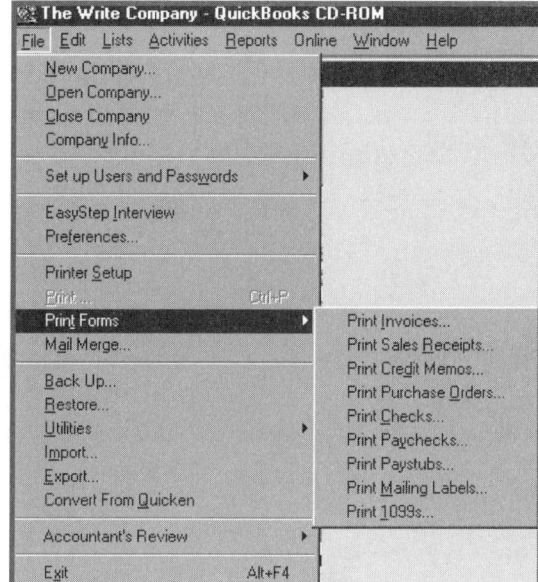

Figure 2.16

The Select Mailing Labels to Print dialog box gives you the options of choosing all customer names, selecting specific names, and printing labels for Ship To addresses.

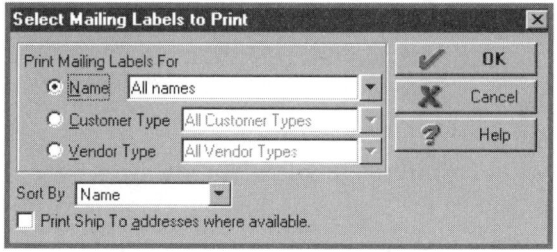

TIP You also can print labels for selected names. In the Select Mailing Labels to Print dialog box, click on the down arrow to the right of the Name field and click on Selected Names. The Select Names dialog box appears. You can then click on the names you want to include. A check mark appears to the left of each name. Click on OK when you've selected all necessary names.

4. Select how you want the labels sorted—by name or by postal code.

5. If you want the Ship To address to be printed in place of the company address, click on the check box in front of Print Ship To Addresses Where Available.

6. Click on OK. The dialog box closes and the Print Labels dialog box appears (see Figure 2.17).

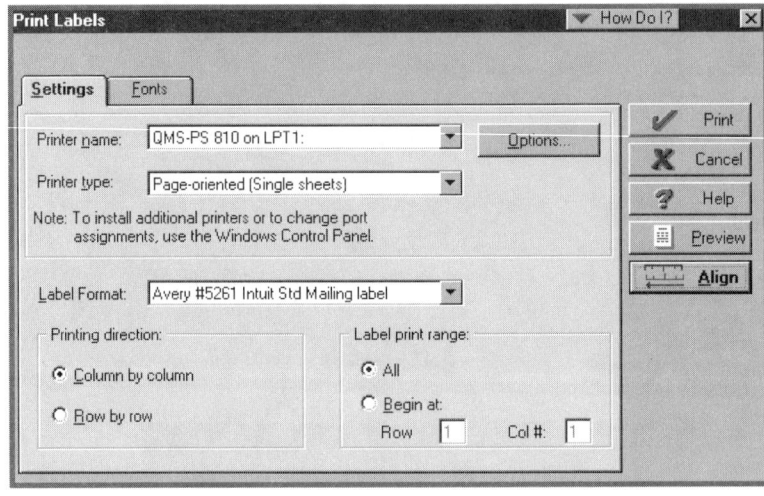

Figure 2.17

The Print Labels dialog box gathers the necessary information about the type of labels you are printing and the printer you are using.

7. Choose the printer you will use by clicking on the name in the Printer Name list.

8. Click in the Label Format field and choose the type of labels you have loaded in your printer. If you are unsure about the type of labels you are using, check the label package to look for the identifying number.

9. Choose the printing direction for the labels. If you choose Column by Column, QuickBooks first prints the columns down the page and then starts back up at the top of the second column and continues down the page. If you select Row by Row, QuickBooks prints

SATURDAY MORNING **Tracking and Recording Sales**

the labels across the page from left to right and then starts the second row at the left edge of the labels sheet.

10. Choose the range for the labels you want to print. In most cases, selecting All is sufficient. If you have a partial page of labels, you can elect to begin printing at a specific row and column. But good luck! Printing labels can be a challenge even under the best conditions. Be prepared to waste a page or two on a test run.

TIP Always do a print test on a regular sheet of 8 ½ × 11 inch paper to check the position of the labels and make sure that they are printing in the right width and depth. After the page prints, hold it up against your mailing labels to do a quick check that all the information will fit the way you've set it up in QuickBooks.

11. When you are ready, click on Preview. QuickBooks prepares the page for you and displays it on your monitor. Use the various tools in the Preview window to navigate in that view. Click on Close when you've finished previewing the labels.

12. Click on Print to begin printing. After a moment or two, your labels are done and ready to be affixed to the outgoing invoices. Next you will print the invoices you prepared in the preceding sections.

NOTE You can change the font used to print the labels if you like. When the Print Labels dialog box is displayed, click on the Fonts tab and click on the Font button. You can then choose the font you want to use and click on OK.

Aligning Labels

Even with all this preliminary planning, it's possible that once you preview or print the labels, they won't be exactly where you want them. You can use QuickBooks' Align feature to fine-tune the placement of the text on the labels.

WORKING WITH PREVIEW MODE

Printing doesn't have to be a risky business. You can make fairly certain that your documents will look the way you intend them to by previewing them first. Preview mode is a simple feature that displays your document as it will appear when printed. You display the document in Preview mode by clicking on the Preview button that appears in the Print dialog boxes. When you are working in Preview mode, you will use the following buttons:

- **Print** sends the page to the printer.
- **Prev Page** displays the previous page of the document.
- **Next Page** displays the next page of the document.
- **Zoom In** magnifies the page so that you can see text more clearly. This button changes to Zoom Out when you have magnified the page. (You can also use the mouse pointer to do this; simply point to the area you want to magnify and click on the mouse button. The display zooms in. To zoom out, click on the mouse button a second time.)
- **Help** displays a help window that explains Preview mode.
- **Close** closes Preview mode and returns you to the QuickBooks screen.

CAUTION Before you change the alignment of the labels, be sure you are putting the labels into the printer correctly. If the page was just a little too far to the right or left because of the way you inserted the sheet, the rest of your labels will be off when you print subsequent pages. Make sure the feed is straight and just where you want it before you use Align.

To adjust the alignment of your labels, follow these steps:

1. Display the Print Labels dialog box using the procedure described in the preceding section.
2. Preview the labels to see in which direction they need to be aligned. Close Preview mode when you are finished.

3. Click on the Align button. The Fine Alignment dialog box appears, as shown in Figure 2.18.

4. Make sure your printer is online and ready. Load a sheet of regular 8 ½ × 11 inch paper in it (don't use the labels yet). Click on Print Sample, and QuickBooks prints a grid you can use to determine how much adjusting the page needs.

5. Enter the new values for the alignment. Remember that each point moves the alignment 1/100 of an inch.

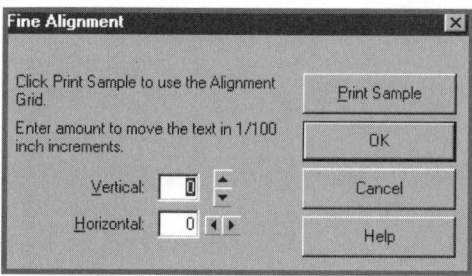

Figure 2.18

The Fine Alignment dialog box helps you fine-tune the placement of your mailing labels so that they print just the way you want them.

TIP For best results, preview the labels again after you make the alignment changes. When the labels are positioned the way you want them, click on Print.

Printing Invoices

Okay, you've taken care of the outside of the envelope—now you need to print the invoices themselves. When you're ready to print the invoices, follow these steps:

1. Make sure the printer is loaded with paper and turned on.

2. Open the File menu and choose Print Forms. The printing submenu appears.

THE SCOOP ON TEMPLATES

QuickBooks includes a number of templates you can use as the basis for forms and documents you print. To see the templates QuickBooks has available, open the Lists menu and choose Templates. By default, QuickBooks comes with the following templates:

- Finance Charge
- Intuit Product Invoice
- Intuit Professional Invoice
- Custom Credit Memo
- Custom Cash Sale
- Intuit Standard Statement

You can use the templates as they are or modify them to suit your needs and resave them as templates you can use over and over again. To modify an existing template, click on the template you want in the Templates list box, click on the Templates button, and click on Edit. You can then use the Layout Designer to change the template to fit your business needs or make changes manually on your own.

Need to know more about templates? To find out more about working with templates in QuickBooks, open the Help menu, choose Help Index, and type *templates*. The section "Templates for business forms" gives you more information on using, editing, and saving templates in QuickBooks.

3. Click on Print Invoices. The Select Invoices to Print dialog box appears, as Figure 2.19 shows. In this figure, all the invoices are currently selected to be printed. All invoices with check marks in the first column will be printed. To deselect invoices, click in the leftmost column to remove the check mark.

TIP Notice that the Print Mailing Labels button is also available in the Select Invoices to Print dialog box. You can prepare the labels from this point if you choose. Click on the button to proceed to the Select Mailing Labels to Print dialog box and make your selections for the labels you want to print.

SATURDAY MORNING   **Tracking and Recording Sales**

Figure 2.19

The Select Invoices to Print dialog box shows you the invoices currently selected to print. Click to remove the check mark if you don't want an invoice to print.

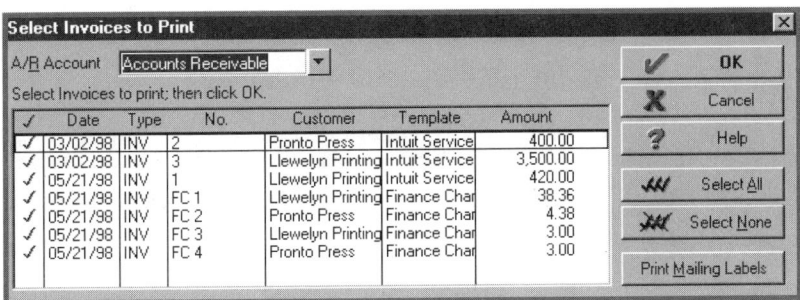

4. Click on OK, and the Print Invoices dialog box appears. Choose the print options you want. The major decisions involve the Printer Name you select (be sure you've selected the printer you're sending the invoices to) and what you plan to print on—preprinted forms, blank paper (this is the default), or your business letterhead.

5. If you select Blank Paper or Letterhead in the Print On settings, the Print Lines Around Each Field check box is enabled, meaning that you can select it. If you want lines to be printed around each field, click on this check box.

6. Click on Preview to see how the page will look when you print. If the page is ready to print, click on Print from Within Preview. If you need to make some adjustments, click on Close to Exit Preview and click on Align to change the alignment of the invoice.

7. When you're ready, click on Print. The invoices are sent to the printer as marked.

TIP When you are printing invoices for the first time, print only one invoice to get an idea of how your particular printer positions the document on the page without printing all invoices the first time through. That way you can make adjustments easily—without a great loss of time or paper—and print the entire batch when you have the printer set up just the way you want it.

Take a Break

Well, you've had quite a workout this morning! You began the day entering your customer information—important pieces of data that will help you serve your clients more professionally and make your business tasks easier. Next you discovered how to prepare and print invoices and mailing labels. All these tasks have been concerned with billing the customer; the next step involves recording the payments once the invoices have done their jobs and the money starts pouring in.

For now though, stand up, stretch, and take a break. Get yourself a cold drink, maybe have a little snack so that your brain is still plugged in for the afternoon. When you've had a few minutes away from your desk, come back and get started entering those payments in your QuickBooks system.

Recording Payments

Making money may not be the only reason you're in business, but chances are it's right up there on the list. After all, you've got to make money to stay in business, and the more money you have to work with, the better. This session helps you enter and keep track of the payments you receive.

Receiving Payments from Your Invoices

The next stop on the Sales and Customers tab is Receive Payments. This part of the program enables you to record and track customer payments. Here are the steps for receiving and recording payments:

1. Make sure the Sales and Customers tab is selected.

2. Click on Receive Payments. The Receive Payments dialog box appears, as Figure 2.20 shows.

3. Click on the down arrow beside Customer Name and choose the customer who is making the payment. Outstanding invoices appear in the window at the bottom of the dialog box.

4. Change the date if the date for which you are entering payments is different from today's date.

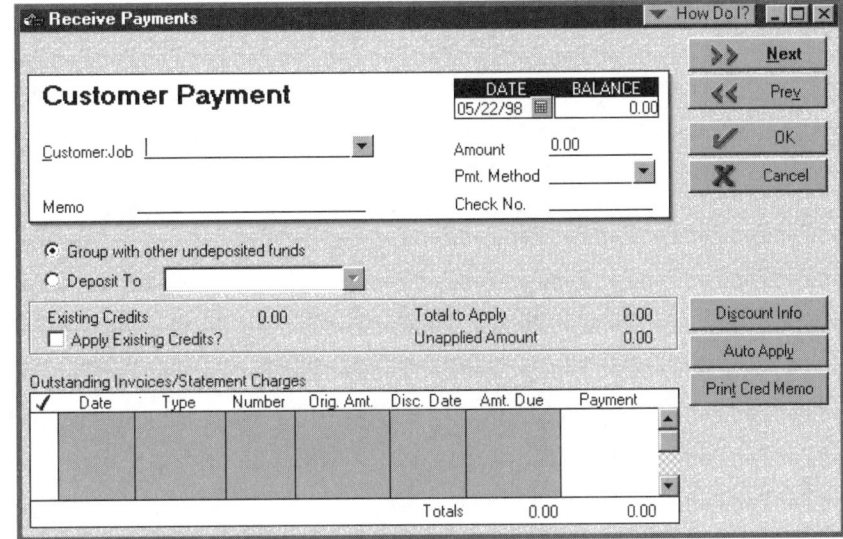

Figure 2.20

When you receive a payment from a customer, you use the Receive Payments dialog box to record the payment and apply it to outstanding balances.

5. Enter the amount of the payment. Press Tab. The cursor moves to the Pmt. Method field.

6. Click on the down arrow. QuickBooks gives you the choice of American Express, Cash, Check, Discover, MasterCard, or VISA. If the customer paid in a method other than one of those, click on Add New and specify that method of payment. In this example, The Write Company chooses Check as the method of payment. Press Tab.

7. Enter the check number if the customer paid with a check.

8. If you want to enter a memo notation about this payment, click in the Memo field and type the text; otherwise, move on to the deposit settings.

9. You can choose to group the payment with other undeposited funds, or you can go ahead and choose to deposit the payment to a specific account.

TIP Use the Group with Other Undeposited Funds option when you plan to deposit several payments at once. You then use the Make Deposits command in the Activities menu to deposit the entire amount. You learn to make deposits later in this morning's session.

10. If you want to set up a discount amount for the customer (perhaps the client paid for his service six months in advance to get a special discount), click on the Discount Info button and enter the pertinent discount information in the dialog box that appears.

11. You can choose to Apply Existing Credits if you have other credits, returns, or refunds due the customer. Click on the Apply Existing Credits check box.

12. If you want to clear payments you've entered, click on Clear Payments.

13. If you want to print a credit memo, click on Print Cred Memo. A credit memo, which you can give to your customer as a receipt, is sent to the printer.

14. Click on Next and continue entering payments for other customers. When you are finished entering payments, click on OK.

Entering Cash Sales

Handling cash and credit transactions is slightly different from handling purchases paid for by check. In the Sales and Customers tab, you see that Cash Sales has its own graphic. Click on it now, and the window shown in Figure 2.21 appears.

1. If you want the name and address of the client to appear in the Sold To box, click on the Customer: Job down arrow and select the client who just made the payment.

2. Enter the date for the transaction in the Date field.

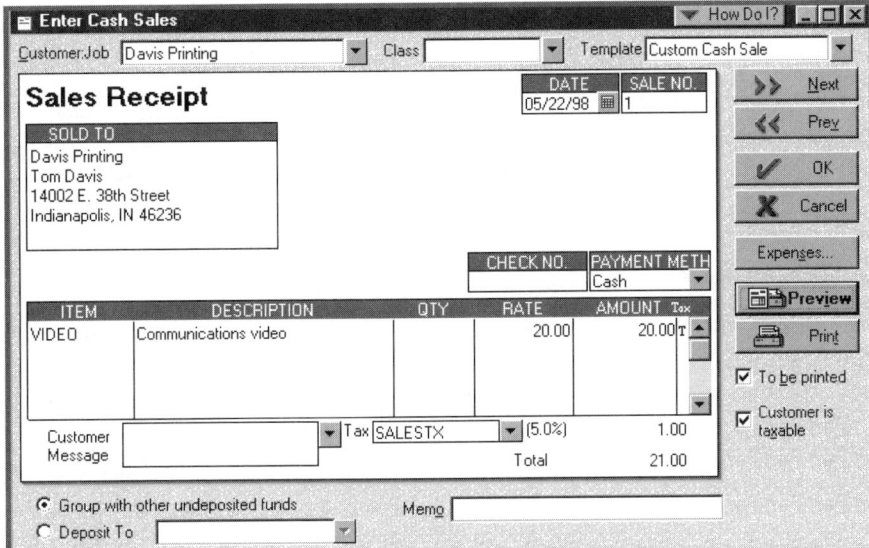

Figure 2.21

The Enter Cash Sales window displays a cash sales receipt you can print and give to your customers when they pay by cash or credit.

3. Click on the Payment Method field down arrow and choose how the customer made the payment.

4. Enter the Item (or select it from the list); QuickBooks fills in the rest of the information for that item.

5. Choose a Customer Message if you want one by clicking on the down arrow and making your choice or typing a new one.

6. Choose whether you want the payment added in with other undeposited funds or deposited into an account. By default, QuickBooks assigns the cash payments to undeposited funds.

7. Add memo text if necessary; click on the Customer Is Taxable check box if tax is added to the purchase.

8. Click on To Be Printed if you want the receipt to be queued for the printer. Then click on Preview to see how the receipt will look when printed.

9. If you want to print the receipt immediately, make sure that To Be Printed is *not* selected and then click on Print to send the receipt to the printer.

10. Click on Next if you want to enter other cash or credit payments; Click on OK when you want to close the Enter Cash Sales dialog box.

Making Deposits

If you select Group with Other Undeposited Funds when you record customer payments, you need to make the deposit to the appropriate account. Here's how:

1. In the Sales and Customer tab, click on Deposits. The Payments to Deposit dialog box appears, as you see in Figure 2.22.

2. Click in the leftmost column to add a check mark beside those payments you want to deposit. When you're finished, click on OK. The Make Deposits dialog box appears, showing you the payments you have elected to deposit.

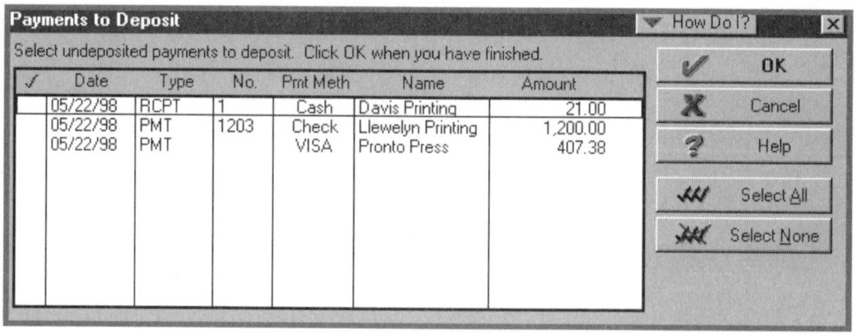

Figure 2.22

When you click on Deposits in the Sales and Customer tab, QuickBooks shows you the payments you have entered that have yet to be deposited.

3. Choose the account to which you want to deposit the payments. Checking is the account selected by default.

4. Make sure the date is the date you want to record the transaction.

5. Review the deposits listed. You also can add payments at this point by clicking in the Received From column beneath the last entry and typing a new entry.

If you want to edit any of the payment information while the Make Deposits dialog box is displayed, click on the Pmts button. The payments are displayed in the Payments to Deposit dialog box, and you can make your necessary changes. Click on OK to return to the Make Deposits dialog box.

Using Credit Memos

Well, you can't make all of the people happy all of the time. There will be times when a customer wants to return something you've sold or asks for a refund on services he no longer wants. This involves the cash flowing in a direction opposite the one you've explored thus far this morning. Now you need a credit memo. Here's how to create one:

1. Start in the Navigator with the Sales and Customer tab selected.

2. Click on the Refunds and Credits graphic to display the Create Credit Memos/Refunds dialog box (see Figure 2.23).

3. Click on the Customer: Job down arrow and choose the customer name. QuickBooks fills in the address information. Press Tab.

4. Make sure the date is correct.

5. Click on the Item down arrow and choose the item for which the refund is being paid.

6. Type a reason for the return in the Memo field.

7. If you want to write a refund check, click on Refund. The Write Checks dialog box appears. You will learn about writing checks in QuickBooks in this afternoon's session.

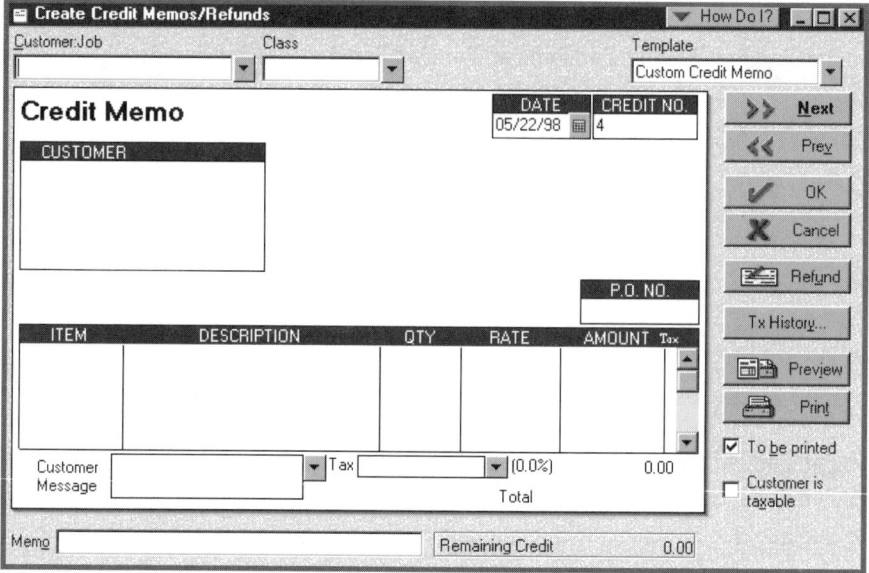

Figure 2.23

You create a Credit Memo to document the transaction when you need to refund a payment or return an item to inventory.

8. Click on Preview to see how the credit memo will look when printed. If you want to print the memo now, click on Print from the Preview window. If you want to add the memo to a print list to be printed later, click on Close to close Preview and then click on To Be Printed in the Credit Memo dialog box.

9. If you want to create additional credit memos, click on Next. To close the Create Credit Memos/Refunds dialog box, click on OK.

Checking the Customer Register

The final stop you'll make in this morning's session is to the Customer Register. You started off this morning with techniques to help you enter and organize your customer data; now you come full circle to the point of reviewing and working with transactions for those customers.

The Customer Register looks similar to a check register. But instead of mixing all customers together in one long columnar display, the Customer Register helps you get a good look at data related to a particular client. One example of the Customer Register appears in Figure 2.24.

SATURDAY MORNING   **Tracking and Recording Sales**

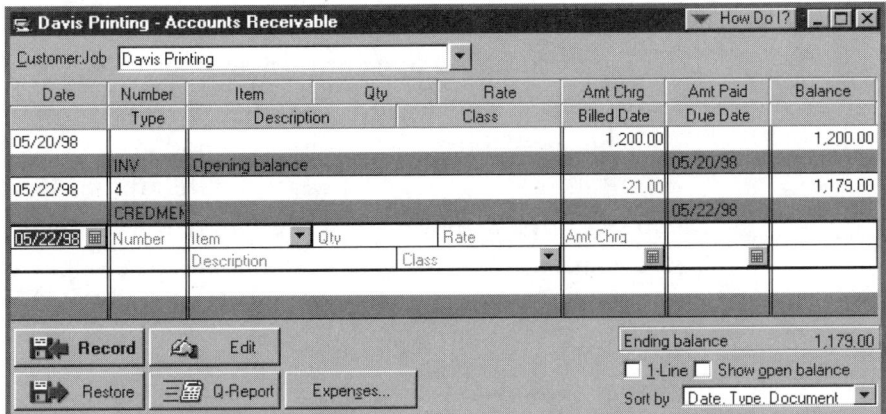

Figure 2.24

The Customer Register lists transactions for individual customers.

The Customer Register for Davis Printing shows the opening balance and, most recently, the credit memo issued when the company returned a duplicate copy of the training video.

To use the Customer Register:

1. In the Sales and Customers tab, click on Customer Register (in the top row of icons). The register appears.

2. Click on the Customer: Job down arrow and choose the name of the client for which you want to display the register. Once the register is displayed, you can add entries, edit existing entries, print a quick report, add expenses, and sort the information in a variety of ways. When you are finished using the Customer Register, click on the Close box.

 Although you can enter all your transactions in the Customer Register, for best results, enter sales using the Receive Payments and Cash Sales icons. This helps make sure you enter all necessary information items.

What's Next?

All right! You've made it through another work session. As you can see, there's a lot to learn and a lot to enter in QuickBooks as you computerize your business. But you should feel good about what you've already accomplished—you've covered essential terrain in the time from that first cup of coffee to now: you have entered and organized your customer information and learned to both bill and receive payments from customers. That's the major part of a successful framework for using QuickBooks effectively.

This afternoon's session focuses on money going out—check writing and bill paying. Specifically, you learn the following things:

- Knowing *when* to write a check
- Adding vendors to your vendor list
- Writing the check
- Managing the checks you write
- Balancing your checkbook
- Understanding accounts payable
- Designing a bill-paying system
- Recording, editing, and deleting bills
- Handling sales tax

Now go fix yourself a sandwich or a salad and do a little stretching and relaxing. When you're ready for this afternoon's work session, come on back and you'll tackle the next big block of QuickBooks tasks.

Enjoy your lunch, and I'll see you shortly.

SATURDAY AFTERNOON

Writing the Check: Paying for Goods and Services

- Adding a New Vendor to Your List
- Writing Checks
- Balancing Your Checkbook
- Creating a Bill System with QuickBooks
- Creating Purchase Orders
- Editing Bill Payments

Business is as much about outgo as it is about income. You've heard the saying, "You've got to spend money to make money"? This afternoon's session focuses on ways you can use QuickBooks to help you organize and track what you spend and how you spend it. You explore the QuickBooks checkbook and learn to reconcile your account this afternoon; you also set up and begin using a bill paying system.

In this morning's session, you used the Sales and Customers tab to enter customer information, create invoices, and record payments. This session makes use of the next two tabs—Purchases and Vendors, and Checking and Credit Cards—to help you understand and organize the way you spend your money.

What Do You Write Checks For?

If you've been in business for a while—or perhaps even if you haven't—you probably have a clear sense of where your money goes. Depending on the nature of your business, you may write only a few checks a month, or you may write hundreds. Whether your check-management needs are simple or complex, QuickBooks can not only help you organize your entire check-writing system; the program can even write the checks for you.

Getting Checks

You can order computer checks from a variety of sources, and after you play around with the alignment in your printer a few times, you'll probably get those to work. But if you're going to be buying checks anyway, your

FIND IT ONLINE

best bet is to purchase your checks directly from Intuit. Simply go to Intuit's Web site at www.intuitmarket.com to check out the checks and learn how to order the ones you want.

There Are Other Ways to Pay

Check writing isn't the only way to pay a bill, of course. QuickBooks provides the means for you to pay using credit cards or cash, as well. And one of the hottest new features in QuickBooks 6.0 is the online component—now you can make payments online, paying and recording them at the same time. The process is fast and easy—and safe. On Sunday afternoon, you'll work through the "Online Banking with QuickBooks" session and discover how to set up and use online banking.

Getting Ready to Pay Bills

Before you get started, you need to get a few things together:

- Your most recent check register
- Your cancelled checks
- Copies of last month's paid bills (for the vendor names and addresses)
- Copies of your credit card bills
- Any accounts payable file you've been using

For the most part, you may need these items only for reference and to cross-check amounts and enter ordering information. Better to have them nearby than to have to go hunting for them in the middle of the session.

Two Ways to Pay Bills

There are two ways to pay bills in QuickBooks. The quick-and-dirty way is to simply use the QuickBooks Check Register to enter the checks you write, write the checks by hand, stick them in an envelope, and mail them. That's what I did for a long time—I simply used the check register and the balancing features to make sure I was accurate and on track with my accounts. Although this worked to help me make sure my account was balanced to the penny each month, I was only using a sliver of QuickBook's talent.

With a little investment of time and effort, you can set up QuickBooks to track an elaborate system of bills and payments for you. This allows you to keep your money in your business as long as possible and also sets up a bill-paying system that will streamline your "bill sessions" every month. You enter the vendor and bill information, and then you can have QuickBooks do the following things:

- Alert you when a bill is due
- Print the check and the mailing label
- Make the payment online
- Balance your checkbook
- Compare the bill and purchase order to make sure everything ordered is received
- Print reports about what's due when and what's been paid

TIP If you seem to have a mental block about paying a particular bill, add the bill to your To Do list. QuickBooks then displays the list when you start the program, reminding you that the bill is a priority item today. To add an item to your To Do list, open the Lists menu and choose To Do Notes. Press Ctrl+N, enter the name of the bill, and choose the date you want to be reminded in the Remind Me On box. Then click on OK.

In this session, you learn to do the quick method first—you will write the checks for bills you owe immediately and learn how to balance your checking account. Then, in the second half of the session (after the break), you will enter bills and set up a bill-paying system that uses the many features QuickBooks offers to get your bill paying in order.

Adding a New Vendor to Your List

The first step in setting up a bill-paying system, whether you're taking the quick approach or the longer road, is to enter the people or companies to whom you pay money. These companies are known as vendors because they sell you either supplies or services. You can add vendors all at once, entering the names and addresses and other pertinent information, or you can add them on the fly as you go along. I've done it both ways, but the best method is to enter the complete set of information, following these steps:

1. Click on the Purchases and Vendors tab in the QuickBooks Navigator.
2. Click on Vendors. The Vendor List box appears, as shown in Figure 3.1.
3. Click on the Vendor button and select New from the submenu. The New Vendor dialog box appears (see Figure 3.2).
4. Type a Vendor name and press Tab to get to the next field. Enter all the information you have for that vendor—including company name and address, contact numbers, and fax.
5. In the Print On Check As box, type the vendor name the way you want it to read on the check.

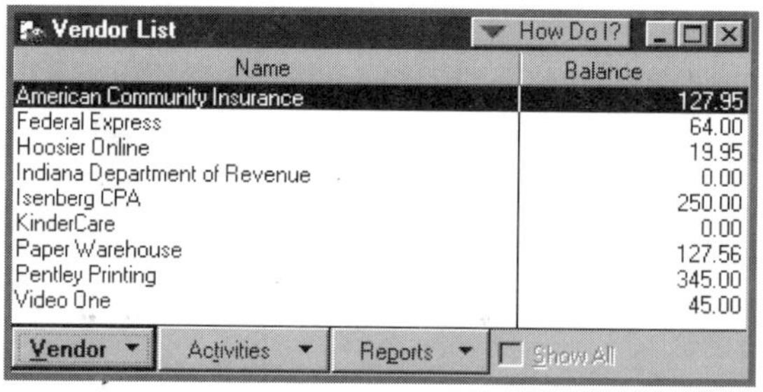
Vendor List
How Do I?
Name
Balance
American Community Insurance 127.95
Federal Express 64.00
Hoosier Online 19.95
Indiana Department of Revenue 0.00
Isenberg CPA 250.00
KinderCare 0.00
Paper Warehouse 127.56
Pentley Printing 345.00
Video One 45.00
Vendor
Activities
Reports
Show All

Figure 3.1

The Vendor List shows all the vendors you set up during the EasyStep Interview. You can easily add vendors to the list.

6. Click on the Additional Info tab. Enter the account number your business assigns to different vendors, and if you are tracking the type of vendor, you can click on the down arrow beside that box and make your selection.

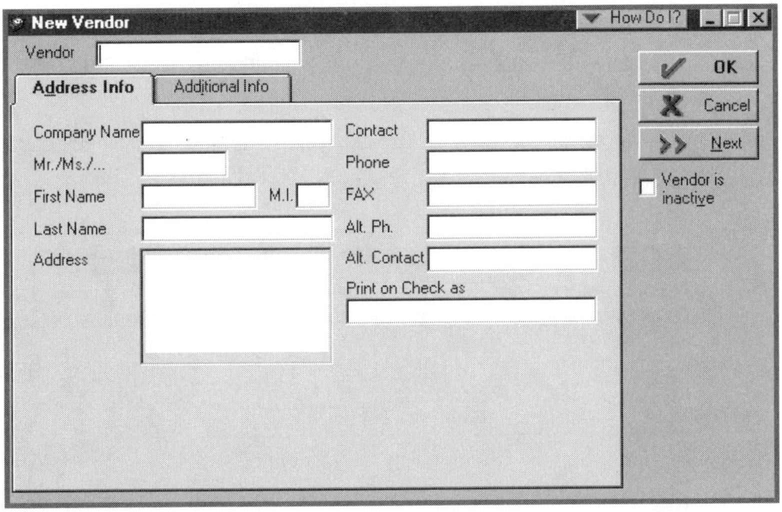

SATURDAY AFTERNOON   Writing the Check: Paying for Goods and Services

Figure 3.2

The New Vendor dialog box gives you the opportunity to enter all kinds of information about the companies that provide goods and services for your business.

> **TIP** In this morning's session, you learned how to define fields in the New Customer dialog box. The process is the same when you are working with the Additional Info tab of the Vendor dialog box; if you want to create your own fields to store information about your vendors, click on Define Fields and enter the field information on the page that appears.

7. To add another vendor, click on Next. To save this vendor's information and return to the QuickBooks Navigator, click on OK.

Writing Checks

The Check Register in QuickBooks resembles the old-fashioned one you are probably accustomed to using, with a few bells and whistles added. To begin writing checks, follow these steps:

1. Display the Vendor List box by clicking on Vendor.

2. Click on the Activities button at the bottom of the box. Choose the first option, Write Checks, from the submenu that appears. The Write Checks dialog box appears, as Figure 3.3 shows.

> **TIP** You can also display the Write Checks dialog box by clicking on the Checking and Credit Cards tab and clicking on Checks.

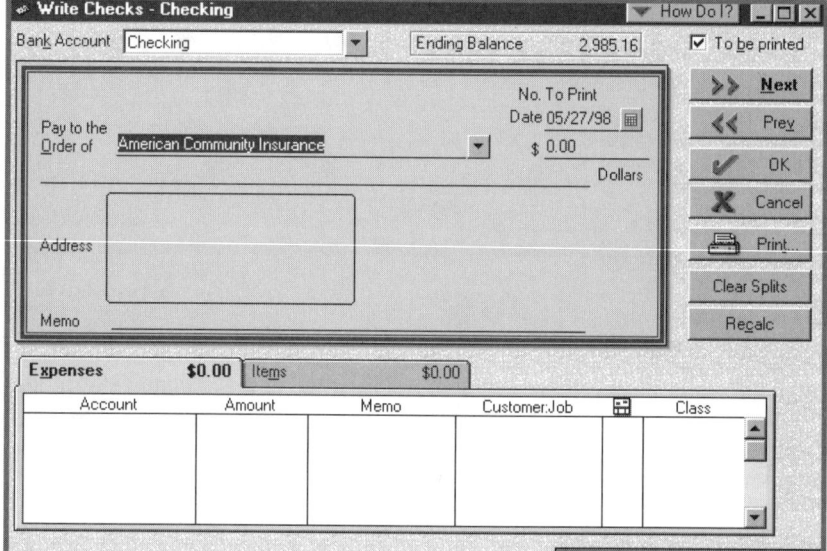

Figure 3.3

In the Write Checks dialog box, you make out the check and enter expense and item information.

3. Type in the Pay to the Order Of line the name of the vendor you want to write the check to. QuickBooks joins in and supplies the rest of the name after you enter a few characters. Press Tab.

4. Enter the amount. Press Tab. QuickBooks fills in the amount in longhand form on the line below.

5. If you have entered the vendor's address information, it appears automatically in the Address box. Otherwise, you need to type it in if you want to include it on the check. Press Tab.

6. Add text in the Memo field if necessary. Press Tab.

SATURDAY AFTERNOON Writing the Check: Paying for Goods and Services

7. Choose an account for the payment. The account for American Community Insurance, for example, is Disability insurance.

8. If you need to change the amount, add a memo, assign the amount to a specific Customer or Job, or specify a Class you have defined, click in the appropriate column and make the necessary change.

9. The To Be Printed check box is selected by default at the top of the dialog box; for now, leave it as is.

10. Click on Next to move to the next check or OK to close the dialog box and return to the Navigator.

TIP Later, when you have set up your bills using the Enter Bills dialog box, QuickBooks will alert you if you have a bill due when you open the Check Register and begin writing a check to a vendor.

Printing a Single Check

QuickBooks gives you the option of printing a single check quickly. You might do this, for example, when you're ready to pay a deposit for that new desk you've been wanting, or you decide to give to the charity that showed up on your doorstep.

To print a single check, display the Write Checks dialog box as explained in the previous section; instead of leaving the To Be Printed check box selected, however, click on the box to remove the check mark. Then click on Print; the Print Check dialog box appears (see Figure 3.4). Make sure the check number is correct and click on OK. The check is sent to the printer.

NOTE
FIND IT ONLINE Before you click on OK to send the check to the printer, make sure that your printer is online and ready and loaded with QuickBooks' checks. To find out more about the checks you can order directly from Intuit, see **www.intuitmarket.com**.

Figure 3.4

The Print Check dialog box enables you to print a check quickly, right after you enter it.

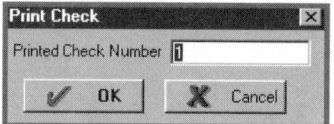

Entering Check Transactions

In the last section, you created checks much as you would write them. You can also enter them directly into the check register. Even if you use QuickBooks' Checking features only for the saving grace of the balancing capability, you can enter the checks you write by hand in the register to keep track of what's going on in the account. The register enables you to enter the checks quickly in a simple format. Here are the steps:

1. In the QuickBooks Navigator, click on Checking and Credit Cards and then click on the Check Register icon. The Open Check Register dialog box appears. Choose the checking account you want to use and click on OK. The Check Register opens, as Figure 3.5 shows.

2. Today's date is already entered for you. If you need to change the date, simply type the new one. Then press Tab.

3. The next check number in the sequence is filled in the Number column. Change this to reflect the number of the check you're recording.

SATURDAY AFTERNOON Writing the Check: Paying for Goods and Services

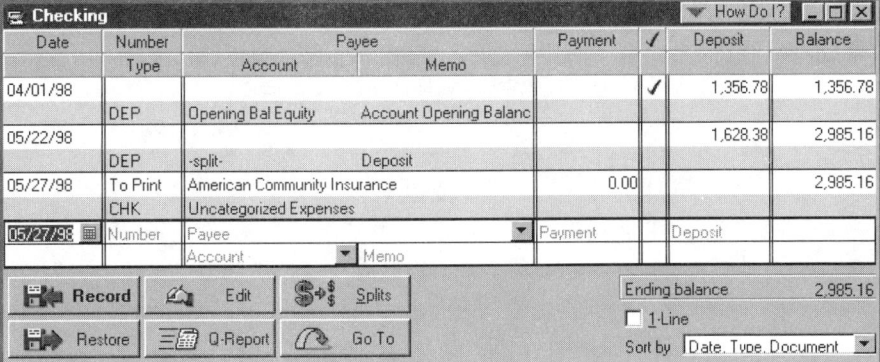

Figure 3.5

The Check Register gives you a quick way to enter checks you've already written out by hand.

 **NOTE** You can enter values other than numbers in the Number column. You might enter **ATM** for a transaction you did at an automatic transfer machine or **PHONE** if you did a phone transaction instead of writing a check.

4. In the Payee area, enter the name of the person or company to whom you're writing the check. As soon as QuickBooks recognizes the name you are typing, the program supplies the rest of the name. You can click on the down arrow and select the name from the list, as well. Press Tab when you're finished.

5. Enter the amount of the check. Press Tab.

6. Choose an expense account for the check. If you are purchasing supplies, for example, you might choose Office Supplies. Press Tab.

7. If you want to enter a memo, enter it in the Memo field. Otherwise, press Enter to record the check. QuickBooks makes a sound like a cash register sale and advances the cursor to the next line in the register.

> **DOES THAT SOUND DRIVE YOU CRAZY?**
>
> In my home office, every time my boys heard the cash-register sound, they would leave their Super Nintendo game and come rushing over, sure that I was playing a computer game. After three or four such trips, I decided to disable the sound. Here's how: Open the File menu and select Preferences. Choose the General icon and display the My Preferences tab. Click on the Beep When Recording a Transaction check box to remove the check mark. Click on OK to close the dialog box.

Adding Vendors As You Go

In the last example, you learned to enter a check transaction in the register. You had the option of typing the vendor name (also called the payee) or selecting it from a list. But there will be those times when you need to enter a check to a person or company just one time—like the time you hired the hauling company to come clear away the old broken TV sets your company needs to dispose of. Here's how to add a vendor quickly:

1. Display the check register. Enter the date and check number as usual. Press Tab.

2. When the cursor is in the Payee field, type the name of the new vendor (I used *Ralph's Refuse*). Press Tab. QuickBooks lets you know that this vendor is not on your Name list (see Figure 3.6). You have three options:

    - You can click on Quick Add if you want to add the name quickly with no additional information (this is what I need to do for Ralph's Refuse).

    - You can click on Set Up to display the New Vendor dialog box where you can enter all the vendor information (do this for vendors you will be working with repeatedly).

    - You can click on Cancel to cancel the operation and enter another name.

Figure 3.6

When QuickBooks sees a name it doesn't recognize, the program gives you the option of filling in complete vendor information for that person

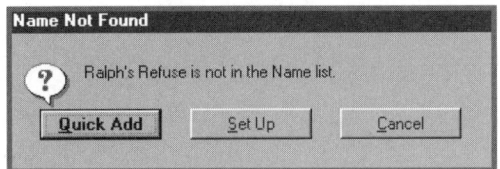

If you choose Quick Add, QuickBooks displays the Select Name Type dialog box (see Figure 3.7). This box displays four categories of name types from which you can choose the category that best describes the name you have entered. Click on the selection that applies and click on OK. QuickBooks adds the name to the list and advances the cursor to the next field in the register.

Figure 3.7

In the Select Name Type dialog box, you choose the category that best fits the name you are adding to your Name list.

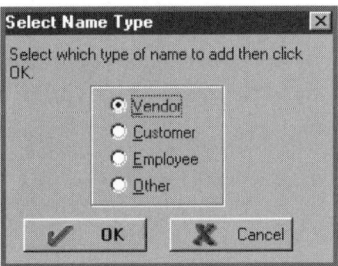

NOTE Most of the names you supply to Quick Add while using the Check Register will be Vendors. When you pay out one-time checks to employees, however, you may select Employees, and when you make contributions to charities, you may select Other.

Splitting Transactions

Sometimes transactions aren't quite as clean-cut as entering a name, an amount, and an Expense category, and then pressing Enter. What about those cases when you pay a vendor for supplies you use in two or more categories? Or an expense that is shared equally between two different jobs?

A *split transaction* is a transaction that is applied to two or more vendors, customers, or jobs. For example, you might pay a vendor both for services (trash removal) and for supplies (trash can deodorant). This would require a split transaction: the total amount of the check is divided into two expense categories: Janitorial and Office Supplies.

◄ ◄

These types of transactions are known as split transactions, and QuickBooks makes it easy for you to enter and track them. Here's how:

1. Display the check register.

2. Enter the date, the check number, the payee information, and the amount, pressing Tab after each.

3. When the cursor is in the Expense account field, click on the Splits button in the bottom portion of the register (refer to Figure 3.5 if you need to locate the Splits button). The Splits window opens so that you can enter the split information.

4. Select the first Expense account for the split (I selected Janitorial expense). Press Tab and enter the amount that needs to be applied to that portion of the check. In this example, I entered 30.00 for the Janitorial expense. The other 5.00 is the charge for the trash can deodorizer.

5. Enter text in the Memo field if you want to remind yourself what the split is all about. Press Tab. Also assign a Customer: Job, if that information applies to your transaction.

6. Press Tab again to move to the next line in the Splits window. Now you're going to enter the second Expense account for the split transaction.

SATURDAY AFTERNOON **Writing the Check: Paying for Goods and Services**

Click on the down arrow and select the account from the list. I chose Office Supplies.

7. Press Tab yet again and enter the amount for this portion of the split. If you enter an amount that doesn't add up to the total entered value for the check, QuickBooks will let you know. Figure 3.8 shows you the Splits window for the example I used. When you close the Splits window by clicking on Close, the word –split– appears in the Expense account field of the transaction.

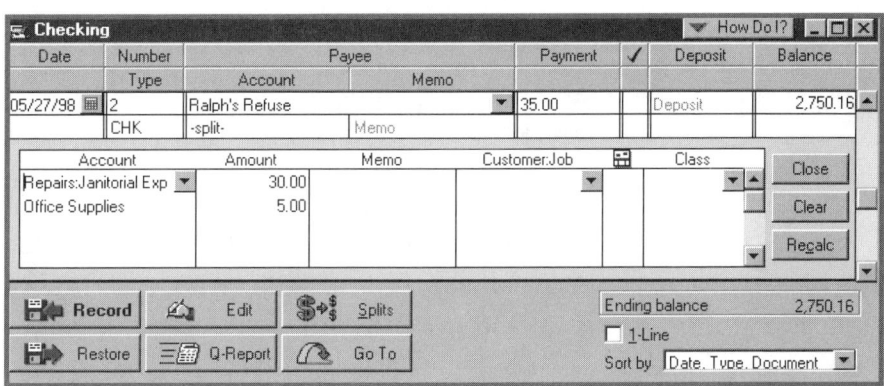

Figure 3.8

When you click on the Splits button, QuickBooks displays the Splits window so that you can divide the amount of the check into the appropriate categories or accounts.

TIP If you haven't yet figured the total amount of the check, you can have QuickBooks figure it for you. Before you enter the amount in the check register, click on Splits. Then enter the account (or job) and the amount assigned to each category. When you click on Close, QuickBooks totals the amounts and enters the value in the appropriate field on the check register.

Editing Transactions

The check register makes it easy for you to change anything you've entered. Whether you need to change an amount, a payee, a date, a check number, or an Expense account, you simply display the check register, select the check you want to change, click in the field where the edits will be made, and make your changes. Press Enter to record the change. QuickBooks will alert you that the data has changed and ask you to confirm that you want to change it. Click on Yes and the change is completed.

Voiding Checks

Who hasn't messed up a check? I know I have. Routinely. Whether you've misspelled a vendor name on a check you wrote by hand, entered the wrong amount, lost a check to a hungry printer, or had some other mishap cost you a check, you will eventually need to void a transaction you've already entered and issue a new check.

Follow these steps to void a check in QuickBooks:

1. Display the check register.

2. Select the check for the transaction you want to void.

3. Open the Edit menu and choose Void Check. QuickBooks zeros out the amount and adds the word VOID: to the Memo field (see Figure 3.9).

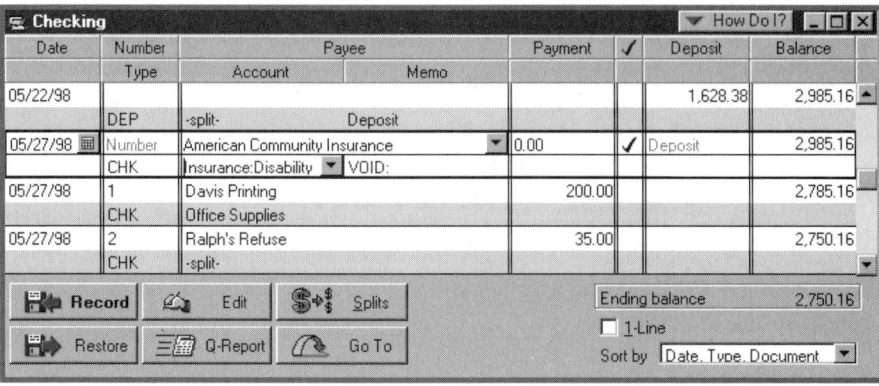

Figure 3.9

When you void a check, QuickBooks leaves the transaction in the register but zeros the amount.

4. Press Enter to record the transaction. Later, when you go to exit the register, QuickBooks will alert you that you changed a transaction and ask you to confirm that you do, indeed, want to make the change. Click on Yes to continue and return to the QuickBooks Navigator.

SATURDAY AFTERNOON   **Writing the Check: Paying for Goods and Services**   **131**

Getting a Reminder

You most likely pay different bills on different days, and you may need some kind of reminder when it's time to issue various checks. QuickBooks has a reminder feature built right in. This is a lifesaver for those likely to get swept away by other details in their business and who could space right through paying important things like light bills, phone bills, and rent.

To use QuickBooks' reminder feature to jog your memory about important bills that must be paid, follow these steps:

1. Open the File menu and choose the Preferences option. The Preferences dialog box appears.

2. Scroll down to the Reminders icon in the left side of the dialog box.

3. Click on the Company Preferences tab. This tab shows you all the reminders you can set in QuickBooks (see Figure 3.10). You can

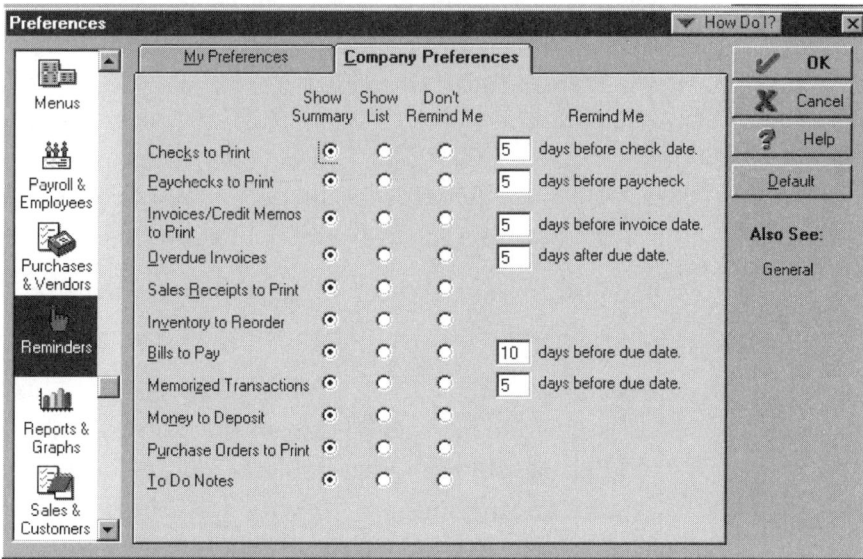

Figure 3.10

You can have QuickBooks remind you about a number of different tasks and specify the number of days in advance you want to be reminded.

choose which items you want to be reminded about, what you want to see as a reminder, and how many days before the date you want to be reminded.

4. Make sure that the Bills to Pay item is selected; then enter the number of days before the due date you want to be reminded.

5. Click on OK to set the reminders and close the Preferences dialog box.

Balancing Your Checkbook

The final task you'll tackle this afternoon before the break is balancing your checkbook. The first time you reconcile (as it's called) using QuickBooks may take you slightly longer than subsequent times, because this first trip through you've got to enter items from your bank statement to get everything started correctly. Even on a bad day, QuickBooks is so much easier than brain-and-calculator balancing that you won't even miss the few extra minutes you spend setting things up.

1. Display the check register.

2. Enter any checks you haven't yet recorded in QuickBooks.

3. Open the Activities menu and choose Reconcile. The Reconcile dialog box appears, as Figure 3.11 shows.

4. First, select the checking account you want to reconcile. If you have only one, this is a no-brainer.

5. Next, move to the Opening Balance field. This first time you balance your checkbook, this amount corresponds to the "real" opening balance of your QuickBooks account. The number you want here is the ending amount of your last bank statement. (This is why QuickBooks suggests you choose your QuickBooks Start Date to correspond with the end of a statement period.) If the number is different, you can go ahead and reconcile and then have QuickBooks adjust the balance at the end of the reconcile process.

SATURDAY AFTERNOON   Writing the Check: Paying for Goods and Services

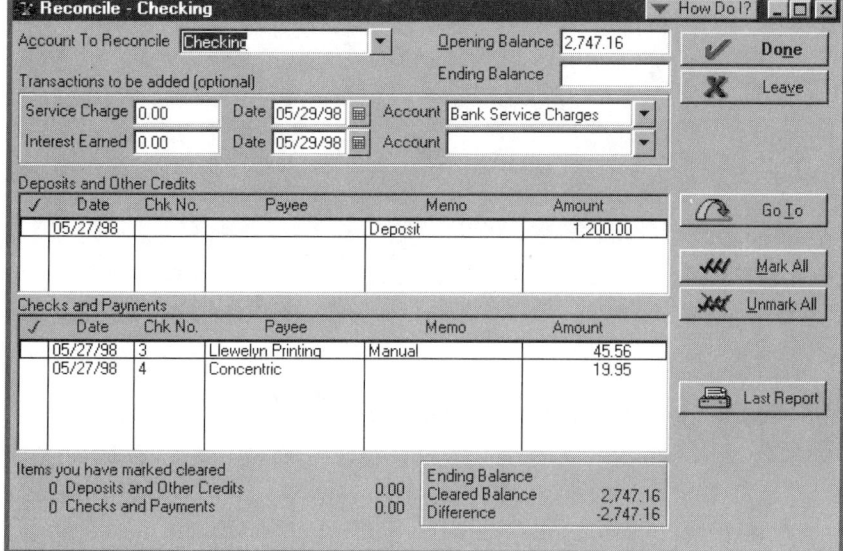

Figure 3.11

The Reconcile dialog box contains everything you need to balance your checking account—from tracking deposits to entering checks and service charges.

6. Enter the ending balance shown on your bank statement. Press Tab.

7. Enter the service charge and interest earned amount, pressing Tab after each. Be sure to enter the date on which the amounts are charged and specify an account for each.

8. In the Deposits and Other Credits area, select the deposits shown on your bank statement. Click in the left column to add a checkmark.

9. In the Checks and Payments area, click to add a check mark for each check that is shown as cleared on your bank statement.

10. When you are finished checking off items from your statement, click on Done.

Figure 3.12 shows the dialog box that appears after you reconcile your checking account and everything balances. Isn't that a nice feeling?

You have the option of printing a summary or a full report. You can also choose not to print a report at this time. Click on your choice and click on OK to return to the check register. Notice that the cleared checks are marked with checkmarks.

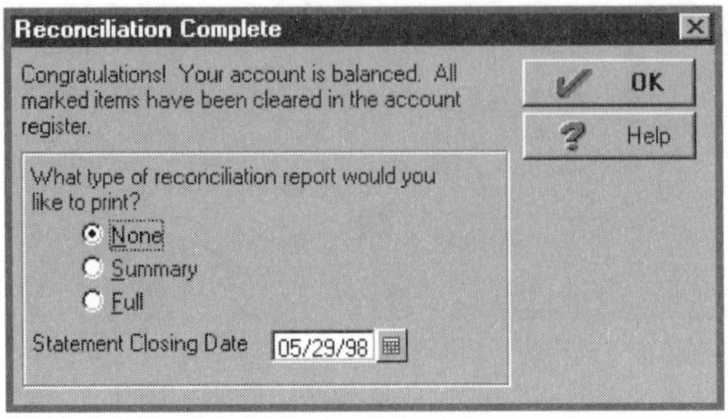

Figure 3.12

When everything balances, QuickBooks congratulates you and offers the option of printing a report.

What If You Need an Adjustment?

There may be times when your checkbook doesn't balance quite so simply. The first time you reconcile using QuickBooks may be such a case. If your Opening Balance needs an adjustment and your books don't balance the first time through, QuickBooks displays the dialog box shown in Figure 3.13 and gives you the option of adjusting the balance. Make your choice and click on OK to return to the check register.

Figure 3.13

If an adjustment needs to be made, QuickBooks tells you how much and gives you the option of returning to the register to try to find the problem.

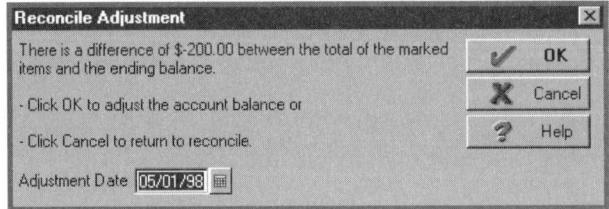

 Although it's not unusual to need to adjust your opening balance the first time you reconcile your account in QuickBooks, for best results, don't get too used to adjusting your balance every time things don't work out to the penny. Try to sleuth out the problem in the check register before you let QuickBooks readjust things for you.

When Things Don't Balance

When you reconcile your checkbook and things aren't balancing, look for these types of errors:

- Do the Opening and Ending Balances not match your bank statement?
- Did you forget to enter the service charge?
- Is there an interest amount you need to enter?
- Did you fail to select all the deposits that appear on your bank statement?
- Did you select *too many* deposits (in other words, you selected one that *isn't* shown on the bank statement)?
- Are the deposit amounts incorrect?
- In the Checks and Payments area, are any check values incorrect?
- Are there any additional automatic withdrawals you have not entered?
- Have there been additional service charges (such as a $0.50 ATM fee) you didn't add in your check register?
- Are you missing any checks?
- Have you selected checks other than those appearing as cleared on the bank statement?

In most cases, errors are simply typos—you transposed an amount, you left off a digit, or you entered an amount twice. (It's impossible to enter the same check twice—QuickBooks warns you about that—but you can erroneously enter the same amount more than once.)

Be prepared to go back to last month's statement (once you've been using QuickBooks for a while) to sleuth out imbalances. You can always go back to your last balanced statement and work forward from there.

Take a Break

Now you've been through the process of entering single checks and editing, voiding, and splitting transactions in the check register. You've also discovered how to balance your checkbook in QuickBooks. That's a lot for an afternoon, and you're only half done!

Take a few minutes now to get up and walk around and clear your head. Maybe play a round of Doom with your son, fix your daughter's flat, or get yourself some chips and a cold drink. When you're ready, come on back and get started creating and using a billing system in QuickBooks.

Creating a Bill System with QuickBooks

Earlier this afternoon, you learned that you can take care of bills two ways in QuickBooks. The first way is to do it quickly—just open the bill, write a check (and record it in QuickBooks), and mail the thing. The second way involves a more elaborate system of entering information and paying bills so that you make the most of the information available to you. The second way also helps you automate a number of things, and it increases the accuracy level of your transactions (meaning that once you get everything set up, there are fewer opportunities for entering things incorrectly).

When you set up QuickBooks' bill-paying feature, you work with purchase orders and bills. The process goes generally like this:

1. You need to buy something for your business. That something might be goods, or it might be services.

2. You create a purchase order for something you need. (In your business, you might call this a *requisition* instead of a *purchase order*.) QuickBooks helps you create, organize, and print purchase orders.

3. You order the item or services.

4. The services are performed or the goods are shipped by the vendor. They arrive with what might be called an *invoice* or a *packing slip*. You check to be sure you've received the services or goods you ordered by comparing what you receive against the information on your purchase order. QuickBooks helps you check the items against the purchase order to determine any missing or outstanding items.

SATURDAY AFTERNOON Writing the Check: Paying for Goods and Services 137

5. The vendor sends a bill to charge for the services or goods. QuickBooks enables you to record, track, and pay the bill after resolving that the services and goods you sought to purchase have been delivered satisfactorily. The remainder of the sections in this afternoon's session show you how to create this type of bill-paying system in QuickBooks. Ready?

Entering Bills

The first step in creating a billing system in QuickBooks involves logging in the bills you've got to pay. Here are the steps for entering your bills:

1. Click on the Purchases and Vendors tab in the QuickBooks Navigator.

2. Click on Enter Bills in the graphic. The Enter Bills dialog box appears, as Figure 3.14 shows.

3. Begin typing the name of the vendor to whom you want to make out the first bill. QuickBooks joins in as soon as the program recognizes the vendor name you're typing.

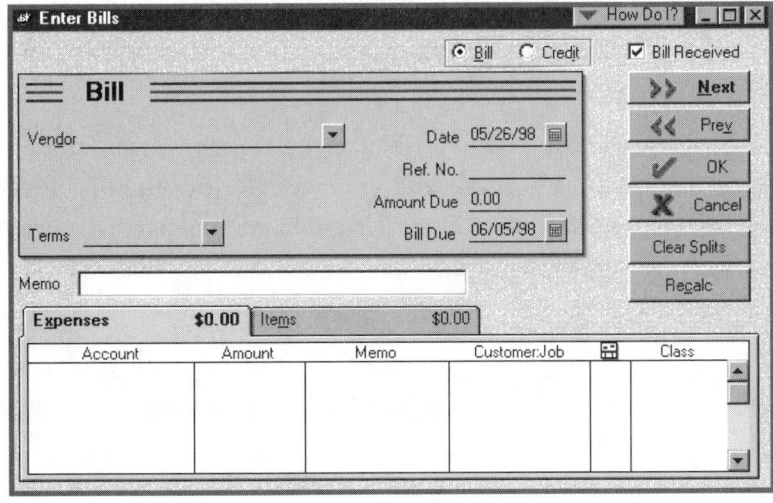

Figure 3.14

The Enter Bills dialog box allows you to track bills and specify when they are due.

TIP

You can add vendors on the fly, as you enter bills. Simply type the vendor name in the Vendor line. When you press Tab, QuickBooks alerts you that the name is not in the vendor list. You can then click on Quick Add to add the name, Set Up to display the New Vendor dialog box so that you can enter the full set of information; or Cancel to back out of the process.

4. Type the date you want to appear on the bill. Press Tab.

5. Enter the ref. no. and the amount due, pressing Tab after each.

6. Choose the terms the vendor has given you; press Tab.

7. Enter the date the bill is due.

8. The amount of the expense is entered in the Expense tab at the bottom of the dialog box. You can assign it to an account by clicking on the Account down arrow and choosing the appropriate account. Click in the Customer: Job column and enter the customer for whom the item was purchased. For example, if The Write Company purchases twelve binders to hold the training materials for the Llewelyn Printing Co., that company name is selected in the Customer: Job column.

9. If you want to itemize the things you purchased, you can click on the Items tab and enter a description, cost, and other information related to your purchase from this particular vendor. If you have a purchase order for this bill, you can select it by clicking on Select PO.

10. Click on Next to move to the next bill you want to enter; click on OK to close the Enter Bills dialog box and return to the QuickBooks Navigator.

Creating Purchase Orders

Once you enter the bills you are going to pay, you create purchase orders to track the services and goods you purchase. This gives you a means of monitoring where your money is going and whether you are getting what you are paying for.

> **BUZZ WORD**
>
> ◄
> A *purchase order* is a document that tracks an item or items you purchase from a vendor. The purchase order lists the number of items you want, the cost per item, and your total purchase amount. When you receive your order, you check the order against the purchase order to make sure everything is received. QuickBooks then marks the purchase order "Received" when all items have been checked in.
> ◄

Ready to create a purchase order? Then follow these steps:

1. Click on the Purchases and Vendors tab in the QuickBooks Navigator.

2. Click on Purchase Orders. The Create Purchase Orders dialog box appears, as Figure 3.15 shows.

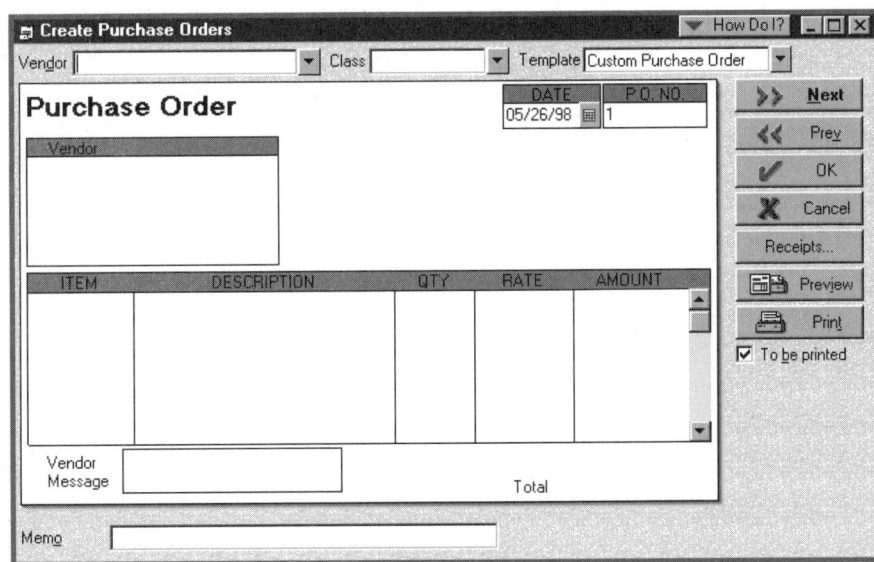

Figure 3.15

You use the Create Purchase Orders dialog box to create purchase orders for items you need in your business.

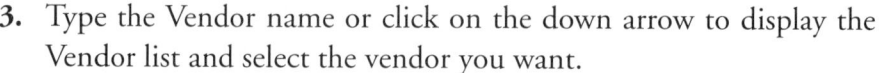

3. Type the Vendor name or click on the down arrow to display the Vendor list and select the vendor you want.

4. Click in the Item column and choose the item related to your purchase. QuickBooks fills in the Description and Rate columns based on the item you select.

5. Click in the Qty column and enter the number of units you want to purchase. QuickBooks recalculates the amount based on what you enter.

6. Click on Preview to see the purchase order before you print it; click on Close to return to the Create Purchase Orders dialog box.

7. Click on Print to send the purchase order to the printer; or, you can click on To Be Printed to have QuickBooks print the purchase order with other documents later.

8. To create additional purchase orders, click on Next. To close the dialog box and return to the QuickBooks Navigator, click on OK.

◂◂◂◂◂◂◂◂◂◂◂◂◂◂◂◂◂◂◂◂◂◂◂◂◂◂◂◂◂◂◂◂
In traditional account practices, you see the term *accounts payable* used to refer to anything you pay for in your business. It's the paying-out part of running your business.
◂◂◂◂◂◂◂◂◂◂◂◂◂◂◂◂◂◂◂◂◂◂◂◂◂◂◂◂◂◂◂◂

Receiving Goods

When you receive the items you ordered, you check them in and issue a receipt. QuickBooks helps you with this. Because different businesses deliver their services and goods in different ways, QuickBooks provides three different methods of receiving goods:

- **Receive Items.** For those times when you received the goods but not the bill.

- **Receive Items with Bill.** For those shipments when the bill and the goods came together.

- **Receive Bill.** For situations in which you received the goods and issued a receipt, and the bill arrived.

Receiving Goods First, Bill Later

When you receive a shipment of materials (for example, those binders you've waited on for weeks finally arrived!), sometimes they arrive with only a packing slip but no bill. You need to check the number of binders received against the number you ordered to make sure you are getting what you ordered, and you need to issue a receipt to the vendor so that you can begin using the items in your own business. Here are the steps:

1. From the QuickBooks Navigator, click on the Purchases and Vendors tab.

2. Click on Receive Items in the center of the Navigator graphic. The Create Item Receipts dialog box appears (see Figure 3.16).

Figure 3.16

When you receive your purchases before you receive the bill, select Receive Items and work in the Create Item Receipts dialog box.

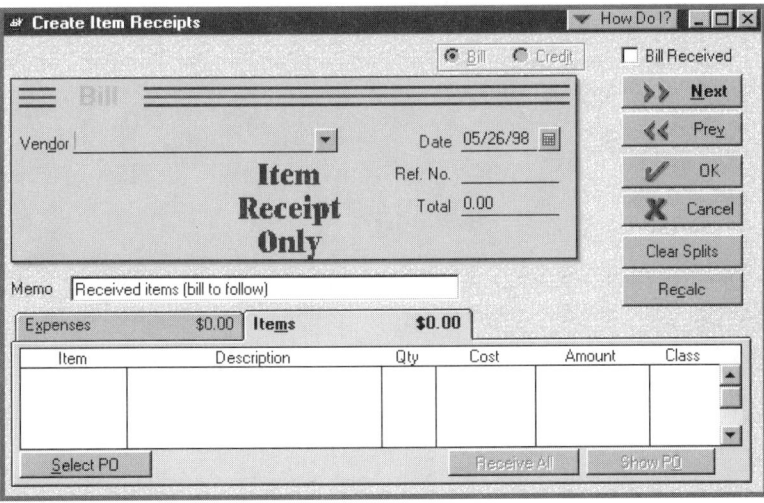

3. Choose the Vendor name. If you have an outstanding purchase order for that vendor, QuickBooks asks you whether you want to reconcile that order now. (See the next section for this process.) For now, click on No.

4. Enter the necessary information in the Expense and Items tabs. When you are finished creating the receipt, click on OK to return to the QuickBooks Navigator window.

NOTE You use Receive Items only when you have received the items but no bill. When the bill is received along with the goods, you use Receive Items with Bill. If you accidentally choose Receive Items and find you already have the bill, simply click on the Bill Received check box in the upper-right corner of the Create Item Receipt dialog box. The box changes to the Enter Bills dialog box, and you can enter the information as needed.

Receiving Goods and the Bill Together

In some cases you receive the items and the bill together. The Lighting Company delivered that shipment of fluorescent bulbs you ordered last Tuesday. Along with the pink packing list is a white bill. You can enter both items now and issue the check in your next check run. Here are the steps:

1. Display the Purchases and Vendors tab.

2. Click on Receive Items with Bill. The Enter Bills dialog box appears (refer to Figure 3.14).

3. Select the Vendor name by clicking on the down arrow and choosing the name from the list. A pop-up dialog box appears, telling you that you have open purchase orders and asking whether you'd like to log in the received goods (see Figure 3.17).

4. Click on Yes. The Open Purchase Orders dialog box appears, showing you the purchase orders that are open (see Figure 3.18).

5. Click on the purchase order you want to show as having been received and click on OK. QuickBooks automatically fills in the info to the Items tab in the Enter Bills dialog box.

Figure 3.17

When you have open purchase orders for a particular vendor, QuickBooks asks whether you want to check in the received goods after you select the vendor name.

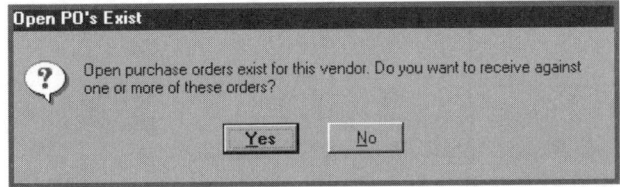

Figure 3.18

The Open Purchase Orders dialog box shows you any open purchase orders you have not checked in with received goods.

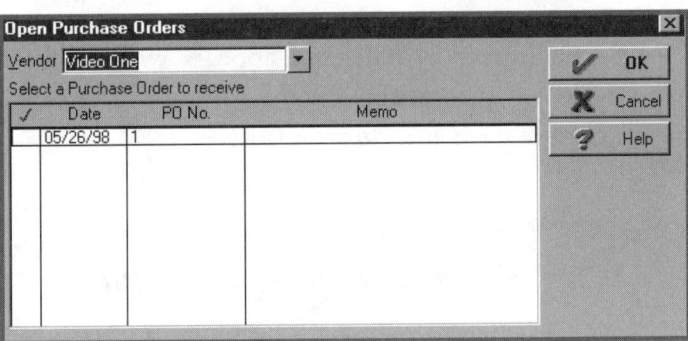

Receiving the Bill

Ah, finally, after you've already used all the binders, Davis Printing sends along the bill to go with the shipment. You need to enter the bill into your system and arrange to pay the bill the next time you print checks. Here's how to enter the bill as received:

1. With the Purchases and Vendor tab selected, click on Receive Bill.

2. The Select Item Receipt dialog box appears.

3. Click on the Vendor down arrow and choose the Vendor from the list. Any outstanding receipts are listed in the box (see Figure 3.19).

144 Learn QuickBooks 6 In a Weekend

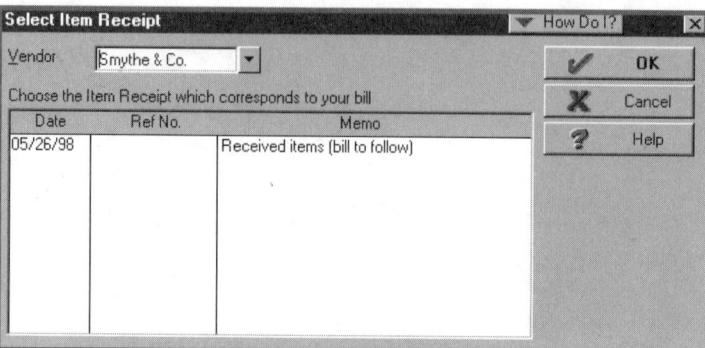

Figure 3.19

The Select Item Receipt dialog box displays the outstanding receipts you have for a particular vendor.

4. The Enter Bills dialog box appears, with the Bill Received check box selected in the upper-right corner of the dialog box. Review the information and click on OK.

TIPS FOR AN EFFECTIVE BILL-PAYING SYSTEM

Print a report of monthly bills. QuickBooks gives you a number of ways to print reports customized to your needs. A printout of monthly bills is a simple thing—but it's also a lifesaver if your data file ever crashes or you need to check something quickly.

Know your routine. If you have some kind of pattern to the way you pay bills, you will be more likely to do it in a timely and thorough manner.

Be clear about who, what, where, and when. If more than one person is responsible for paying bills in your business, make sure those responsible work together to make sure nothing gets overlooked.

Take the time to set up bill paying in QuickBooks. If you use all QuickBooks' features in entering and paying bills, your data will be organized and kept in a form easy to maintain and update.

Make it a habit. If you pay bills on a certain day, at a certain time, following a certain process, you are more likely to pay on time and with fewer mistakes.

Keep paper copies. Electronic files are great, but printouts are a necessary backup. Print your check register every month and print monthly bill payment reports.

Paying Bills

Now that you have entered bills, created purchase orders, checked in the goods and services, and received the bill, you are ready to pay for the items you received. To pay bills in Quickbooks, follow these steps:

1. Display the Pay Bills dialog box (see Figure 3.20) by clicking on the Purchases and Vendors tab in the Navigator and then clicking on Pay Bills.

2. Specify the bills you want to see by choosing either the date in Show Bills Due On Or Before or by clicking on Show All Bills.

3. Determine how you want the bills in the display organized by clicking on the Sort Bills By down arrow and making your choice: You can sort by Due Date (the default), Discount Date, Vendor, or Amount Due.

4. Choose your method of payment. You can choose checking, cash, credit, or online payments.

    - To choose checking, click on Check in the Pay By options. If you want QuickBooks to print the check, click on To be printed. From the drop-down list, click on the name of the checking account you want to use.

    - To choose to pay the bill with a credit card, click on Credit Card in the Pay By options. Choose the name of the credit card you want to use from the drop-down list.

    - To use cash to pay a bill, select Check in the Pay By option. Deselect the To Be Printed option. In the drop-down list, select a cash account.

5. Next, you need to choose the bills you want to pay by clicking in the left column to add a check mark beside those bills.

6. Click on OK to record the payments and return to the QuickBooks Navigator.

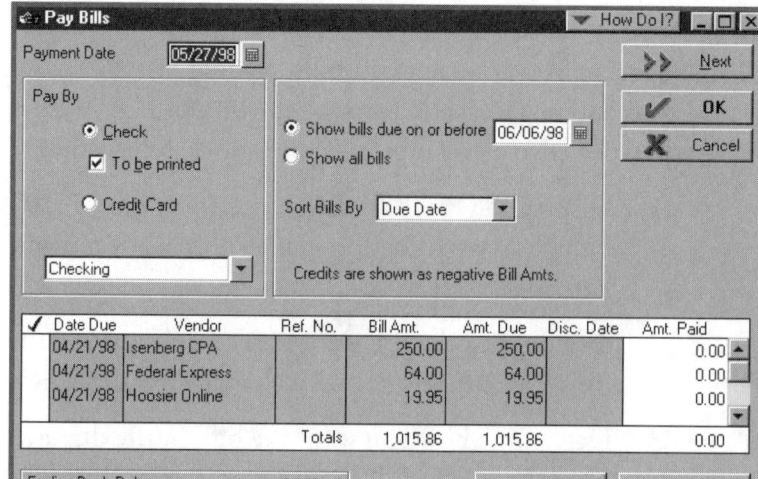

Figure 3.20

The Pay Bills dialog box brings together the bill information so that you can pay items easily.

What did QuickBooks do? As you can see in Figure 3.21, QuickBooks recorded the payments and updated the checking account (if you selected checking) with new entries showing the paid bills. If you elected to use a credit card, your credit card account was updated; and likewise, if you selected a cash payment, your cash account was modified automatically.

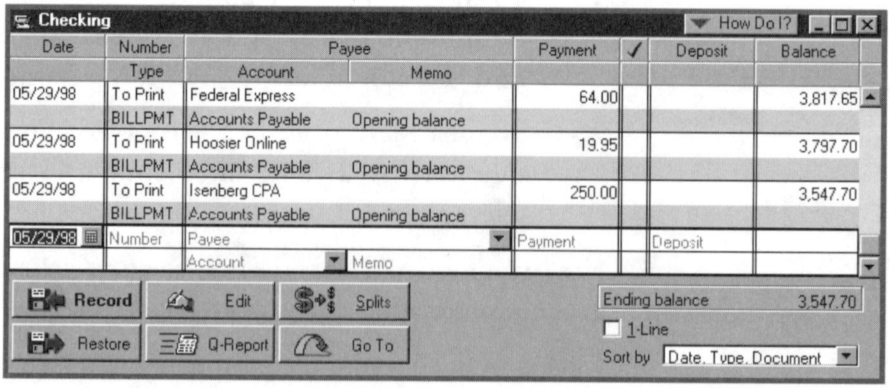

Figure 3.21

QuickBooks pays the bills and adds the payments automatically to the account you selected to pay the bills.

SATURDAY AFTERNOON Writing the Check: Paying for Goods and Services

> **THE SCOOP ABOUT MAKING ONLINE PAYMENTS**
>
> Online payment is a fast and easy way to pay your bills. Now you can record and pay your bills at the same time, all from within QuickBooks. The benefits of paying your bills online include:
>
> - **Instant bill payment.** You can pay your bills online now.
> - **Safe transfers.** Encryption technology makes your transfers secure.
> - **Convenience.** No more running out to the mailbox before the cutoff time.
> - **Control.** You can schedule payments as you like.
>
> You can pay bills online using either the Pay Bills dialog box or the Write Checks dialog box. For more information on how to pay bills online and perform other online transactions, see the Sunday Afternoon session, "Online Banking with QuickBooks."

What about Accounts Payable?

If you are more familiar with traditional forms of bookkeeping, you may be wondering about accounts payable. Where did it go and why aren't you using it?

Actually, you are. Every bill you pay is still regarded, in QuickBooks, as accounts payable. QuickBooks keeps track of accounts payable in a single account set up in the Chart of Accounts.

1. Open the Lists menu.
2. Choose Chart of Accounts. In the Chart of Accounts list box, Accounts Payable is set up as an individual account (see Figure 3.22).
3. To open the Accounts Payable account, double-click on it. Figure 3.23 shows the Accounts Payable register. Once you get into the Accounts Payable register, you can make changes to bills, split transactions, and more, similar to working in the check register window.

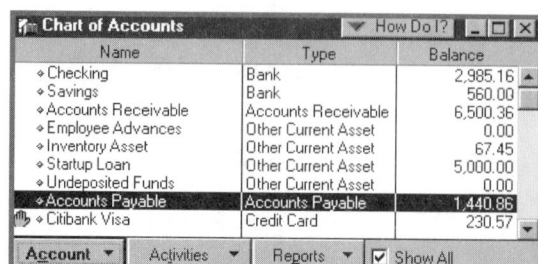

Figure 3.22

QuickBooks sets up your Accounts Payable in the Chart of Accounts.

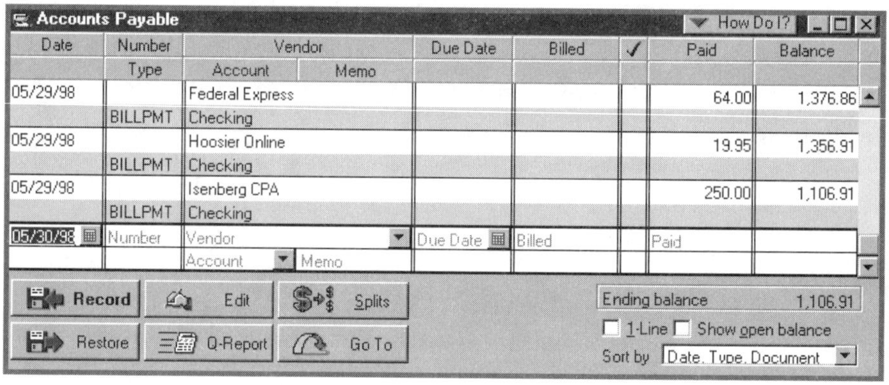

Figure 3.23

The Accounts Payable register tracks the payments you just made using the Pay Bills feature.

Editing Bill Payments

If you need to edit a bill, display the Accounts Payable register, select the bill you want to change, and click on Edit. QuickBooks displays the bill in the Bill Payments dialog box. Make your changes and click on OK to record the change.

NOTE If you make changes to the amount paid, QuickBooks automatically updates your checkbook to show the modifications.

Deleting Bill Payments

When you want to delete a bill payment from Accounts Payable, begin by displaying the register and selecting the bill. Next, open the Edit menu and choose Delete Bill. The entire transaction is deleted from the register, and the balances of both the Accounts Payable account and your checking account (or credit card or cash account, depending on the account you used to pay the bill) are updated to reflect the change.

NOTE In some cases, you might want to void a bill payment rather than delete it. Voiding leaves the bill payment in QuickBooks but changes the amount to zero; deleting removes the entire transaction.

What's Next?

Well, you've completed yet another session of your whirlwind QuickBooks intensive. You've learned a lot in this session—from adding vendors to writing checks to creating a bill-paying system to paying the darned things to editing the payments you made.

Time to take a nice long break, have some dinner, watch a good movie, and relax. Then come back for the evening session, when you'll learn the following things:

- How QuickBooks can help you handle inventory
- How you can set up an inventory system
- Ins and outs of inventory management
- Why payday doesn't have to give you nightmares
- How to track employee information

Sound fun? Don't sweat it—QuickBooks makes it much easier than tackling these issues on your own. Come back soon…

SATURDAY EVENING

Keeping Track of Inventory and Managing Payroll

- Creating Inventory Accounts
- Payroll with QuickBooks
- Entering Employee Information
- Payday! A Step-by-Step Process
- Paying Your Liabilities
- A Payroll Tax Form Primer

It's an old George Carlin routine...we've all got to have our stuff. The older we get, the more stuff we seem to accumulate. If you're in business for yourself, you probably are responsible for more "stuff" than the average person. Depending on the nature of your business, you have materials to track, items to shelve, and goods to organize. This session tackles the QuickBooks-as-inventory-tracker part of your QuickBooks weekend.

Another major source of panic for many business owners is payroll. Luckily, QuickBooks can make payroll easier, helping you organize information, figure deductions, print checks, and do your reporting in a smooth process you can repeat from pay period to pay period and quarter to quarter.

In this evening's session, you'll learn the basics of handling your inventory in QuickBooks and setting up and working through the payroll process—as painlessly and panic-free as possible.

Inventory with QuickBooks

Does your business keep a current inventory? If so, QuickBooks may be able to help you organize, analyze, update, and report on the stock you are tracking and its value. QuickBooks can help track your inventory if you have a business that purchases goods and then resells them, as in the following businesses:

- ✪ A small card shop that purchases cards, posters, candles, and other gifts from wholesalers and resells them at retail price

- An automotive supply company that sells tools, auto supplies, cleaning supplies, and more
- A lighting services and supply company
- A restaurant supply company
- A small furniture store
- A mom-and-pop quick mart

There are, however, types of inventory QuickBooks won't be much help with:

- A craft business that purchases craft items and then assembles them into items for sale
- A manufacturing business that purchases metals for use in assembling a product
- A service business that tracks supplies and materials used in providing its service to customers

In short, QuickBooks does great with inventory you purchase, track, and resell. QuickBooks won't be as much help when the cost of the purchased item is absorbed into another item offered for sale or when the item isn't sold at all, but rather used in support of the business product or service.

NOTE If your business inventory needs are more sophisticated than QuickBooks can handle, consider checking into other inventory or database management programs to give you the flexibility you need. You may want to contact a QuickBooks online advisor to find out about the best types of programs to help you track your specific business inventory.

What Does Inventory Look Like?

With everything you've done in QuickBooks up to this point, it may be hard to imagine what inventory in QuickBooks would look like. After all, you've worked with lists and list boxes, checks, forms, and purchase orders.

An inventory would seem to require a more database-like approach, with columns and rows set up in a table format.

Figure 4.1 shows an inventory screen in QuickBooks. As you can see, it looks more like a simple data-entry screen that gathers information about items you have in stock. If you look closely, however, you'll see that this screen includes everything you need to know about the inventory item—a description, the number in stock, the cost, the price, the number on order, and more.

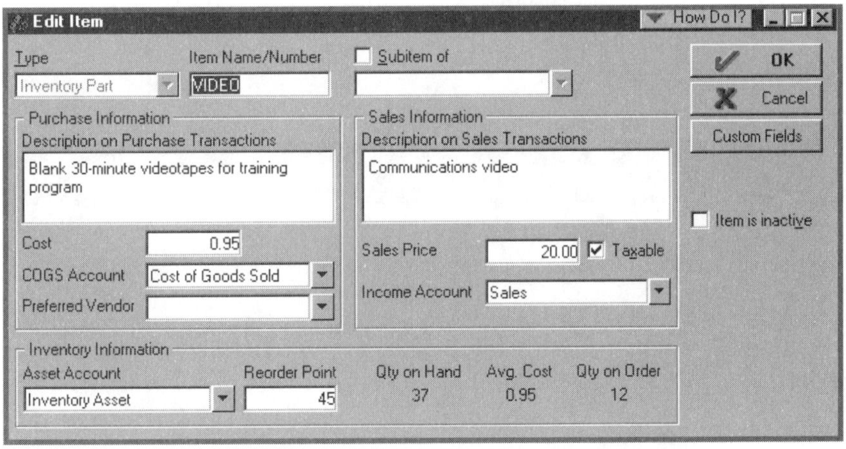

Figure 4.1

QuickBooks keeps track of your inventory information in the Edit Item dialog box. You can display inventory items by opening the Lists menu and then choosing Items.

Turning on the Inventory Features

When you went through the EasyStep Interview, QuickBooks asked you whether you wanted to set up the inventory features at that time. If you selected Yes, QuickBooks added the inventory options to the Activities, Lists, and Report menus. If you chose No, QuickBooks reserved those items. The first step in setting up your inventory system in QuickBooks involves turning on the inventory features, if you did not do that during the interview.

To turn on the inventory features, follow these steps:

1. Open the File menu and choose Preferences. The Preferences dialog box appears.

2. Click on the Purchases & Vendors icon in the left side of the dialog box.

3. Click on the Company Preferences tab (see Figure 4.2).

4. Make sure that all the options in Purchase Orders and Inventory are selected. (If check marks don't appear in all three check boxes, click on the boxes to add the check marks.)

5. Click on OK.

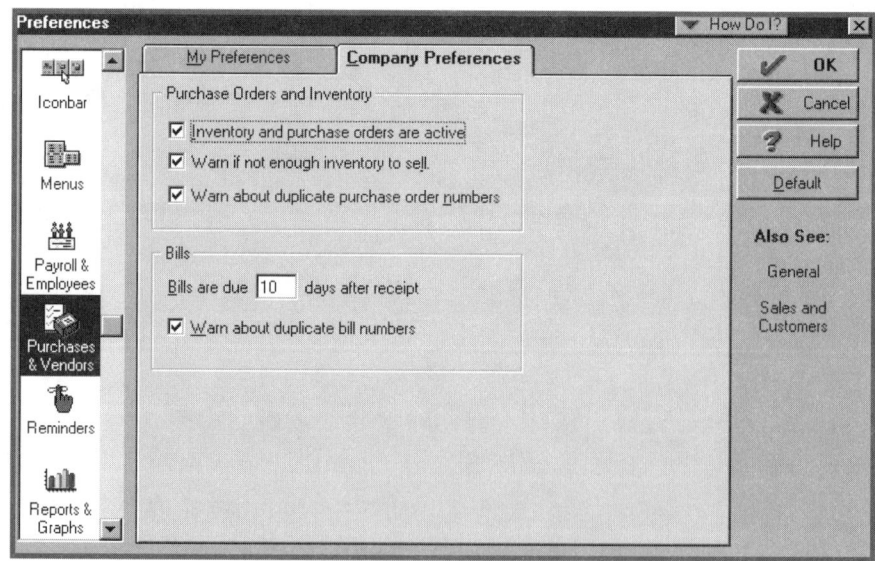

Figure 4.2

You turn on the inventory feature by displaying the Preferences dialog box and choosing the Purchases & Vendors icon.

Creating Inventory Accounts

Once you enable the inventory features so that QuickBooks will know you want to keep track of inventory information, you need to set up an inventory account. An inventory account is an account set up in your chart of

> **WHAT DO THE PURCHASE ORDERS AND INVENTORY OPTIONS DO?**
>
> When you turn on the inventory features, you select three options using the Purchases & Vendors icon in the Preferences dialog box:
>
> The Inventory And Purchase Orders Are Active option actually enables the inventory feature and makes it possible for you to track inventory, create inventory items, and create purchase orders for items you add to inventory.
>
> The Warn If Not Enough Inventory to Sell option tells QuickBooks to display a warning if you attempt to sell more of an item than you currently have in inventory.
>
> The Warn about Duplicate Purchase Order Numbers option lets you know if you duplicate the purchase orders you've created for purchases you add to inventory.

accounts that records inventory information. You might find this information valuable for several reasons. For instance, you might track the value of your inventory so that you can keep track of how much you have invested in your current stock. Also, if you are keeping track of inventory information, you could easily follow the resale of the inventory you purchase and produce reports that show how well your stock is selling. Or you might track how much the inventory costs for you to sell it—in other words, the per-item cost involved in each sale.

NOTE During the EasyStep Interview, if you told QuickBooks you wanted to track inventory, the program created an inventory account for you. In the Chart of Accounts, the account is called Inventory Asset and is set up as the Other Current Asset account type.

To create a new inventory account, follow these steps:

1. Open the Lists menu and choose Chart of Accounts.
2. Click on the Account button.
3. Choose New. The New Account dialog box appears, as Figure 4.3 shows.

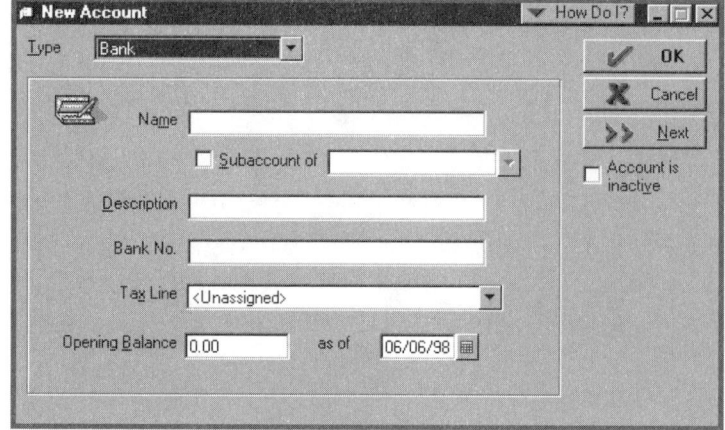

Figure 4.3

Use the New Account dialog box to create a new inventory account.

4. Choose the Type of account (for example, choose Other Current Asset).

5. Enter the name for the account (such as GBC Inventory).

6. If you want to create a subaccount of a main inventory account (such as the one QuickBooks set up for you during the EasyStep Interview), click on the Subaccount check box and select the account name from the list. For this example, I chose Inventory Asset.

7. Enter a description for the account and press Tab.

8. Enter bank information if you need to, such as a routing number, a PIN number, or other pertinent data so that you don't have to look it up separately.

9. For now, leave the Tax Line unassigned as an inventory account.

10. In the Opening Balance box, enter the value of your current inventory. Press Tab.

11. Enter the date the inventory was completed.

12. Click on OK. The account is added to the Chart of Accounts. If you created the account as a subaccount of something else, the account is shown beneath the other account (see Figure 4.4).

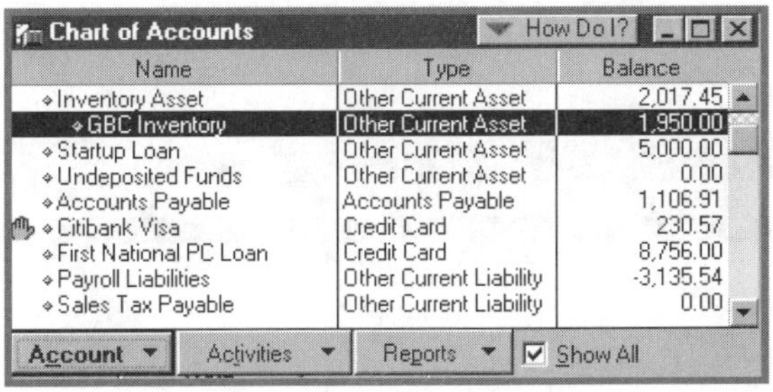

SATURDAY EVENING Keeping Track of Inventory and Managing Payroll **159**

Figure 4.4

The new inventory account is added to the Chart of Accounts.

NOTE In order to get the opening balance to enter in the New Account dialog box, you need to have completed some kind of inventory analysis so that you know how much you've got wrapped up in stock. QuickBooks includes a sheet you can print and then use in tracking your existing inventory. See "Taking Inventory" later in this session for information on how to gather the information you need about the value of your business inventory.

Adding Inventory Items

Inventory items help you keep track of items you purchase and then resell. While they are in inventory, you can keep an eye on how much you have, how much money you have invested, what you have on order, and the cost of the order. When you set up QuickBooks to track inventory information, you create an inventory item for each item in your inventory.

First, open the Lists menu and choose Items. The Item List box appears, as Figure 4.5 shows. As you can see in the figure, The Write Company has only one inventory item set up—this one is for the videotapes the company sells to accompany its training sessions. The Item list shows that the VIDEO item is set up as an Inventory Part type, in a Sales account, and that there are 71 videos currently in stock at a cost of $20 each.

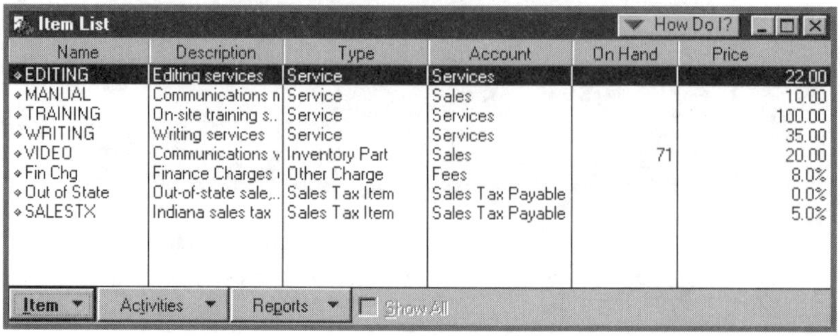

Figure 4.5

The Item List box shows information about all the items you have set up in QuickBooks. If you set up QuickBooks to track inventory during the EasyStep Interview, the inventory part(s) you set up will appear here.

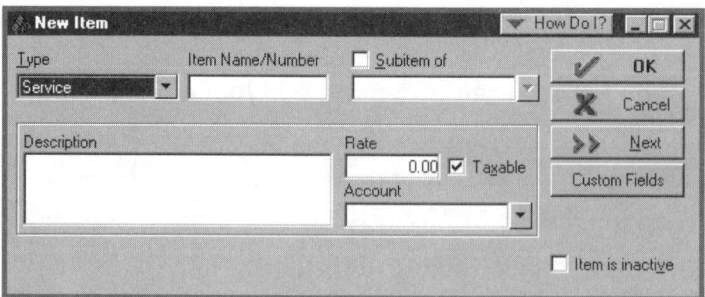

To create a new inventory part item, follow these steps:

1. Open the Lists menu and choose Items. The Item List box appears.

2. Click on the Item button in the lower-left corner of the list box. A submenu appears. Click on New. The New Item dialog box opens (see Figure 4.6).

Figure 4.6

The New Item dialog box provides the space for you to enter pertinent information about the inventory item you want to track. First choose Inventory Part in the Type box.

3. First click on the Type down arrow and choose Inventory Part. The dialog box changes, as Figure 4.7 shows. Now you've got even more information to enter. Start by entering the Item Name/Number of

the part you're tracking. The Write Company enters VIDEO because the item being tracked is a videotape it is selling. You can use names or numbers to help you organize the data according to your business needs.

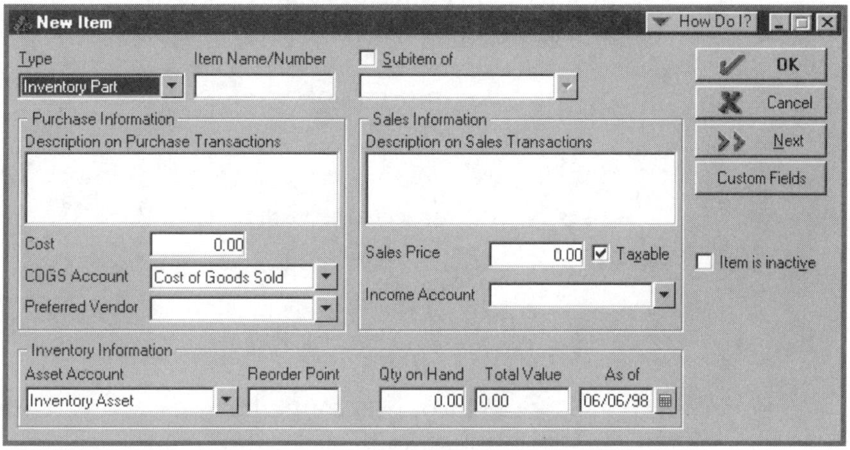

Figure 4.7

When you choose Inventory Part in the Type box, the dialog box changes, asking for more information.

4. If you want to create the item as a subitem of something else, click on the check box in front of Subitem Of and then click on the down arrow to choose the item you want to use. Only those items that are the same type as the one you are creating appear in the list.

5. In the Purchase Information area, enter a description the way you want it to appear on your purchase orders. In other words, when you create a purchase order to buy this particular item, what do you want to appear on the order to remind you of the purchase? The Write Company enters "Blank 30-minute videotapes for training program" in this box. Press Tab.

6. In Cost, enter the per-unit cost for the inventory item. (The blank videotapes cost $0.95 apiece, so enter .95.) Press Tab.

7. The COGS Account is the Cost-of-Goods account—that is, the account used to track how much each inventory item costs and to track the invested inventory cost. The Cost of Goods Sold account is probably appropriate here. Press Tab.

8. In Preferred Vendor, if you have a vendor you like dealing with for this particular inventory item, click on the down arrow and choose the vendor name from the list. Press Tab.

9. In the Sales Information area, type a description for the item that you want to appear on the customer receipts you print when a customer purchases the item from your inventory. The Write Company uses "Communications video" here. Press Tab.

10. Enter the sales price for the item. The video from The Write Company is $20. If the item is taxable, click on the Taxable check box. Press Tab.

11. Choose an Income Account that receives the payment when the goods are sold (for example, Sales). Press Tab.

12. In the Inventory Information area, choose the Inventory Asset account that tracks the inventory for this item.

TIP If you set up inventory tracking during the EasyStep Interview, QuickBooks has already created the Inventory Asset account for you. If you added another inventory account in the previous section, the original inventory account and any additional accounts will be shown in addition to all the other accounts in the drop-down list in the Asset Account list box.

13. When do you want QuickBooks to prompt you to reorder? Enter the number of units in the Reorder Point box. Press Tab.

14. Enter the quantity you have on hand. Press Tab.

15. Enter the total value of your inventory for this item. (If this value is different from the one QuickBooks automatically figures using the number on hand and the purchase price, you can adjust it by entering the corrected amount here.)

16. Choose the date that reflects the current inventory information.

17. When you're finished entering the inventory part item, click on Next if you want to enter more items, or click on OK to return to the Item list.

Setting Up Items for Later

If you are setting up inventory items you plan to use in the future, you can enter the data in the New Item dialog box and click on the Item Is Inactive check box to make the item inactive. When you are ready to use the item in your active inventory, click on the check box to deselect it and then enter the Qty On Hand, the Total Value, and the As Of date to begin inventory tracking.

At any point you can edit an inventory part item you have added by selecting the item in the Item List box and pressing Ctrl+E. The Edit Item dialog box appears, displaying all the information you entered for the inventory part item. Make your edits as necessary and click on OK.

Setting Up Custom Inventory Fields

Even though QuickBooks automatically enables you to track a number of important pieces of inventory information, there may be others unique to your business that aren't covered here. You can add your own fields by clicking on the Custom Fields button in the New Item dialog box. If no custom fields are defined for this item, QuickBooks alerts you to that fact and tells you to click on the Define Fields button in the dialog box that is displayed. When you click on Define Fields, the small dialog box shown in

Figure 4.8 appears. Here you can enter the names of the fields you want to create and click on the check box in the Use column to the left of the names to make them active. When you're finished, click on the OK button to return to the New Item dialog box. When you click on the Custom Fields button, a small pop-up dialog box appears, giving you the option of adding the additional information, as Figure 4.9 shows.

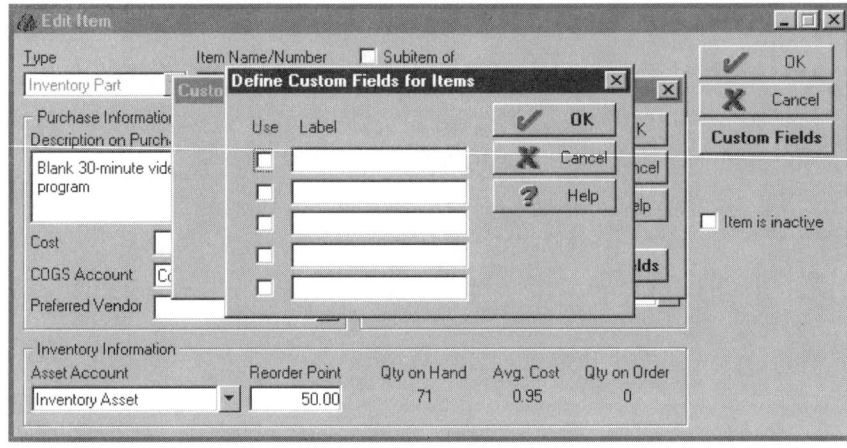

Figure 4.8

You can easily set up custom fields to track information QuickBooks doesn't ask for right off the bat.

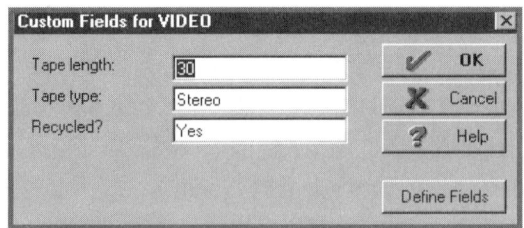

Figure 4.9

After you set up custom fields, you enter the information by clicking on the Custom Fields button.

Working with Inventory

Once you've set up the different inventory part items so that you know what you're tracking, you are ready to take a physical inventory and figure the value of your stock. The first time you come up with the hard numbers for QuickBooks, you're going to have to count boxes and units to come up with a total. Then you can determine the amount of money you've got invested in the inventory and plug the numbers into QuickBooks. From that point on, you can update the files electronically, figuring out how many units have been sold and how much money your business has spent to make the money it's made.

TIP Even though QuickBooks gives you the means to organize and monitor inventory information electronically, the good old eyeball-and-count method is a good way to cross-check your numbers. Periodically you should do a full inventory of your stock. Some businesses do inventories yearly; others do them twice a year or quarterly. Adjust the numbers as needed in your QuickBooks file by opening the List menu, choosing Items, and pressing Ctrl+E to display the Edit Item screen.

Taking Inventory

After you get QuickBooks ready to record your inventory data, you've got to gather it. QuickBooks includes a form you can print to help you pull the necessary information together. Here's how to print the form and start your inventory:

1. Open the Reports menu and choose Inventory Reports. A submenu appears.

2. Click on Physical Inventory Worksheet. The report is created and displayed in a window, showing all the inventory part items you have created and displaying the number you have entered as the Qty on Hand (see Figure 4.10).

3. You can modify the report as needed by changing the font, adjusting the column size, or showing additional information (see tomorrow morning's session, "Tracking Results: Reporting Your Financial Data," for information on creating, printing, and customizing reports).

Figure 4.10

The Physical Inventory Worksheet shows you the inventory part items you've set up and the number you show on hand.

4. When you are ready to print the worksheet, click on the Print button, fill in the options you want in the Print Reports dialog box, and click on Print.

 Print one Physical Inventory Worksheet as a master copy and then have it copied so that others can help in the actual counting process. Remember to keep a master copy on hand for when you compile all the numbers later.

A Quick Inventory QuickReport

While the Physical Inventory Worksheet is displayed on the screen, you may have a question. "Wait a minute," you might think, "I don't remember having 71 videotapes on hand. Could that be wrong?"

There's an easy way to see the history of that particular inventory part item if you're wondering about something. Simply double-click on the item in the Physical Inventory Worksheet. A QuickReport is displayed showing you all recent transactions regarding that item (see Figure 4.11). After you've reviewed the account, you can print the report by clicking on Print and choosing the print options you want, or you can close the QuickReport by clicking on the Close button in the upper-right corner of the window.

INVENTORY TIPS

As a former retail store manager, I react to the word "inventory" the way a football player reacts to "Super Bowl." Most managers I knew hated inventory time—the physical counting of the stock was a nightmare, helpers were hard to find unless threatened, and the inevitable erroneous results could be threatening (you could lose your job if your numbers were too far off) or at least fear-inducing. But for some reason I loved the challenge. Each year was an opportunity to make inventory go a little smoother, a little more accurately, a little happier. Each year I revised my system and tried to improve on the year before. And each year something seemed to work just a little better.

Your business may not require the inventory-intensive care that a retail operation requires, but here are some tried-and-true tips for taking a relatively painless inventory:

- Start planning months before. Several years ago I took a job managing a museum shop that was part of a major art gallery. Two weeks after I started, the chairman of the board stopped by to see me. "By the way," she said, "We're counting on you to pull off inventory smoothly. The last manager really botched the last one." I swallowed hard and asked when the next inventory was scheduled. "Next Saturday," she said with a smile. For best results, be thinking about inventory—how you'll count what you've got, what sections group logically together, how your stock is physically organized—long before you've got to explain to people how to pull all the data together. Knowing what you've got is the first major step to tracking it accurately.

- Enter all your information in QuickBooks ahead of time. When you set up your inventory part items in QuickBooks, you have a great opportunity to use Items and Classes to organize the various items you'll be tracking in QuickBooks. In my museum store, we had Original Art, Prints, Books, Jewelry, Stationery, Clothing, Glassware, and Miscellaneous.

- Draw a store map. Know the physical layout of your store or supply room and make a map helpers can refer to for sections that still need to be inventoried. Keep a master map to mark off those sections that have been assigned and completed.

- Color code your printouts. I used different color printouts for each section in the store so that I could easily tell where the sheets for one section ended and those for another began. This also kept us from mixing sheets from the Books area with sheets from the Glassware area and enabled me to tally each area separately.

INVENTORY TIPS (CONTINUED)

- **Keep one master printout.** Things get lost, shuffled, or thrown away. Especially if you are not doing a store-closed inventory when everyone joins in for two or three hours after closing on a weekend night, it's possible for people to mix the inventory pages in with order forms, magazines, or wrapping paper.

- **Organize helpers in shifts.** Although I have done store-open inventories in which employees count stock items while the store is open, it is generally most effective—and more accurate—to close the store (or do the inventory after hours) and organize your helpers in shifts. An employee who might grumble about working "until we get done" on a Friday night might be a lot happier about working a two-hour shift of his choosing on Sunday evening. The demands of your business and your open hours will determine how best to organize the actual time of your inventory. But giving workers a choice and a time limit helps them keep to their own schedules and priorities.

- **Make it a party (or at least a team effort).** Sure, order pizza. But make sure you do it after the work is done, or the inventory will drag on forever. If you organize things in shifts, you might want to have something for those who have just completed their work time; then they won't need to come back for the big shebang when the whole inventory is finished.

- **Have a troubleshooter.** Invariably there will be questions about what fits where. Those types of questions can cause you to spin off course and begin searching for the answer to the question rather than continuing to count inventory items. To avoid this kind of distraction, assign one of the workers the role of "troubleshooter" to go sleuth out this kind of issue without taking away from the general inventory going on.

- **Debrief afterward.** When the inventory is complete (not the same evening but within a week after the inventory is completed), have a meeting that involves everyone who was involved in the inventory. What did the workers like? What was difficult? What could have been done better or differently? Collect all the comments and incorporate them in next year's (or next quarter's) inventory.

- **Don't panic.** When you begin tallying up the numbers, don't panic. Even if things come out way off balance, you are going to be totaling those sheets several times. A cool head leads to more accurate numbers. Another good idea to keep the worry quotient down is to ask for a volunteer "checker," a fresh pair of eyes, who will add the same numbers and validate your totals or point out any miscalculations you have made.

SATURDAY EVENING Keeping Track of Inventory and Managing Payroll **169**

> ### INVENTORY TIPS (CONTINUED)
>
> ✦ Write a report. When you get a clear picture of your inventory results, write them up in report form. Summarize what you found, what areas have seen the largest growth since your last inventory, how that equates to your sales, and so on. Using the data in this way will help you get a better picture of where your money is invested in your business and whether it is invested in the most profitable way. (For example, if your sales show that you make most of your money on book sales but your book inventory is the lowest in the store, you know you can make changes to increase your book inventory and perhaps boost sales even more.)
>
> ✦ Plan for next year. While this year's inventory is still fresh in your mind, brainstorm about things you want to do differently next year. Use the comments from your debriefing with the staff and make your own notes and plans about how things can be improved. This will help you reduce your inventory dread for next year and maybe even help you start looking forward to it.

Figure 4.11

You can move directly from the Physical Inventory Worksheet to the QuickReport for a particular inventory part item by double-clicking on the item you want to find out more about.

Adjusting Inventory Information

Now that you've tallied the numbers and know how many of each item you've got on hand, you may notice some disparity between the Qty on Hand value and what you actually counted on your shelves. You can adjust the inventory information by following these steps (be sure to have your completed Physical Inventory Worksheet handy):

1. Open the Lists menu and choose Items.

2. In the Item list, choose the first item you want to update.

3. Click on Activities. A submenu appears. Click on Adjust Quantity/Value on Hand. A dialog box appears for you to make the necessary adjustments, as Figure 4.12 shows.

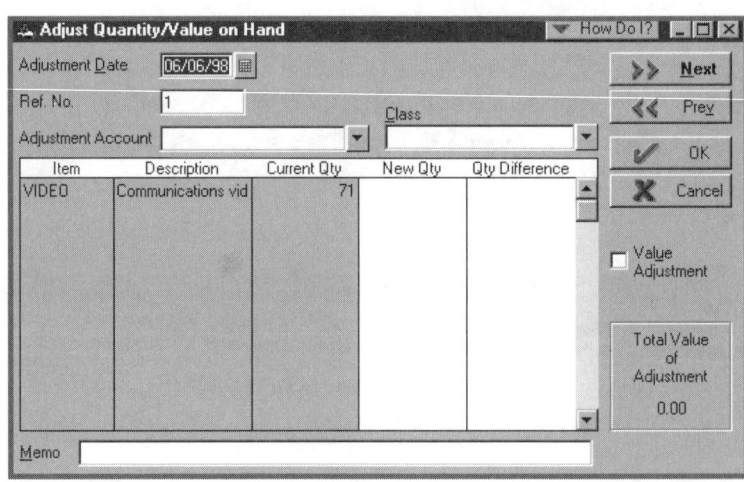

Figure 4.12

After you complete the Physical Inventory Worksheet, you may want to adjust your QuickBooks inventory information.

4. Choose an account to track the adjustment. If you donated a case of videos to a nonprofit organization that offers school-to-work training, for example, the account would be Contributions.

5. Enter the Class if you are tracking class categories.

6. Click in the New Qty column and type the number on hand you show on your Physical Inventory Worksheet. QuickBooks figures the Qty difference and enters it for you.

7. If you have other adjustments to enter, click on Next. If you want to return to the Item list, click on OK.

NOTE QuickBooks also gives you the option of adjusting the value of your inventory without changing the number of items you have on hand. Click on the Value Adjustment check box to have QuickBooks display the Current Value and New Value columns so that you can enter the value adjustment.

Selling Stock

Once you have the various items entered in your inventory, you know not only how many of a particular item you've got, but also how much the items cost you and how much you have invested in the inventory. When you make a sale, QuickBooks subtracts the items sold from the quantity you show on hand.

In this morning's session, you learned about entering sales. The process of selling something out of inventory is no different from recording an actual sale. When you issue the customer a receipt, QuickBooks updates your inventory information to reflect the sale of the inventory item.

1. Pronto Press is purchasing three of The Write Company's videos. To record a cash sale, click on the Lists menu and choose Items. The Item list appears.

NOTE You can also enter sales by opening the Lists menu and choosing Customers: Jobs, selecting the customer name, clicking on Activities, and choosing Enter Cash Sales.

2. Click on the Activities button and when the submenu opens, select Enter Cash Sale. The Enter Cash Sales dialog box appears, as Figure 4.13 shows.

3. Complete the Sales Receipt as usual and click on To Be Printed if you want to print the receipt with others when you are finished entering sales.

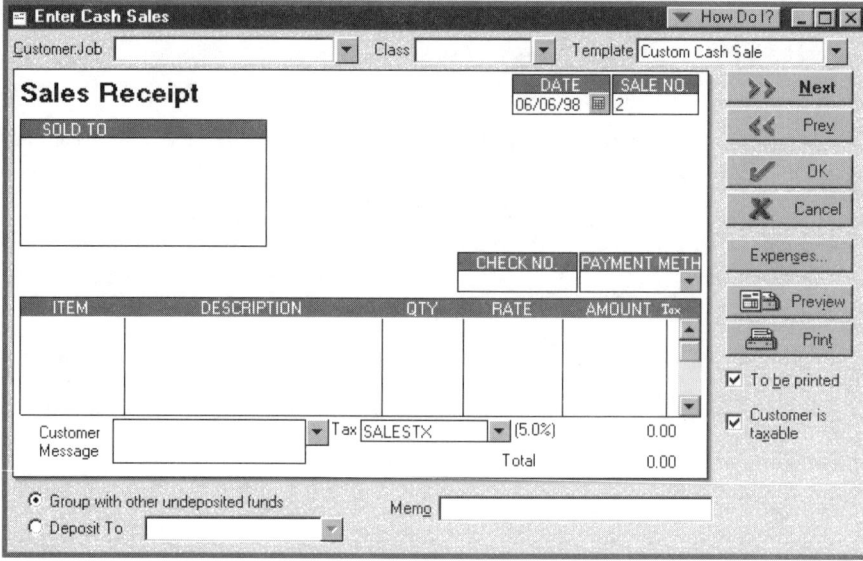

Figure 4.13

When you sell something from inventory, you fill out a sales receipt and QuickBooks subtracts the items from the Qty on Hand total.

4. If you want to enter other sales, click on Next. To close the Enter Cash Sales dialog box and return to the Item list, click on OK.

 **NOTE** If you need a refresher on entering sales and creating receipts, see Saturday morning's session, "Tracking and Recording Sales."

Ordering Stock

When you filled out the New Item screen, you entered a Reorder Point in the Inventory Information area of the dialog box. When QuickBooks records a sale that takes a particular stock item to a number lower than the number you entered in Reorder Point, the program alerts you by adding the item to your Reminder list.

When you are ready to reorder, fill out a purchase order as usual. First display the Item list by opening the Lists menu and choosing Items. Then click on the item, open the Activities menu, and choose Create Purchase

Order. The Purchase Order dialog box appears, and you can enter the information about the purchase. Choose the vendor name and, in the ITEM column, select the item you want to order. The description and per-item cost appear automatically. Fill in the QTY you want and click on Next if you want to create a purchase order for another item or click on OK to return to the Item list.

Reordering Reminders

QuickBooks will alert you in the Reminders list to order more inventory items if you have it set up to do so. To turn on Reminders, follow these steps:

1. Open the File menu and choose Preferences.

2. Click on the Reminders icon in the left side of the dialog box. You may have to scroll down to get to it.

3. Click on the Company Preferences tab. A whole list of reminders QuickBooks offers is displayed. The item concerning inventory is halfway down the list.

4. Click on the Inventory to Reorder button.

5. Click on OK to close the dialog box and return to the QuickBooks Navigator.

TIP When you are choosing Reminder preferences, you have three options: you can choose to see a summary of the task you are being reminded about, you can request to see a list of tasks to be done, or you can opt not to be reminded at all. The summary is selected by default, but you may want to try the list option to see which you prefer.

Receiving Items into Inventory

When the order comes in, you need to check it in. The traditional method of checking in items, issuing a receipt, and paying the bill works the same way for inventory items that it does for noninventory items; however, QuickBooks provides the means for you to receive inventoried goods separately.

When you want to check in an order that will be reflected in your inventory data, follow these steps:

1. Open the Activities menu and choose Inventory. A submenu appears.

2. Choose one of the three options that fits what you're doing (Receive Items and Enter Bills for those times when you receive both the goods and the bill together; Receive Items when you have only the goods; and Enter Bill for Rec'd Items for situations in which you have already received the goods and now need to enter the bill).

3. Complete the dialog box that appears (each option presents a different dialog box) and click on OK when you're through. QuickBooks logs the change into the system and updates your inventory totals.

Analyzing Your Data Using Inventory Reports

As you learned when you were gathering the information from your Physical Inventory Worksheet, the basically simple task of counting your stock can give you quite a bit of information about your business. From your inventory, you can determine important things like whether you are putting your money in the place where it is likely to get the most return. Other items you can discover from inventory information include how much you are paying for individual items, whether you are staying current in ordering, and whether you are carrying enough stock to support your sales demand.

You can use QuickBooks to analyze the inventory information you have gathered. Several reports can help you do these types of analyses, and you can invent your own as you go along.

What's Your Inventory Worth?

One of the most helpful inventory reports QuickBooks offers is the Valuation Summary report. This report gives you a quick look at where you are spending your money: How much have you invested in your stock and how evenly is your money distributed?

To create a Valuation Summary report, follow these steps:

1. Open the Reports menu and choose Inventory Reports.

2. Choose Valuation Summary. The report lists a number of columns that detail not only the items themselves and the quantity you have in stock but the total percentage of assets the items represent. Figure 4.14 shows The Write Company's Valuation Summary, but notice that the report itself isn't very helpful: The company has only one item tracked in its inventory system, so a report like this doesn't do much good. In my museum shop, however, when there are a hundred or more items to track, this type of inventory report summary shows where the money is going, how it's spent, and how it relates to the overall percentage of income in the business.

3. Click on Print to display the Print Report dialog box and choose your options.

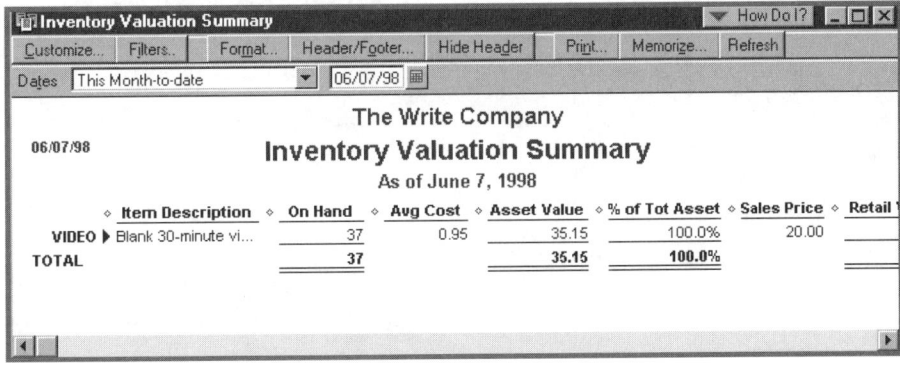

Figure 4.14

The Valuation Summary report shows you how many of your assets you have invested in your current inventory.

TIP Tomorrow morning's session, "Tracking Results: Reporting Your Financial Data," explores the various options involved with printing quick and customized reports. You'll learn to format, change fonts, reorder columns, filter, and more. For now, just getting a simple report with the data you seek is the point. Stay tuned for tomorrow morning's session to learn about the ins and outs of printing reports.

Getting a Detailed Report

You can get a detailed report of transactions that affect a particular inventory part item by choosing Reports, Inventory Reports, and Valuation Detail. The Valuation Detail report shows all the transactions that changed the quantity of the item you selected during a specified period. The default time frame is one week, so when you choose Valuation Detail, QuickBooks shows you the activity for that item for the preceding workweek (see Figure 4.15).

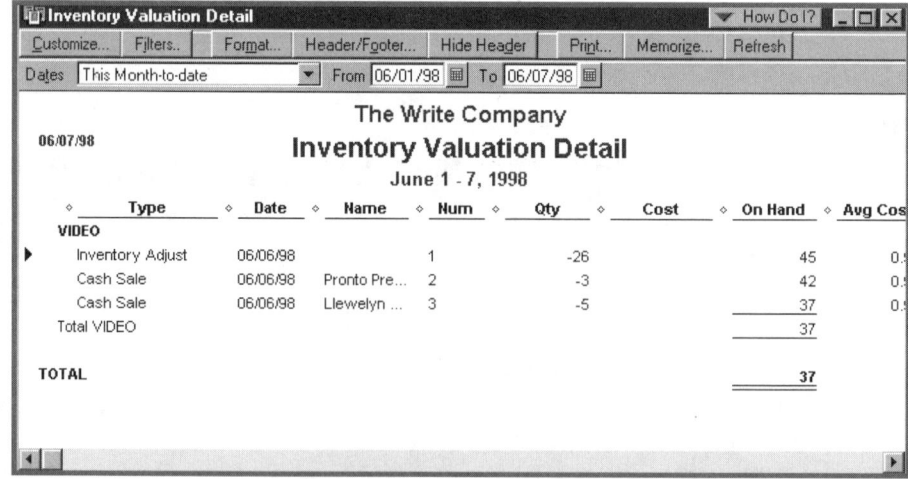

Figure 4.15

The Valuation Detail report lists the transactions that have affected your inventory for a specified period.

Printing a Stock Report

The stock report shows you information about a particular inventory part item. For example, suppose that you want to see how many videotapes The Write Company has in stock, how many are on order, and when that next order is expected to arrive. The Stock Detail report can show you these things. To create the Stock Summary report, follow these steps:

1. Open the Reports menu and choose Inventory Reports.

2. From the submenu that appears, choose Stock Status by Item. The report shown in Figure 4.16 appears. The Write Company shows only a single item in stock; however, other inventory items would be listed following the VIDEO item if more were inventoried as part of this company.

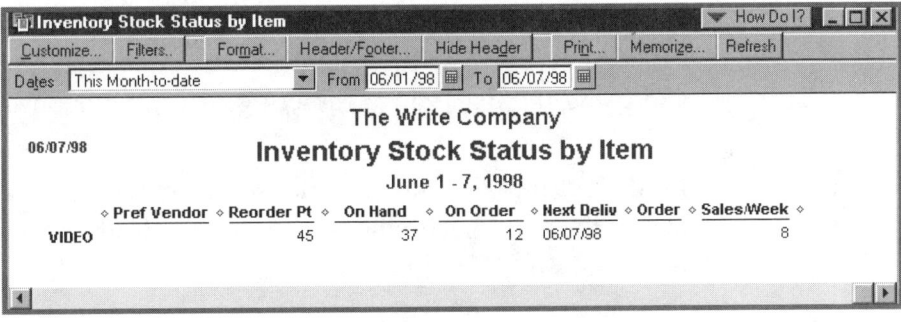

Figure 4.16

The Stock Status by Item report shows ordering information for each inventory part item.

Reporting Vendor Status

The final report type in the Inventory Reports groups information by vendor. If you have specified Preferred Vendor in the Purchase Information area of the New Item or Edit Item dialog box, QuickBooks uses this vendor to display the results of the report. For example, if you purchase binders, folders, and dividers from Llewelyn Printing, paper from Paper Warehouse, and videotapes from Video One, QuickBooks would list the items, including ordering status, such as reorder point, number on hand, number on order, and when the shipment is expected:

Llewelyn Printing
  Binders
  Dividers
  Folders
Paper Warehouse
  Paper
Video One
  Videotapes

Take a Break

Thus far this evening, you have learned the ins and outs of inventory in QuickBooks. As you can see, it's a fairly simple process, but there are a number of steps involved. And like anything else in QuickBooks, once you get past the data entry part and begin using the system you've set up, it gets easier and easier. Then it is simply a case of maintaining what you've done and using the data you're gathering to run your business more productively.

Ready for a break? Stand up, walk around, check on the kids, go outside and look at the stars for a minute. Clear your head. The next issue is one that can roll some stumbling blocks at your feet, but take heart—it is also one of those necessary evils that gets much less insidious in QuickBooks: payroll.

Payroll with QuickBooks

Payroll is a hassle for many owners of small businesses, because so many small things can go wrong, and because owners operating on a shoestring often sweat blood right around payday. In a small and struggling company, payday is continually a question of "Are we going to make it this month?" For a larger, more established company, payday may not induce panic, but it is still a potential hotbed for technical and financial woes.

QuickBooks makes the payroll process easier by automating many of the tasks you do repeatedly. Once you enter the basic payroll information—

employee data and deductions—QuickBooks does the calculations for you and will even write the checks. And when it's time to file the 940s and 941s, QuickBooks helps you generate them and can even submit the forms for you online.

The process of doing payroll in QuickBooks looks like this:

1. Turn on payroll features.
2. Enter employee information.
3. Track payroll information.
4. Enter deductions.
5. Payday!
6. Report payroll and pay payroll taxes.

Turning on Payroll Features

During the EasyStep Interview, you had the option of enabling the payroll features. If you chose No during that important juncture, you can reverse your decision now and turn on the payroll features by opening the File menu, choosing Preferences, and selecting the Payroll & Employees icon in the left side of the Preferences dialog box. Click on the Company Preferences tab. A number of payroll features appear, as Figure 4.17 shows.

The QuickBooks Payroll features are the most important when you are first getting started. Make sure that Full Payroll Features is selected. This enables you to use all the payroll features—from tracking, to calculating, to reporting—available in the program. If you want only the payroll reporting features, you can select Payroll Reports Only. Check any other options you want (see the next section for more detail on the Preferences options) and click on OK when you're through.

Choosing Your Payroll Preferences

Figure 4.17 shows a number of preferences that come into play when you begin thinking about payroll. What type of information do you want printed on the checks? How do you want the employee names sorted? Do you

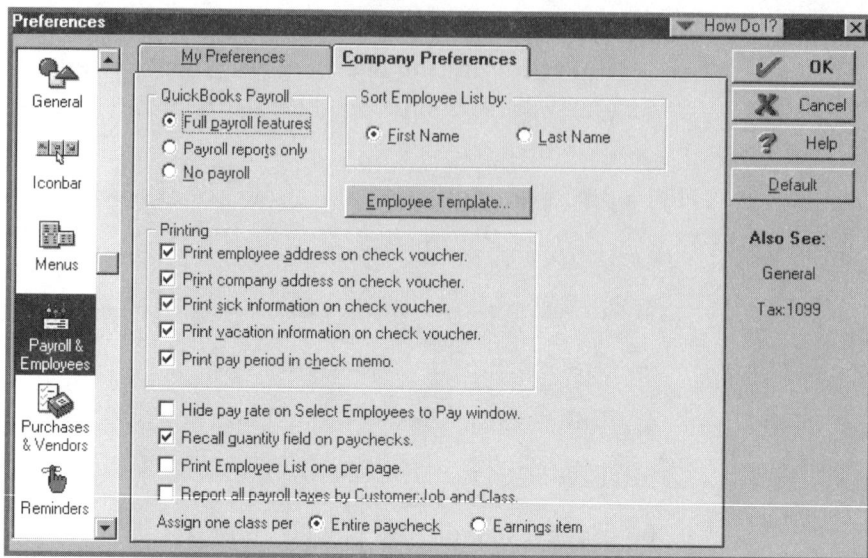

Figure 4.17

QuickBooks includes a whopping number of payroll features meant to streamline payroll tasks and reduce your headaches.

want to display what might be sensitive information? (This is important if someone other than you may be preparing payroll.) Click on the options that affect your particular business and click on OK when you are finished. You are returned to the QuickBooks Navigator window.

WHAT IS AN EMPLOYEE TEMPLATE?

In the Company Preferences tab is a button labeled Employee Template. This template assists you in setting up new employees. For example, if you know that all your employees are paid an hourly rate on a biweekly schedule, you can enter that information so that when you go to set up a new employee record, those items are selected by default. You can enter other items, too, such as number of sick days and vacation days, common tax information, and more.

What Do You Need to Set Up Payroll?

Once you turn the QuickBooks payroll feature on, you need to set up the information you need. First, you'll need to gather several documents to help you enter the right information right off the bat:

- **Know what taxes you pay.** Make a list of all the payroll taxes you pay in your business. This list should include both employee taxes and company liabilities.

- **Have your personnel data together.** Get your updated employee files, including each employee's full name, address information, social security number, W-4, start date, salary, sick days available, and vacation time.

- **Get your payroll totals ready.** You'll need to know what your company has paid in payroll up to this point in the current year. Have the figures for social security contributions, Medicare, county and state taxes, and any additional payroll expenses (such as the Daycare Co-Pay that The Write Company pays) you may have.

- **List any other deductions.** If your employees have any other deductions taken out, have those totals, percentages, and amounts ready.

- **Gather a list of benefits your company pays for employees.** If there are any other benefits—such as membership to a health club or a private medical program—your company pays, know the information for those payments, including vendor, amount, percentage of employee's pay, and such.

- **Know your insurance amounts.** For payroll, this means the state unemployment insurance (SUI) and state disability insurance (SDI) rates.

Entering Employee Information

When you are ready to begin entering payroll information, start by clicking on the Payroll and Employees tab in the QuickBooks Navigator. The Navigator displays the screen shown in Figure 4.18. Here you can see the process of managing payroll in QuickBooks. Start by entering employee information. Click on the Employees icon in the top icon bar to begin the process. The Employee List box appears, as shown in Figure 4.19.

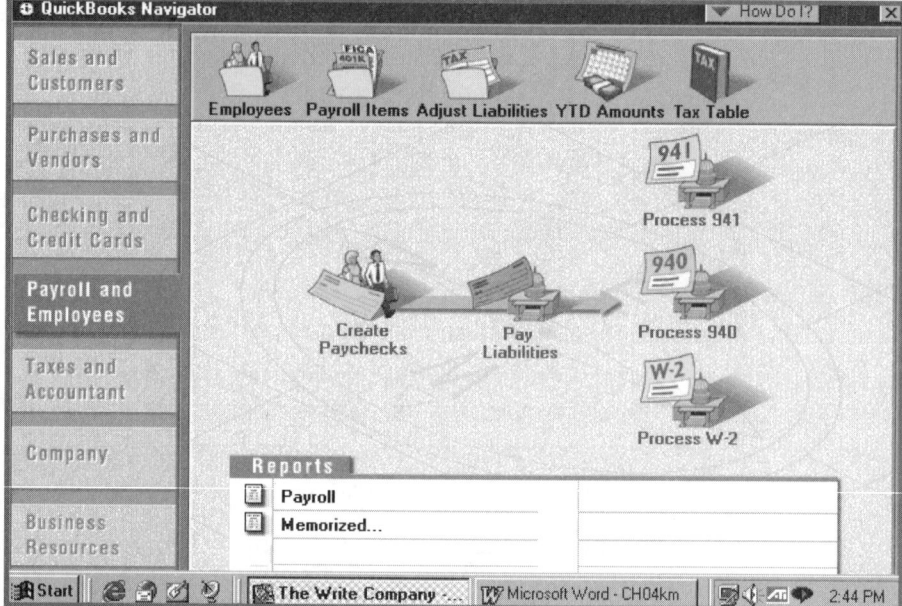

Figure 4.18

Begin the process of entering payroll in QuickBooks by clicking on the Payroll and Employees tab in the Navigator window.

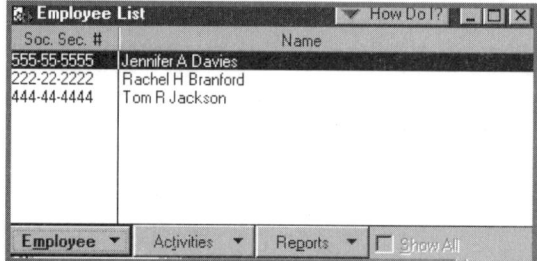

Figure 4.19

You enter and update employee information using the Employee list.

The Employee list shows any employee information you entered during the EasyStep Interview, if you set up payroll with that feature. If you are just now setting up payroll for the first time, this list will be blank.

 TIP You can also display the Employee list by opening the Lists menu and choosing Employees.

NOTE Each time you hire a new employee, be sure to get Form W-4, "Employee's Withholding Allowance Certificate," and keep it on file for each employee. This form tells you how many deductions to withhold for each employee. If an employee wants to change his or her deductions at some point, have the person fill out another W-4 as an addendum to the original one.

Adding an Employee

To add an employee to the list, click on the Employee button and click on New. The New Employee dialog box appears, as Figure 4.20 shows. Here you can add all your basic employee information—name, address, hire date, and so on. Click in each field and type the information. In the Print As field, type the name of the employee as you want it to be printed on paychecks and in reports.

TIP Double-check all employee information after you enter it to be sure you've entered the name, the address, and especially the social security number correctly. Once you've entered the information in QuickBooks, the program will use what's already there, so you won't be entering the social security number again unless someone points out that it is incorrect in the program.

The Additional Info tab allows you to enter an account number (your own company's internal referencing information) and add any custom fields you might want to track. The Payroll Info tab enables you to enter the payroll information you need in order to figure withholding rate, exemptions, and more.

Click on the Payroll Info tab. The screen shown in Figure 4.21 appears. Here you work through each option systematically, entering the information from your payroll records for each employee.

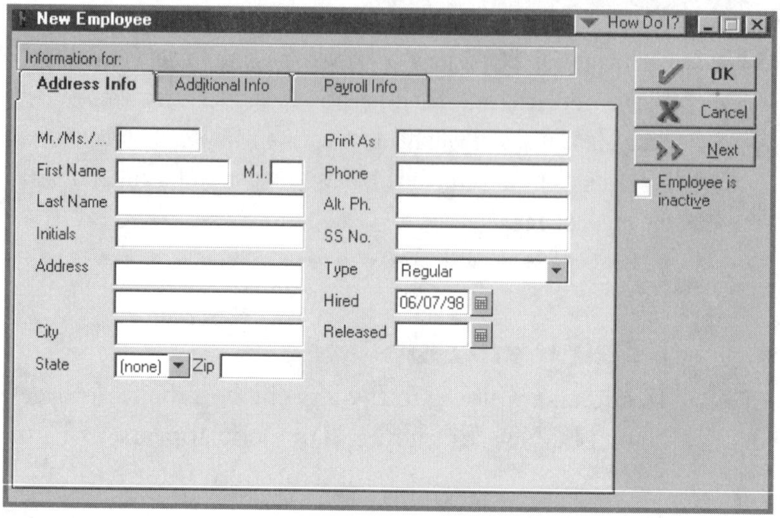

Figure 4.20

The New Employee dialog box gathers all the pertinent information about the employee for tracking purposes.

NOTE If you used the Employee Template to set up common items for all employees, those settings will be reflected in the Payroll Info tab of the New Employee dialog box.

Figure 4.21

The Payroll Info tab of the New Employee dialog box enables you to enter and track information about the way the employee is paid, how many sick days are available, deductions and company contributions, and more.

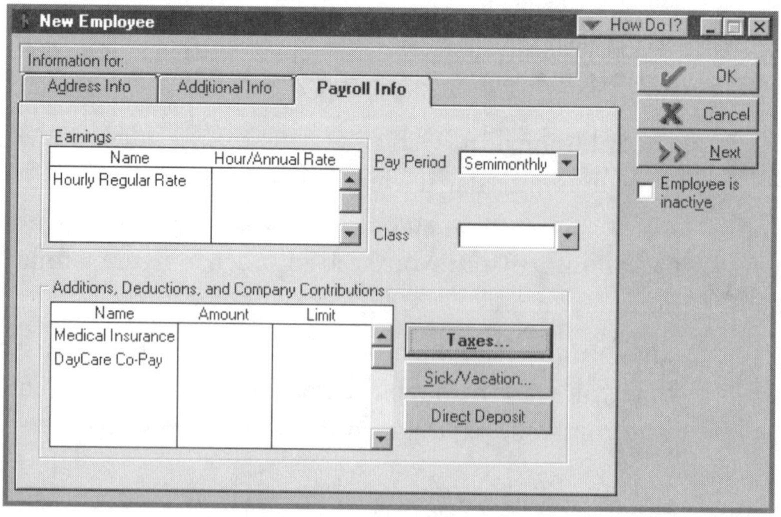

1. In the Earnings area, check to make sure the correct pay type is selected. The Write Company pays an hourly regular rate for employees. Your business might pay a salary or pay by commission, however. Click on the down arrow and choose the option that best suits your business.

2. In the Hour/Annual Rate area, enter the amount the employee is paid.

3. In Pay Period, click on the down arrow and choose the period your company uses for payroll.

4. If you are using a Class category for payroll, select that from the list displayed when you click on the Class down arrow.

5. In the Additions, Deductions, and Company Contributions area, make sure the items displayed apply to the current employee. Enter the amount and limit for each item.

6. Click on the Taxes button. The Taxes dialog box appears, as Figure 4.22 shows. The Federal tab is showing. Using the employee's W-4

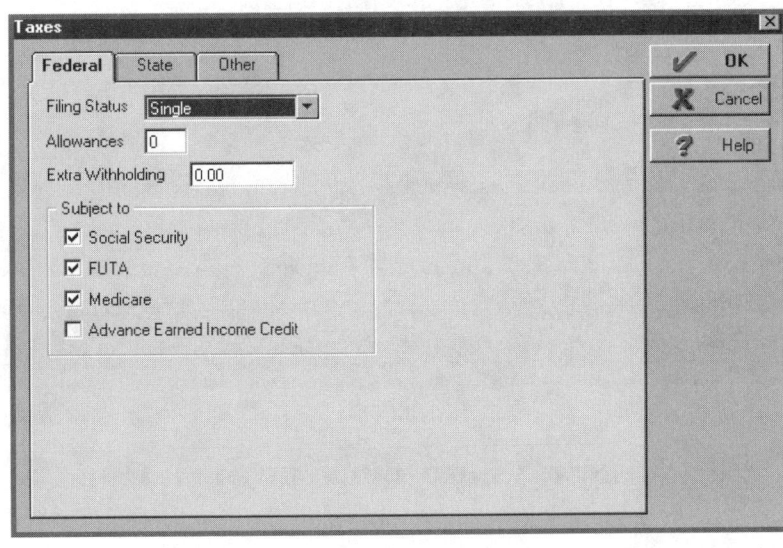

Figure 4.22

In the Taxes dialog box, enter the information you have gathered for the employee through the W-4 or other personnel information.

(if this is a new employee) or your personnel file for the employee (if you are setting up a QuickBooks record for an employee who's been around for a while), enter the information for the Federal and State tabs. Click on OK when you're finished entering tax information.

NOTE If an employee has special circumstances that need to be tracked tax-wise, use the Other tab in the Taxes dialog box to set up those fields and track the information. QuickBooks will ask whether the current employee is subject to county tax, as well—if so, QuickBooks will add county tax to the Other tab and track the tax needed for that area.

7. Click on the Sick/Vacation button in the Payroll Info tab. Enter the necessary information for sick and vacation days. How many hours of sick and vacation time do you make available to employees? Are the hours available at the beginning of the year or after a certain number of hours worked? Do you reset the hours at the beginning of the year or can employees carry the unused hours with them from year to year? The answers to these questions go in the Sick & Vacation dialog box. After you enter your information, click on OK to return to the Payroll Info tab.

WHAT ABOUT ONLINE PAYROLL?

QuickBooks allows you to set up online payments—and that includes payroll—for your QuickBooks accounts. When online payroll is enabled, you can make direct deposits to your employees' accounts. When payday rolls around, the funds are transferred from your account to the employees' accounts electronically. Direct Deposit will allow you to deposit funds in up to two accounts per employee. For more about online payroll, see tomorrow afternoon's session, "Online Banking with QuickBooks."

Changing Employee Information

Probably not long after you get all the employee information entered, somebody will need to change something. Don't stew—making changes is simple in QuickBooks. Just display the Employee list by clicking on the Employees icon in the Payroll and Employees tab, click on the Employee button, and select Edit. (You can bypass the menu selection by pressing Ctrl+E when the Employee list is displayed, if you prefer.) The Edit Employee information is displayed, and you can click on the necessary tab(s) and make your changes as needed.

TIP As you begin working with employee information, you may notice other items you'd like to add to the Employee Template. You don't have to go all the way back to Payroll Preferences to add the items; just display the Employee list, click on Employee, and click on Template. Add the items as needed and click on OK. The next time you add an employee, the template will be updated.

Entering Year-to-Date Amounts

Now that you've entered the employees you plan to pay using QuickBooks' payroll features, you are ready to enter the year-to-date amounts for your existing payroll totals. You can do this two ways: by entering all the payments you've made since the beginning of the year (to both employees and tax agencies) or by entering a YTD adjustment that tells QuickBooks your current totals and gives the program an accurate starting point. Entering the YTD adjustment is the faster route:

1. Click on the YTD Amounts icon in the Payroll and Employees tab of the Navigator.

2. The first page of the Set Up YTD Amounts Wizard appears (see Figure 4.23). Click on Next.

3. What date do you want to begin? QuickBooks recommends using your start date and displays that date by default. Choose the date and click on Next.

4. On which date do you want to begin affecting your bank and liability accounts? Again QuickBooks displayed your start date by default. Enter the date and click on Next.

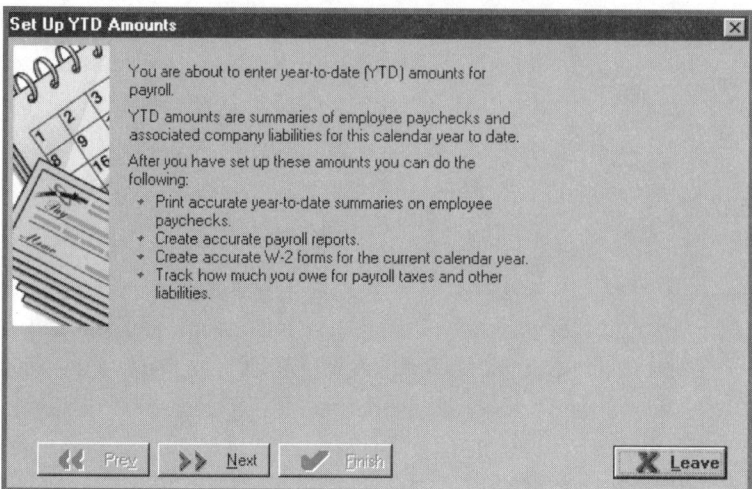

Figure 4.23

The Setup Up YTD Amounts Wizard walks you through the process of entering year-to-date amounts for payroll and tax liabilities.

> **NOTE** Why are your YTD amounts important? Your YTD payroll amounts affect payroll totals printed on checks, on W-2s, on payroll reports, and on tax forms submitted to tax agencies.

5. Enter the date you want to begin using QuickBooks for payroll; click on Next.

6. The list of your current employees appears. To enter the YTD information for each employee, click on an employee name and click on Enter Summary. The YTD Adjustment window appears, as Figure 4.24 shows.

> **NOTE** If you entered this information during the EasyStep Interview, data will appear in the fields. If this is the first time you have used QuickBooks' payroll, the fields will be blank.

7. Using your past payroll records, enter the totals for the pay periods between your QuickBooks start date and the date you plan to begin payroll. Click on Next Period to move to the next pay period or Prev

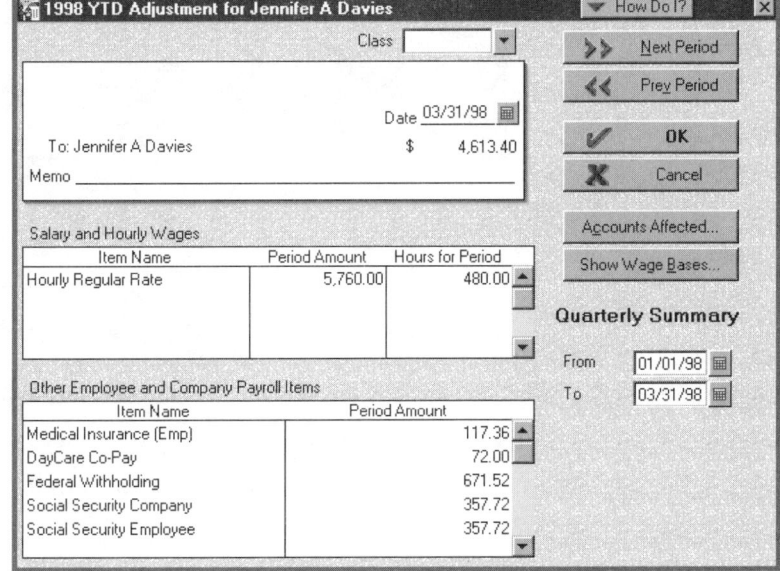

Figure 4.24

In the YTD Adjustment window, you enter past payroll information for each individual employee.

Period to move to a preceding payroll period. When you're finished entering the YTD amounts for the current employee, click on OK to return to the Set Up YTD Amounts dialog box.

8. Repeat step 7 for each of your remaining employees. When you're finished entering the YTD amounts, click on Next.

9. QuickBooks displays a window to tell you whether you have payroll payments you need to enter from the period from the start of the year through the QuickBooks' start date. If so, click on Create. Otherwise, click on Finish. If you click on Create, the Prior Payments of Taxes and Liabilities window appears (see Figure 4.25). Enter the taxes you have paid through your QuickBooks' start date.

10. Click on the Accounts Affected button to display a dialog box that gives you the choice of adjusting your liability accounts, your bank accounts, or both. Make your selection and click on OK.

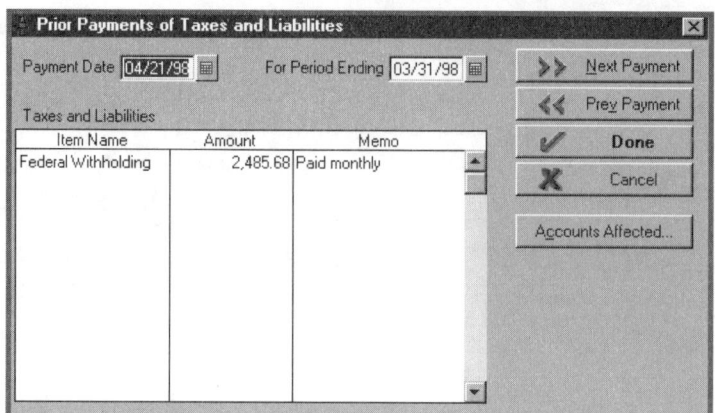

Figure 4.25

The Prior Payments of Taxes and Liabilities window is for entering the tax payments you've made between the beginning of the year and your QuickBooks' start date.

11. Click on Done to leave the Prior Payments of Taxes and Liabilities window.

12. Click on Finish to end the Set Up YTD Amounts Wizard.

Your year-to-date amounts are entered and should print correctly on your employees' paychecks, on payroll reports, and on tax reporting forms. The first time you run payroll, however, go ahead and total everything by hand to make sure you entered correctly and that QuickBooks is doing the necessary calculations.

Keeping Track of Payroll Expenses

There's more to payroll than writing a check. You are also working with data that can be very valuable in the management and planning of your business. You can break down your salary expenses by job or by class, allocating employees' time to various projects as well as determining which jobs are the most cost-effective and which are the most draining of your resources (in which case, you may want to increase your rates).

You can track payroll two ways:

- **By Customer and Job.** This enables you to assign employees' time to a specific customer or project.

- **By Class.** This enables you to categorize employees' time by classifications you've set up. For example, if you have classes for EDITING, WRITING, MANAGING, and VIDEO PRODUCTION, one employee might have time allocated to EDITING while another might have time allocated to MANAGING.

To turn on payroll tracking:

1. Display the Accounting Preferences by choosing File, Preferences and clicking on the Accounting icon.

2. Click on the Customer Preferences tab.

3. Make sure Track Expenses by Customer: Job is selected if you want to track payroll that way. Similarly, make sure Use Class Tracking is selected if you want to follow payroll by class. You can have both options selected at once.

4. When you create the paychecks (which you'll do in a moment), be sure to specify the Customer: Job or Class Tracking settings so that QuickBooks can categorize the expense.

Taking the Duh Out of Deductions

Do deductions mystify you? Anything that takes away from gross or net pay is technically called a *deduction*. This includes taxes, medical expenses, payments to a pension or 401(k) plan, and more. To specify deductions for your employees, follow these steps:

1. In the Payroll and Employee tab of the QuickBooks Navigator, click on the Payroll Item icon.

2. Click on the Payroll Item button at the bottom of the Payroll Item list and click on New. (Alternatively, you can press Ctrl+N to bypass the menu selections.) The first page of the Add New Payroll Item Wizard appears (see Figure 4.26).

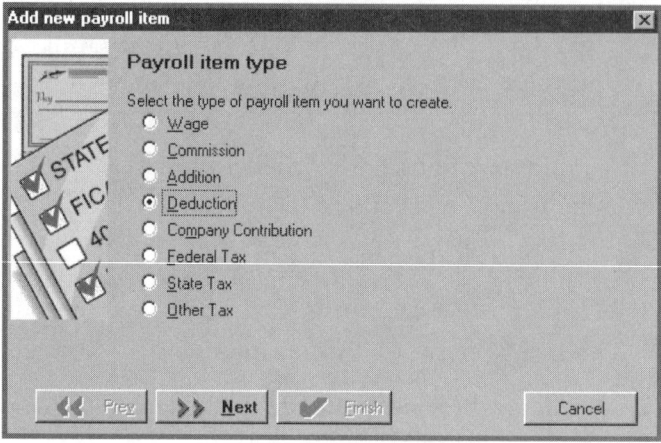

Figure 4.26

The Add New Payroll Item Wizard steps you through adding a new deduction to your payroll system.

3. Enter the name for the deduction you want to add. Click on Next.

4. Enter the name of the agency to which you pay the deduction. If it is ABC Insurance, for example, enter that name. Press Tab and enter your account number with that company. Press Tab again and choose an account for the deduction. Click on Next.

5. Enter the tax tracking type if one applies to your deduction. Click on Next.

6. Click on the payroll taxes that should be deducted *before* the new deduction is subtracted. Click on Next.

7. If the deduction has anything to do with a certain number of units sold, click on the Based on Quantity check box in the next screen; otherwise, leave the box blank. Click on Next.

8. In the Default Rate and Limit screen, enter a percentage rate if the same rate applies to all employees. In other words, if the deduction is two percent of gross wages for all employees, you enter 2% in the top field. In the bottom portion of the screen, enter a limit for the deduction if there is one. If you pay two percent of gross pay up to a total of $1,000, enter the 1000 in the bottom field. Click on Finish. The wizard finishes, and the dialog box closes.

Payday! A Step-by-Step Process

After you've set up everything you need in the payroll process, you're ready to run the checks. Start out, as usual, in the Payroll and Employees tab of the Navigator. Click on Create Paychecks. The Select Employees to Pay dialog box appears, as shown in Figure 4.27.

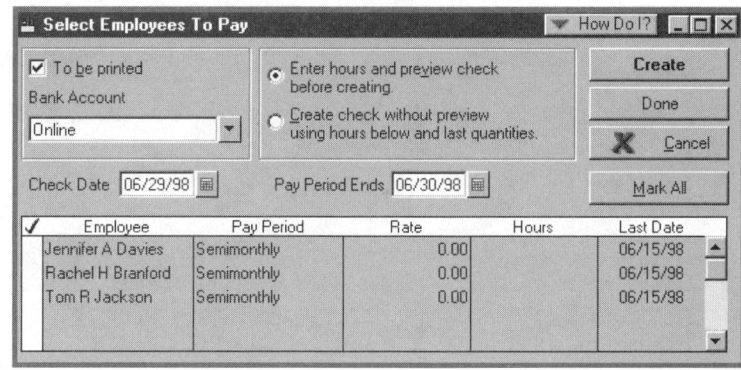

Figure 4.27

The first screen of the paycheck process asks you to choose the names of the employees you want to pay.

Follow these steps to issue the paychecks:

1. Do you want the checks to be printed in a batch? If so, make sure that the To Be Printed check box is selected (it is already selected by default).

2. Choose the account from which you want the checks to be drawn.

3. Enter the date for the paycheck. Press Tab.

4. Enter the end date for the pay period. Press Tab.

5. Select the way you want to figure the check amounts. You can choose either to enter the number of hours worked and preview the check or to run the check using the number of hours shown in the columns in the bottom of the dialog box.

NOTE Select the option that enables you to use the number of hours shown, only if the hours have stayed the same from the previous pay period or you are paying salaried employees.

6. Click to the left of the names of employees you want to pay.

7. Click on Create. The Preview Paycheck dialog box appears, as shown in Figure 4.28.

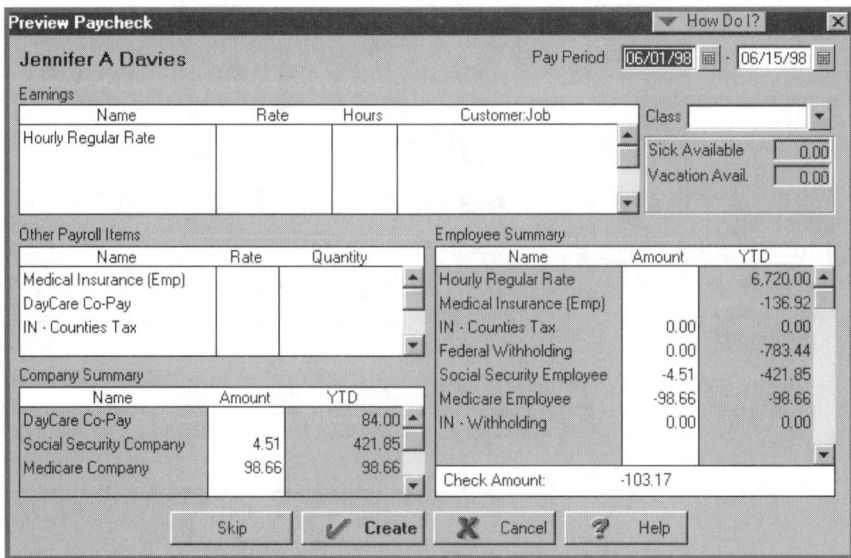

Figure 4.28

In the Preview Paycheck dialog box, you enter the amounts for the current check and review YTD totals.

8. In the Earnings area, choose the pay type, the hourly rate, and the number of hours worked. Assign a Customer: Job if one applies. As you enter the amounts, the Employee Summary at the lower right of

the dialog box changes to reflect the values you enter. QuickBooks keeps a running total to show you what the net pay is for the employee (see Figure 4.29).

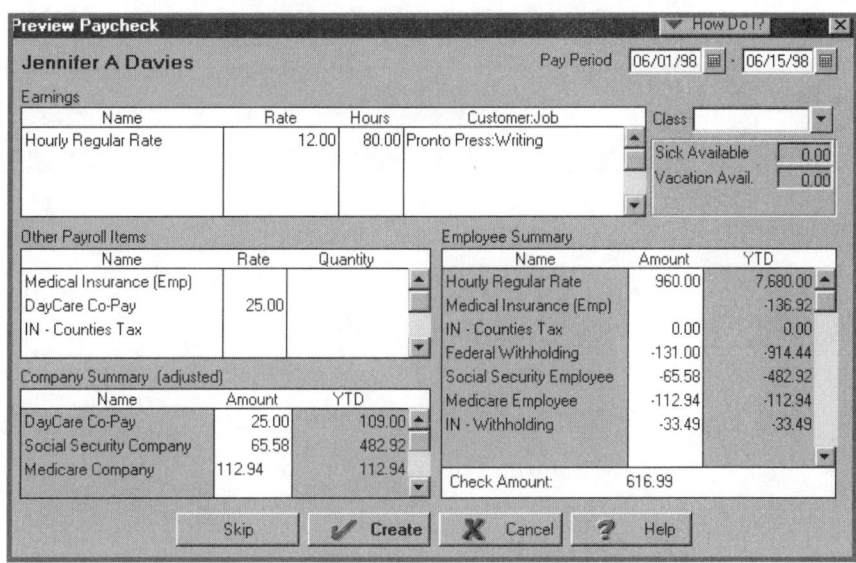

Figure 4.29

As you enter information in the Preview Paycheck dialog box, QuickBooks updates the Employee Summary area to show you the net pay after deductions.

9. When you are finished entering the amounts, click on Create. QuickBooks displays the Preview Paycheck dialog box for the next employee selected in the Select Employees to Pay dialog box.

10. After you finish entering information for each employee, the Select Employees to Pay dialog box is displayed again. Click on Done to close the dialog box and return to the Navigator.

Okay, but where are the checks? Perhaps you were expecting to see real checks in the Preview Paycheck dialog box, but rest assured they have been prepared. You can look in your checkbook to make sure. Just click on the Checking and Credit Cards tab and then click on the Checkbook Register icon. The payroll checks have been written and appear as PAY CHK in your checkbook register (see Figure 4.30).

Figure 4.30

The paychecks are written and ready to print. Look for PAY CHK in the Type column to see which checks QuickBooks has issued as payroll checks.

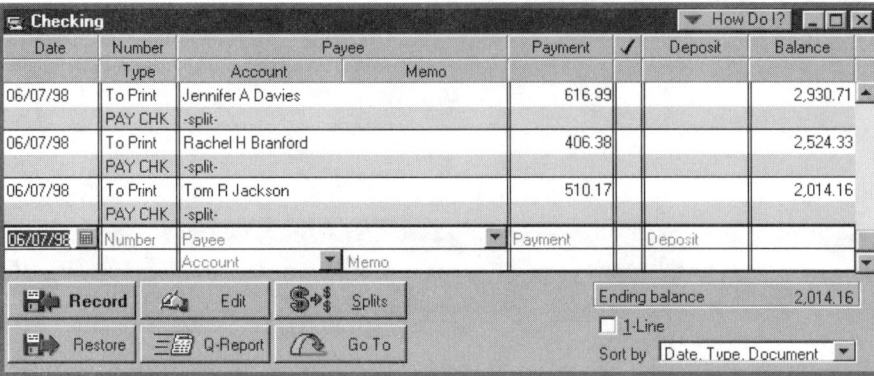

After you finish filling in the Preview Paychecks dialog box, QuickBooks writes the checks and puts them in the queue to be printed. You can print the checks (assuming, of course, you've ordered printer checks and they are loaded in the printer and ready to roll) by following these steps:

1. Open the File menu and choose Print Forms. A submenu appears.

2. Choose Print Paychecks. The Select Paychecks to Print dialog box appears, as shown in Figure 4.31.

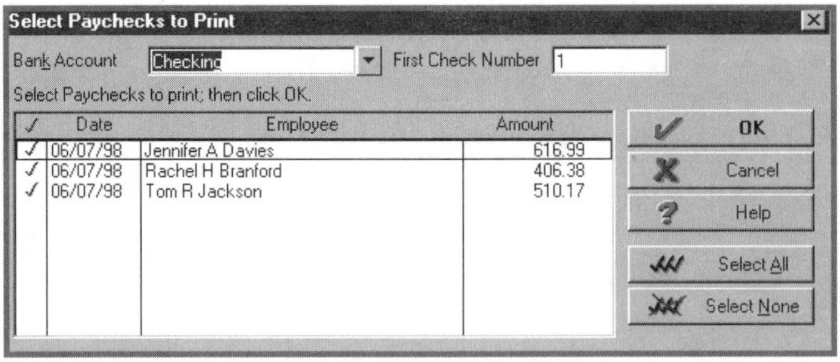

Figure 4.31

The Select Paychecks to Print dialog box displays the checks you created in the Preview Paychecks window.

3. Choose the account you want to print checks from. The columns list the paychecks you issued in the Preview Paychecks window.

4. Make sure the paychecks you want to print are selected. Click on OK, and QuickBooks sends the checks to the printer.

You can order checks online directly from Intuit. Open the Activities menu, choose Other Activities, and select the Order Checks/Forms/Software Online option. When the Connect dialog box appears, type your password and click on Connect. QuickBooks takes you online to Intuit's order site so that you can order the checks you need.

Paying Your Liabilities

Once you've set up all the various payroll items and have cut your paychecks, you know what deductions you pay and to whom. But it's still nice to let QuickBooks do the figuring for you at the end of the month, the quarter, or the year.

When you are ready to pay your liability accounts, click on the Payroll and Employee tab in the Navigator and click on Pay Liabilities. The Pay Liabilities dialog box appears, as Figure 4.32 shows.

If you don't have a vendor or agency listed in the Payable To column, QuickBooks will prompt you to enter that information for each liability

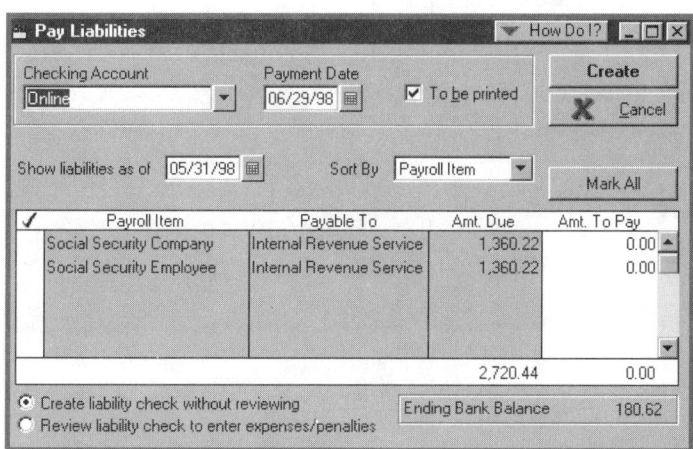

Figure 4.32

The total amounts are entered in the Pay Liabilities dialog box. Select the ones you want to pay, verify the amounts, and click on OK to have QuickBooks issue the check.

item listed. Follow the onscreen prompts and enter the information as requested.

Click on the liabilities you want to pay and verify the amounts. Finally, click on OK. QuickBooks writes the check and puts the check in the queue to be printed.

> **FIND IT ONLINE** QuickBooks gives you the option of filing your taxes online. This service, which is available for a subscription fee from Intuit, electronically pays federal and state payroll taxes, prepares W-2s for your employees and W-3s for your company, and automatically sends you updated tax tables via e-mail. For more about paying taxes online, see "Online Banking with QuickBooks," the Sunday Afternoon session.

A Payroll Tax Form Primer

In the Payroll and Employee tab of the Navigator window, you see three remaining icons: Process 941, Process 940, and Process W-2s. What are these forms and why do you need to worry about them? And perhaps most important—how can QuickBooks help you with them?

- Form 941 is a form you submit quarterly showing the amount of federal tax, social security tax, and Medicare you paid for the quarter.

- Form 940 is the form you submit at the end of the year on which you report your company's FUTA (Federal Unemployment Tax) liability.

- The W-2 is the form you supply to each employee showing the gross amount earned and the amount of federal, state, and local taxes that have been deducted from the gross.

- The W-3 is a form that summarizes all the individual W-2 forms you create for your employees.

Creating the 941

When you're ready to tackle the 941, display the Payroll and Employee tab of the Navigator and click on Process 941. The Form 941 dialog box appears, as Figure 4.33 shows. In this dialog box, you can choose to create, edit, print, or preview the form.

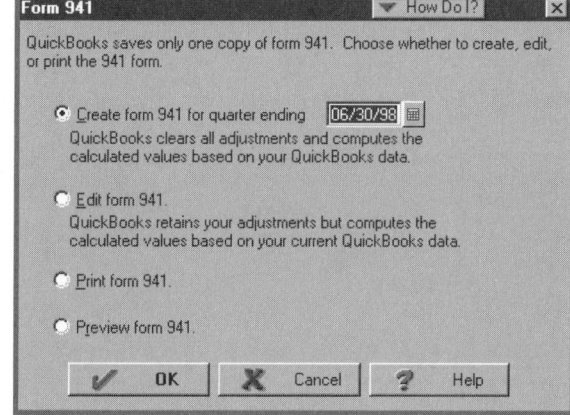

Figure 4.33

In the Form 941 dialog box, you can create, edit, print, or preview your 941.

Make sure that the first option is selected and choose the end date for the quarter you are reporting on. After you click on OK, an information screen appears showing you the data you have entered for your business, including the company name, the federal ID number, the address, the state code, and the end date of the quarter. Verify that all the information is correct; then click on Next.

If you will be exempt from filing the 941 in subsequent quarters, click on the Click Here check box. Additionally, if you are a seasonal employer, click on the appropriate option. Click on Next.

Fill in the information requested in each of the subsequent screens, clicking on Next after each one. If you have a question about how to respond to any of QuickBooks' questions, look up your previous 941s or call your accountant for clarification.

At the end of the process, you have the option of either printing or previewing the Form 941. Figure 4.34 shows the previewed form. If you want to go ahead and print the form, click on Print.

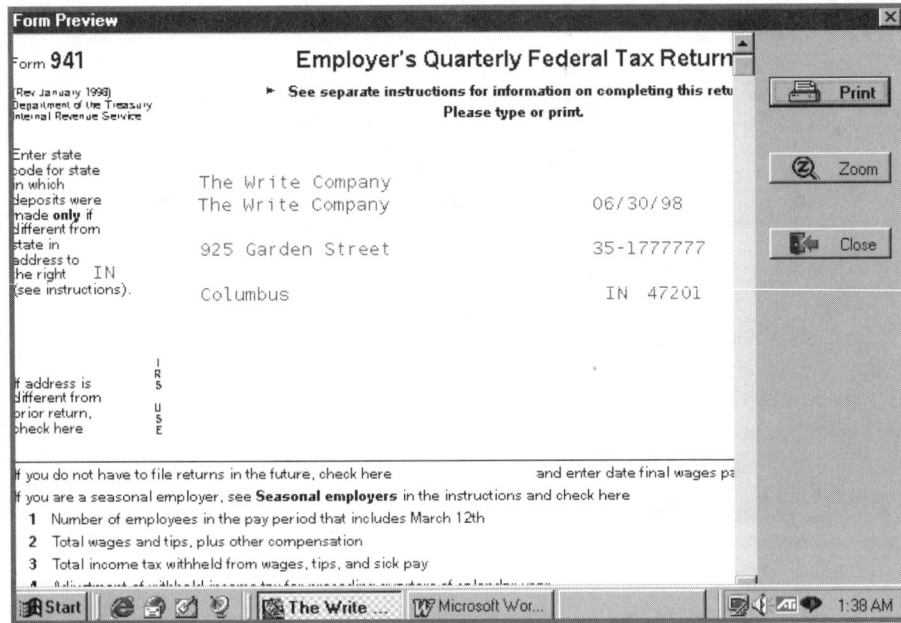

Figure 4.34

QuickBooks walks you through the process of creating the 941. At the end of the task, you can either preview or print, or both

Creating the 940

Creating Form 940 is a simple task as well. Begin in the Payroll and Employee tab of the Navigator window; click on Process 940. Again you have the option of creating, editing, previewing, or printing the report. Click on Create, enter the date for the ending of the period, and click on OK to continue.

The information window appears, showing you the data QuickBooks has gathered about your business, including name, address, and year-end date. Verify the accuracy of the information and click on Next.

The next screen asks you several questions about the way your company files unemployment taxes. Fill in the appropriate answers and click on Next.

Answer all questions as they are displayed; verify amounts and click on Next. The next-to-last screen displays your 940 liability broken down by quarter. When you click on Next, you are given the option of printing or previewing the 940. If you decide to preview first, you can print the form by clicking on the Print button while the document is displayed in Preview mode.

W-2s Made Simple

We all know what W-2s are. We've known for years, since we had our first jobs and had to file our first taxes. W-2s, which employers are supposed to get to us by January 31 every year, tell us how much we made and how much of a cut the government got (see Table 4.1).

As an employer, the pressure is on you to deliver the W-2s your employees need accurately and on time. QuickBooks can help you do that. Here's how:

1. Start in the Payroll and Employee tab.

2. Click on Process W-2s. The Process W-2s dialog box appears so that you can select the employees for whom you want to create W-2s.

3. Click on the column to the left of each employee for whom you want to print W-2s.

4. Preview the W-2 for a selected employee by clicking on the employee's name and clicking on Review W-2. The W-2 is displayed in Preview mode, as Figure 4.35 shows.

5. Click on Next to see the next W-2 or click on OK to close the display and return to the Process W-2s dialog box.

6. When you're ready to print the W-2s, click on Print.

Figure 4.35

Take a look at a QuickBooks-generated W-2.

> **TIP** A W-3 is a summary form that incorporates all the individual W-2s you need to print. To create a W-3, begin with the Process W-2s icon in the Payroll and Employee tab. Select all the employees for which you want to print W-2s, print the W-2s, and then go back and print the W-3 by clicking on Print W-3 in the Process W-2s dialog box.

4.1 WHEN TO FILE WHAT		
Form	**When**	**To Whom**
940	January 31	IRS
W-2s	January 31	Employees
1099s	February 28	Contractors
941	April 30	IRS

SATURDAY EVENING   **Keeping Track of INVENTORY and Managing Payroll**

What's Next?

See—that wasn't so bad, was it? Even though payroll can be a complicated process, once you get the information entered, QuickBooks does the rest. From organizing your employee information to helping you figure deductions and pay your liabilities—even to allowing you to create and submit your tax forms online—QuickBooks takes much of the sting and worry out of tax time.

You must be tired! It's time to shut the PC down for the night and give your eyes and brain a well-deserved rest. But tomorrow morning when you are ready to get going again, you've got a fun topic to tackle: "Tracking Results: Reporting Your Financial Data."

Whether you're giving a presentation to potential investors or simply talking up your new line of products, being able to show in black and white (and maybe color) how your company is thriving is a good thing. And being able to communicate with your accountant—with reports and charts he understands—can help you make sure your business is being represented in the best possible way. Specifically, tomorrow morning's session will introduce you to the following:

- Knowing when you need a report
- Choosing the right report for the job
- Understanding profit and loss
- Creating and printing a simple report
- Printing your balance sheet
- Formatting your report
- Working with report filters
- Memorizing reports
- Creating custom reports
- Adding graphs to spice things up

So tomorrow will be a fun change of pace—rather than focusing on input, you'll play around a little with output and see how good your business can look on the printed page.

For now, though, get some rest. And come back tomorrow refreshed and ready to finish up your QuickBooks-in-a-weekend course.

Good night!

Sunday Morning
Tracking Results: Reporting Your Financial Data

- Choosing the Right Report
- QuickReports on the Fly
- Formatting Your Report
- Working with Report Filters
- Adding Graphs

You've mastered many of the main features of QuickBooks. You've set up your company; entered customer information and recorded sales; set up a billing system and starting cutting checks with QuickBooks. You've discovered how you can use QuickBooks to organize and maintain inventory information and tackled what can be a major headache for many people—payroll—in one evening session. This morning you are ready to discover how you can print reports and graphs that help you communicate how your business is doing and where you want it to grow. Specifically, this session walks you through the following procedures:

- Knowing when you need a report
- Choosing the right report for the job
- Understanding profit-and-loss
- Creating and printing a simple report
- Printing your balance sheet
- Formatting your report
- Working with report filters
- Memorizing reports
- Creating custom reports
- Adding graphs to spice things up

Ready? If your Sunday morning schedule is cleared, get yourself a fresh cup of hot coffee, put a Mozart CD in the drive, and get started reporting in QuickBooks.

When Do You Need a Report?

You first set up and became used to QuickBooks as you fed data into the program. After all, you've got lists to create, checks to write, employee information to track, and bills to pay. Reports are probably pretty far from the top of your priority list.

But once you begin to get comfortable with your QuickBooks tasks, you will start to consider how you can show off your business data. When you go to a meeting, you'll want to be able to show potential investors your active client list. When you make that trip to the accountant's office, you'll be eager to wow him with the slick layouts and organized data QuickBooks can provide.

And you're not too far from being able to produce such a thing—quickly, easily, and in color.

Checking Out Available Reports

Throughout these sessions, you've worked with the QuickBooks Navigator. You've used the tabs along the left edge of the Navigator window to move from task to task. You've worked with the graphics in the center of the window to choose different options and work with various features. But I've ignored one part of the Navigator window that has been present in every session: the Reports area. For example, take a look at Figure 5.1.

TIP Different tabs show different reports in the Reports area of the Navigator window. For example, when you select the Sales and Customers tab, the available reports are Profit & Loss, Accounts Receivable, Sales, Budget, and Memorized. When Checking and Credit Cards is selected, Transaction Detail, Other, Custom, and Memorized reports are available.

SUNDAY MORNING Tracking Results: Reporting Your Financial Data

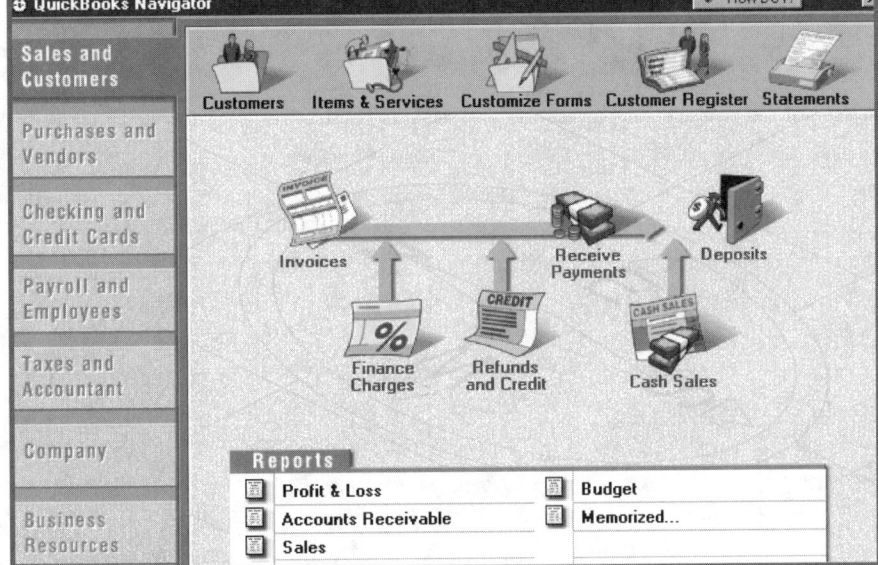

Figure 5.1

The Reports area in the Navigator window shows you the preset reports you can create and allows you to create custom reports as well.

Display the Navigator and click on the different tabs to see the reports that are available. Table 5.1 describes the basic reports (although you can create variations of each and invent your own custom reports as well).

Where Do You Find Reports?

One place to look for reports is obvious: the Navigator window. But you can create reports from two other places in QuickBooks as well: from some list boxes and from the Reports menu. First take a look at the reports available in list boxes:

1. Click on the Sales and Customers tab.
2. Click on the Customers icon. The Customer: Job List box appears.
3. Click on the Reports button at the bottom of the Customer: Job List. A submenu appears, as Figure 5.2 shows.

Table 5.1 Reports Available in QuickBooks

Report Type	Description
Profit & Loss	Shows you, over the amount of time you specify, the big picture of your company's income and expenses.
Balance Sheet	Portrays the financial health of your business by listing your company's assets, liabilities, and equity.
Accounts Receivable	Tells you what monies will be coming in—which invoices are outstanding and how much your customers owe you.
Accounts Payable	Lets you know what monies will be going out—who you owe, how much, and when the payments are due.
Sales	Shows you what items you have sold, who you sold the items to, and how much you sold them for.
Budget	Compares the actual income and expense information with your budgeted, or planned, amounts.
Payroll Reports	Enables you to produce reports using the payroll data you have entered and calculated. (Note: You must be using QuickBooks' payroll features in order to print payroll reports.)
Inventory Reports	Produces reports using inventory information you are tracking; you might report on vendors, transactions, inventory items, or a combination.

You can also create reports from the Reports menus. Logical place, yes? Take a look at the report types housed there (see Figure 5.3).

Wow! What are you going to do with all those reports? Not only are you faced with a huge variety of report types, but within each type there are a number of *other* options you can select. Yes, the choice is astounding, but

SUNDAY MORNING Tracking Results: Reporting Your Financial Data 211

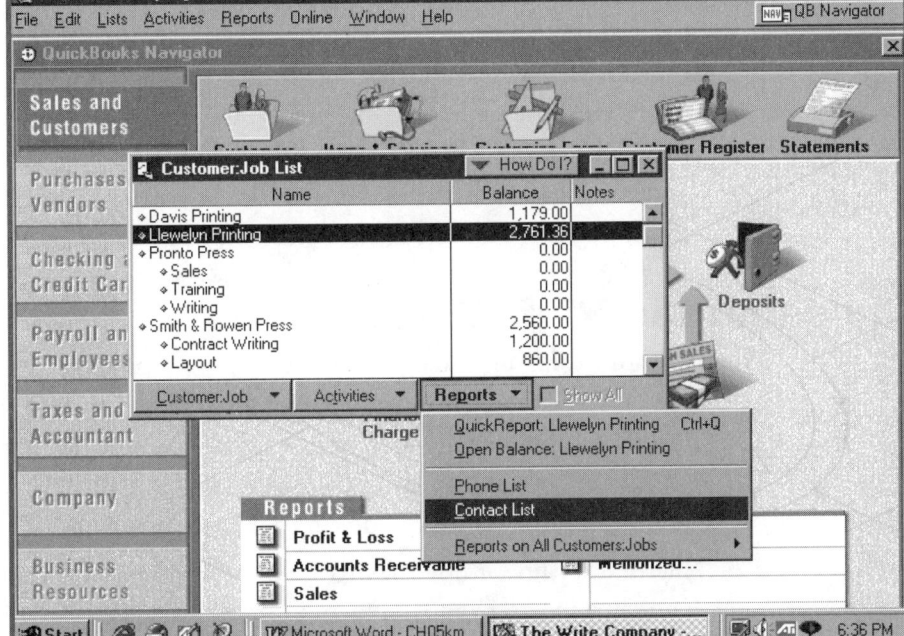

Figure 5.2

You can choose reports from different list boxes. This report list is available when the Customer: Job List is displayed.

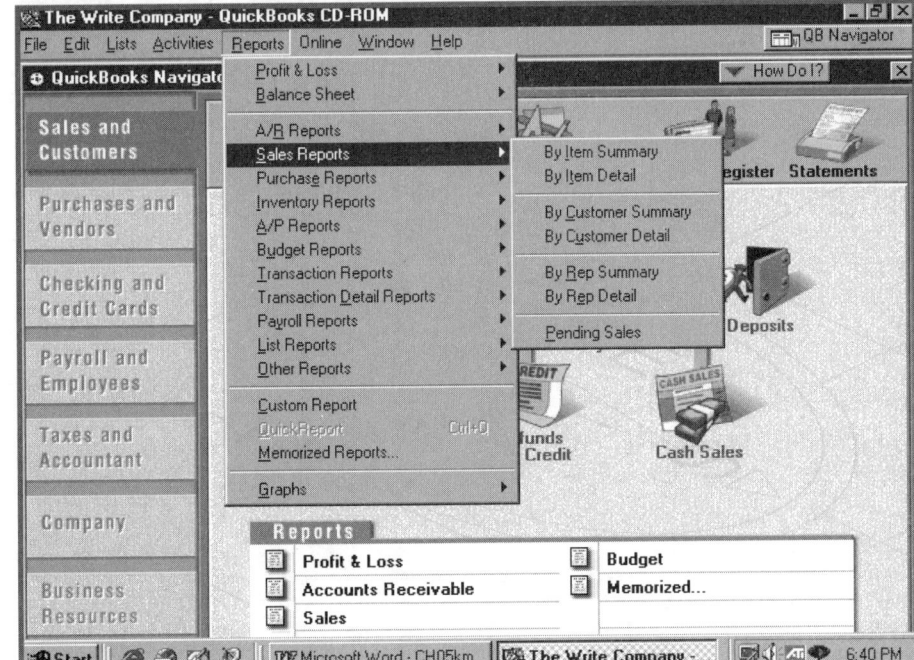

Figure 5.3

In the Reports menu are a number of report styles and options that control the way your QuickBooks data is displayed.

don't panic. Finding the right report isn't as hard as you might think. And QuickBooks makes it so easy to create a report quickly that if it isn't just exactly what you want, it's no big deal to delete the report and start again. Once you get the hang of it, you'll be creating reports in a matter of minutes—maybe less. And after you hit on a report style you especially like, you can have QuickBooks memorize it so that you can use it again and again without reentering the settings you selected to create it.

Choosing the Right Report

Part of exploring the QuickBooks' report repertoire is simply experimenting. What do you want to show? How do you want to show it? Your first task is to narrow the choices of reports until you know basically the one you want—then you can customize it to use the fonts, columns, colors, graphs, and styles you're looking for.

Here are a few guidelines to help you choose the right report for what you're trying to show:

- If you want to show the results of company sales over time, create a *Sales* report.

- If you want to show the transactions in a specific account, create a *Transaction Detail* report.

- If you want to show whether your business is profitable, do a *Profit & Loss* report.

- If you want to take a look at where the money goes, create an *Accounts Payable* report.

- If you want to get an idea of what money will be coming in, do an *Accounts Receivable* report.

- If you want to see whether your actual expenses and income are close to what you planned, print a *Budget* report.

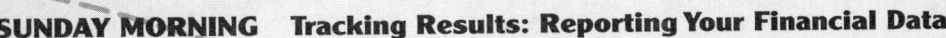

SUNDAY MORNING   Tracking Results: Reporting Your Financial Data

- If you want to analyze whether the money spent on inventory is going to the right items, create an *Inventory* report and choose Valuation Summary.

- If you want to get a transaction history with a certain vendor, create an *Inventory* report and select Stock Status by Vendor.

> ### What About Other Reports?
>
> QuickBooks includes a number of other reports that don't fit into any particular category—hence the name "Other Reports." You'll find this option two-thirds of the way down the Reports menu. Because these reports might be just what you are looking for, I include them quickly here so that you can see what you're (not) missing:
>
> - The *Cash Flow Forecast* report shows what to expect your income to be and projects your account balances so that you can get an idea of how much money you expect to have.
>
> - The *Check Detail* report lists the accounts the checks were taken from and to whom they were paid.
>
> - The *Deposit Detail* report lists details about the deposits you specify.
>
> - The *General Ledger* report lists the transactions in a specified period of time.
>
> - The *Income Tax Summary* report lists the amount of tax for each tax line on the form you select. (The *Income Tax Detail* report shows the individual transactions that make up the summary information.)
>
> - The *Missing Checks* report lists checks, invoices, and payments in numerical order, spotlighting missing and duplicate numbers.
>
> - The *Journal* report separates transactions into debits and credits.
>
> - The *Trial Balance* report does a balance of your accounts using the debit and credit double-entry method.
>
> - *Transaction Journal* and *History* reports show debits and credits as well as list the transactions that have taken place, along with payments and invoices.

NOTE You can also use the Audit Trail report, but first you've got to open the File menu, choose Preferences, click on Accounting, and select Use Audit Trail. Audit Trail reports show you any transactions that were changed during the specified period; they can also display deleted transactions.

Creating, Previewing, and Printing a Simple Report

Ready? Then put some of this theory into action. The process is so simple you may miss it if you look away.

Open your company file if you haven't already done so. With the QuickBooks Navigator displayed, click on the Sales and Customers tab. Now follow these steps:

1. In the Reports area, click on Profit & Loss. A submenu appears.

2. Click on Income by Customer Summary. Figure 5.4 shows the report that results from The Write Company's data.

3. Now, assuming that this report is just what you hoped for, you are ready to print it. (For most of your reports, you will do at least a little "tweaking"—change the fonts, rearrange things, add headings, whatever. For the sake of this example, though, this is *just* what you wanted.) To start the printing process, click on the Print button in the Report toolbar. The Print Reports dialog box appears, as shown in Figure 5.5.

4. Choose the printer you plan to use by clicking on the down arrow and selecting the printer name from the displayed list.

NOTE Different printers have different printing options. You can display—and change—the options for your particular printer by clicking on the Options button to the right of the Printer selection box.

Figure 5.4

The Income by Customer Summary report displays income totals by customer. With two clicks of the mouse, the report is created.

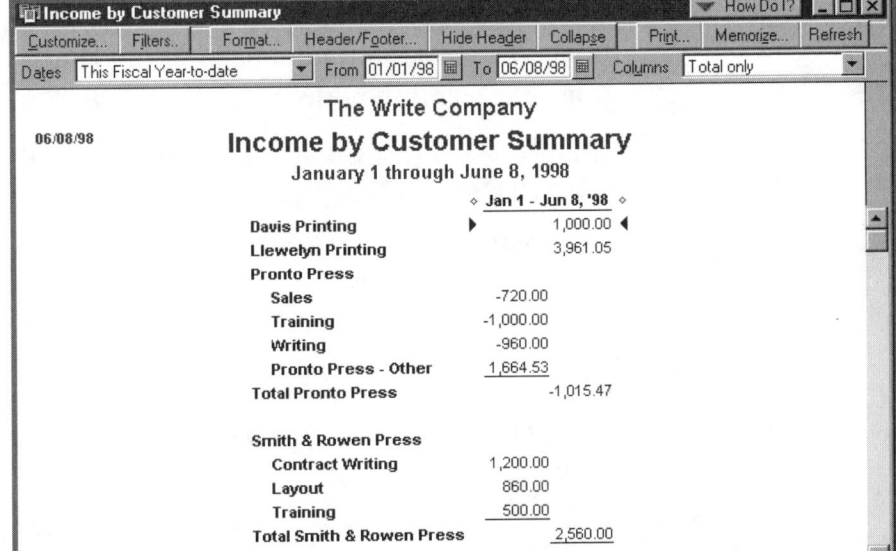

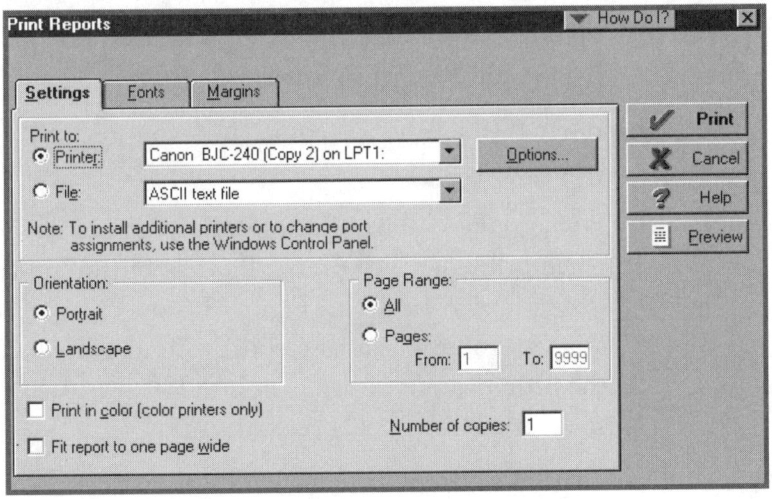

Figure 5.5

Once you display the report in the Report window, you can print it by clicking on Print, choosing your print options, and clicking on Print once again.

5. Choose the orientation—portrait or landscape. Portrait orientation prints the report in traditional 8 ½ × 11 inch format. Landscape prints the report in horizontal, 11 × 8 ½ inch format.

TIP A feature of QuickBooks 6.0 enables the program to "remember" which orientation you prefer. If you always print reports in landscape mode, for example, QuickBooks will recall that setting the next time you create a report.

6. Choose the Page Range. You can choose to print a single page or selected pages (enter the page numbers in the text boxes) or to print All.

7. If you have a color printer and want to print in color, click on the Print in Color check box. (If you have not selected a color printer in the Printer box, this option will be unavailable.)

8. If you want to print the entire report on one page, click on the Fit Report to One Page Wide check box.

9. Enter the number of copies in—you guessed it—the Number of Copies text box.

10. Finally, take a look at this puppy in Preview mode. How will it look when printed? Click on the Preview button on the right side of the dialog box to find out. Figure 5.6 shows you the resulting screen. You can zoom in on the report to find out what's what by clicking the little magnifying glass pointer on the place you want to see; to zoom back out, click a second time.

11. To go ahead and print, click on Print while still in Preview mode. (If you want to print without previewing a report, you can simply click on Print in the Print Reports dialog box to begin printing.) If you'd rather close the Preview window instead, click on Close to return to the Print Reports dialog box.

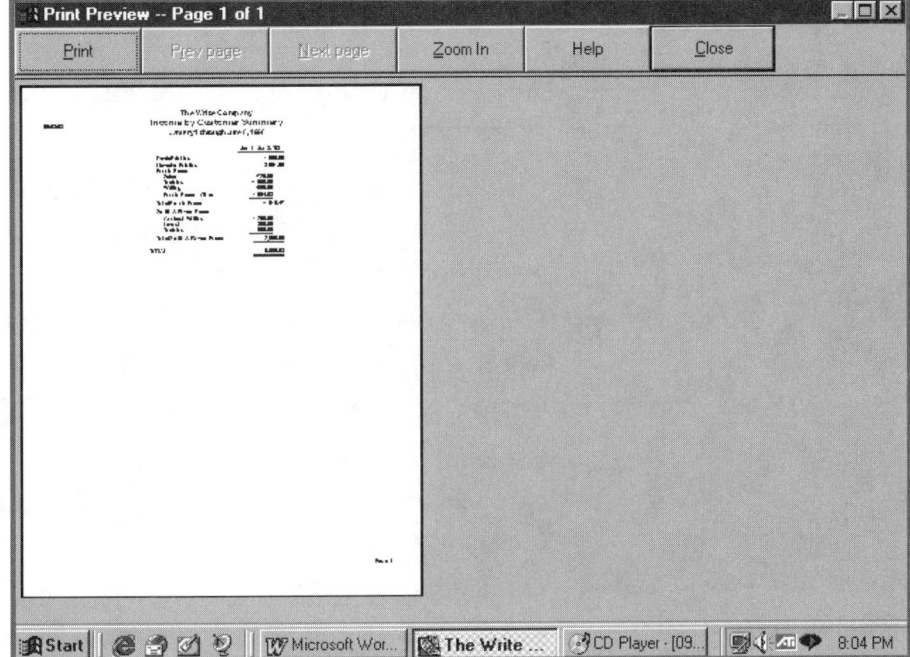

Figure 5.6

Preview mode shows you—in big-screen view—how the report will look when you print it.

 **NOTE** You may notice that you only explored the first tab in the Print Reports dialog box. Two others—Fonts and Margins—contain options you will explore when you begin modifying and formatting reports. The idea here is to get through the process once quickly. Stay tuned for more coverage of the Print Reports dialog box.

Checking Out the Report Window

The process of creating a report took you to a new place in QuickBooks: the Reports window. You got a look at it in Figure 5.5. Look back there now and check out the various screen elements:

- **Title bar.** Nothing new here, except that the title of the report shows up in the title bar. This is helpful when you're not sure which report you selected or whether it's the one you really intended to create.

- **Reports toolbar.** The Reports toolbar—also called the Reports button bar—contains the major tools you'll use as you modify, format, and enhance the reports you create. The buttons available in the toolbar are these:

    - **Customize.** Displays the Customize Report dialog box, which allows you to make changes such as report date, reporting method, and column content.

    - **Filters.** Allows you to specify what kind of data is shown in the report. Filters help you net out the information that isn't needed in order to show the data result you're trying for.

    - **Format.** Controls all kinds of format issues, including the way numbers are displayed, the font used, the header and footer used, and more.

    - **Header/Footer.** Enables you to set up, control, and print header and footer information. You choose what you want displayed, where you want it, and how you want it to look.

    - **Hide Header.** With one click on this button, you can hide the header you created in the Header/Footer dialog box. After you click on the button, the name on the button itself changes to Show Header so that you can redisplay the header again.

    - **Collapse.** This is another single-click button—this one collapses the subitems in the report. For example, see what happens in Figure 5.7 to the report shown in Figure 5.5 when I click on Collapse. The subordinate items disappear, and the Collapse button changes to Expand. To return the report to full display, click on Expand.

    - **Print.** You've already seen this one—the button displays the Print Reports window. You can choose your print options and click on Print or Preview.

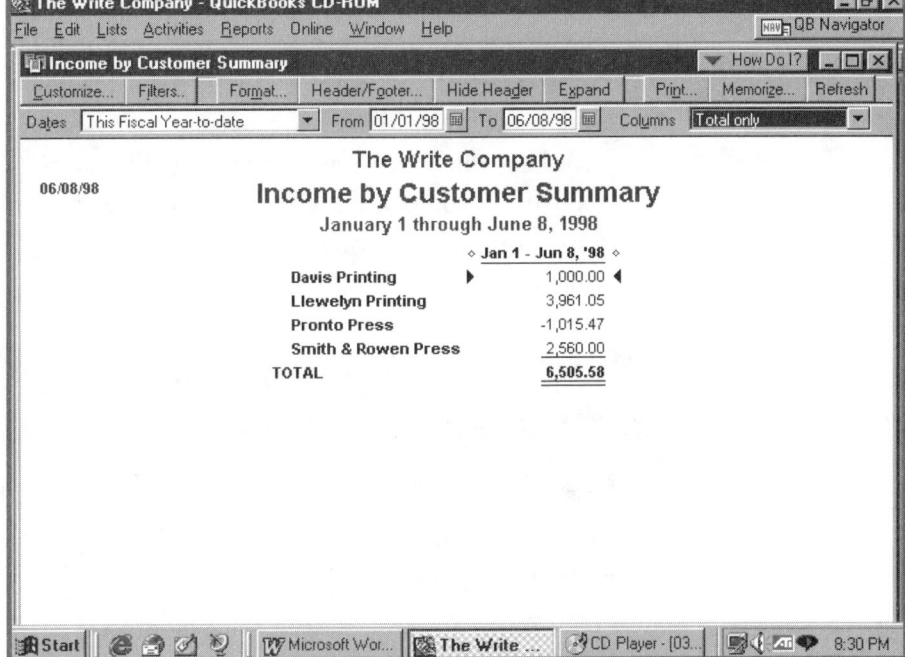

Figure 5.7

Collapsing a report in the Reports window removes subordinate items, although the totals remain the same.

- ✦ **Memorize.** When you click on Memorize for the first time, QuickBooks lets you know about the new memorize-the-orientation feature. Click on OK and a pop-up box appears so that you can enter a name for the report you want to memorize. Memorizing a report is a great idea after you've spent some time getting it just the way you want it—this feature saves you time and trouble and tweaking later.

- ✦ **Refresh.** This button simply repaints or refreshes the screen, redisplaying the report after any changes you've made. Click on this button when you're not sure things are displaying properly after edits.

- ✦ **Help button.** Click on How Do I? to see a list of topics you can get help with regarding report issues. You can even watch two videos—one on tips for printing, and another on tips for filtering reports.

✦ **Dates and more dates.** The date you choose for your report has everything to do with whether you get the kind of result you were hoping for. If you want to show the sales results from last quarter and you choose the wrong dates, what have you got? A bunch of numbers that don't mean anything. The Dates setting is an important one—when you are creating your report, think carefully about what you want to choose for this item. Figure 5.8 shows the amazing list of choices that are available.

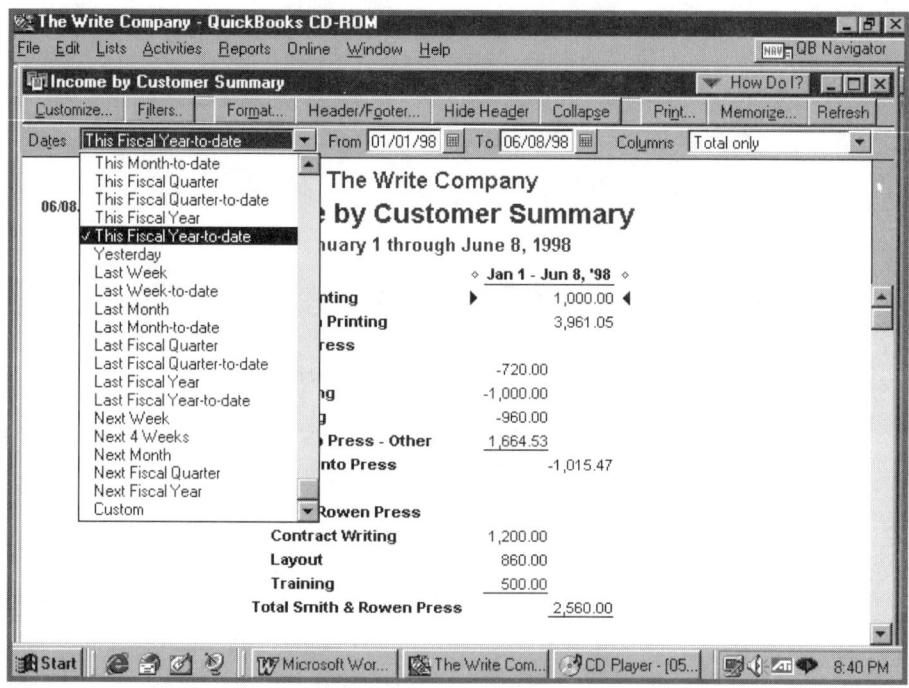

Figure 5.8

Dates, dates, and more dates— important considerations when you're creating a report.

✦ **From and To dates.** Not only can you enter the Dates information by clicking on it from the list, but you can pinpoint the specific dates between which you want to gather the information. Want to show the transactions you had with Pronto Press between May 2 and June 10? Enter the dates in the From and To boxes; then move the magnifying glass pointer to the total for Pronto Press and double-click. QuickBooks instantly displays the Customer Detail report that shows you all the transactions for Pronto Press between the dates you specified (see Figure 5.9). Wow. Pretty simple, eh? Simple and powerful.

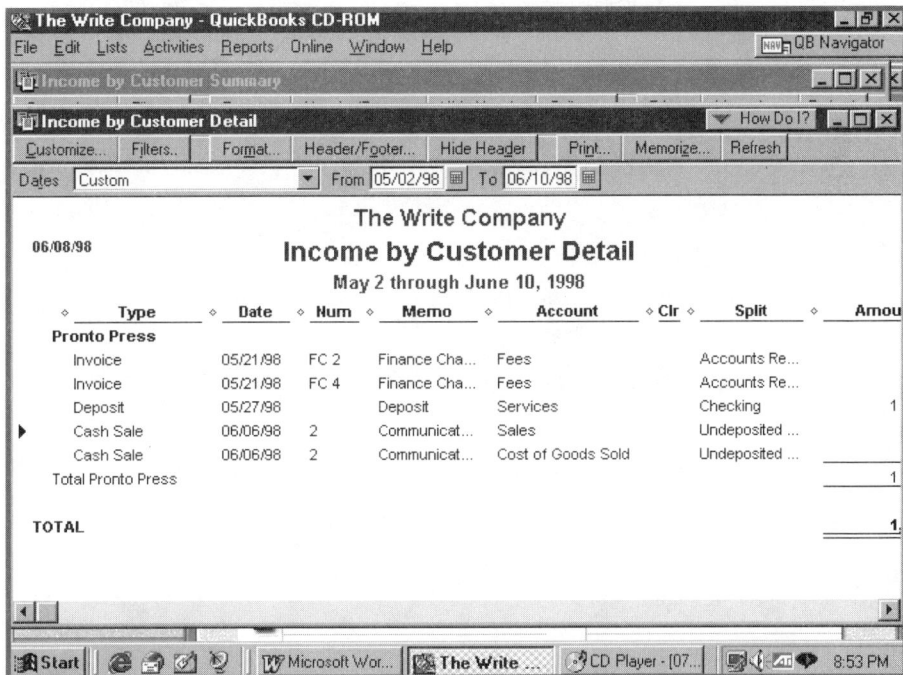

Figure 5.9

You can use the From and To dates to get even more closely targeted information about a specific vendor, customer, employee, or item.

NOTE When QuickBooks takes you from one report to another, the program leaves the first report open on the screen. To return to it, click on the Close box in the most recently displayed report. (Of course, you can minimize the report if you simply want to see the previous report and maximize it after you've done your check.)

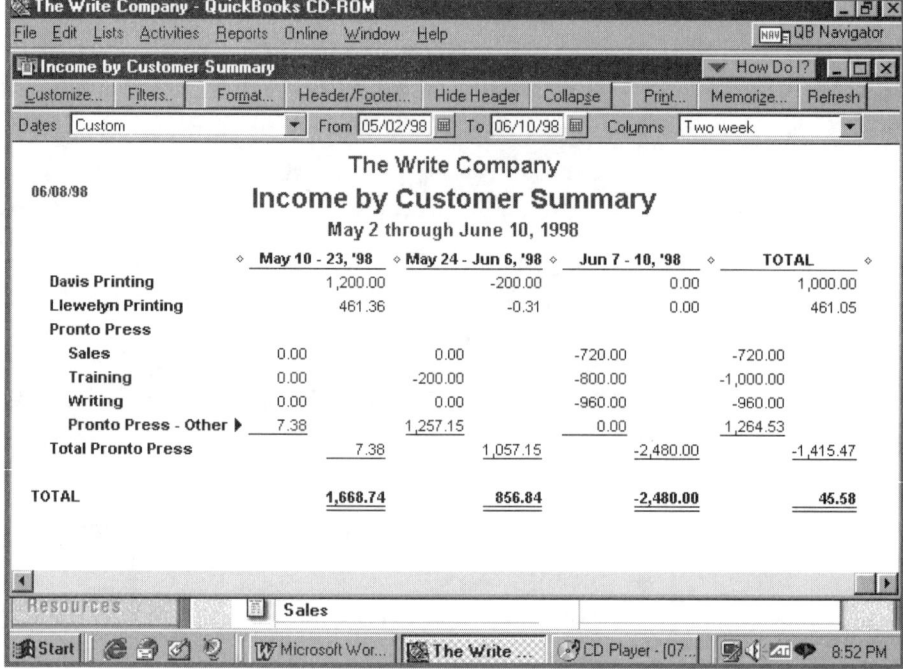

Figure 5.10

Changing the Columns setting drastically changes the way the report looks and the type of data that is displayed.

- **Selecting column content.** The last stop on the Reports window tour is the option that controls the columns that are displayed in the report. By default, the report in Figure 5.5 shows Total Only, meaning that only the totals are shown for the customers in the report. Other choices include Day, Week, Two Week, Four Week, Half Month, Month, Quarter, and Year. To see what kind of a difference the Columns setting makes, check out Figure 5.10, where I've selected Two Week instead of Total Only.

QuickReports on the Fly

In the last section, QuickBooks created a report on the fly when you changed the dates in the From and To boxes and double-clicked on the total for Pronto Press. That speedily generated report is a QuickReport.

QuickReport is an option available to you whenever you are working with lists in QuickBooks. You can do a QuickReport by clicking on an item in the list and pressing Ctrl+Q. It's that simple. Of course, you can also click on the Reports button and choose the QuickReport option if you prefer.

TIP To get a quick QuickReport, select a list item (Vendor, Customer, Item, or what have you) and press Ctrl+Q.

When would you want to use a QuickReport? When you have a clear picture of the type of data you want to see and aren't interested in doing it with a lot of bells and whistles. No hefty filters necessary.

To generate a QuickReport, follow these steps:

1. Open the Lists menu and choose the list you want to work with. (You can choose from Chart of Accounts, Items, Payroll Items, Classes, Customers: Jobs, Vendors, Employees, or Other Names.)

2. When the list is displayed, click on the item you want to use in the report.

3. Press Ctrl+Q. Figure 5.11 shows a QuickReport generated when I chose the first customer in The Write Company's Customer: Job list.

TIP Don't see the data you expected? Check the Dates setting and the From and To dates. Still not showing what you need? Maybe the Columns selection needs to be changed, too. QuickReport uses your most recent report settings to generate the report quickly, so the settings you selected for your last report will be in effect for this one until you change them.

Project Reports You Can Create

I think it may be a good idea to walk through a few of the specific project reports you would want to create for your business with QuickBooks. This

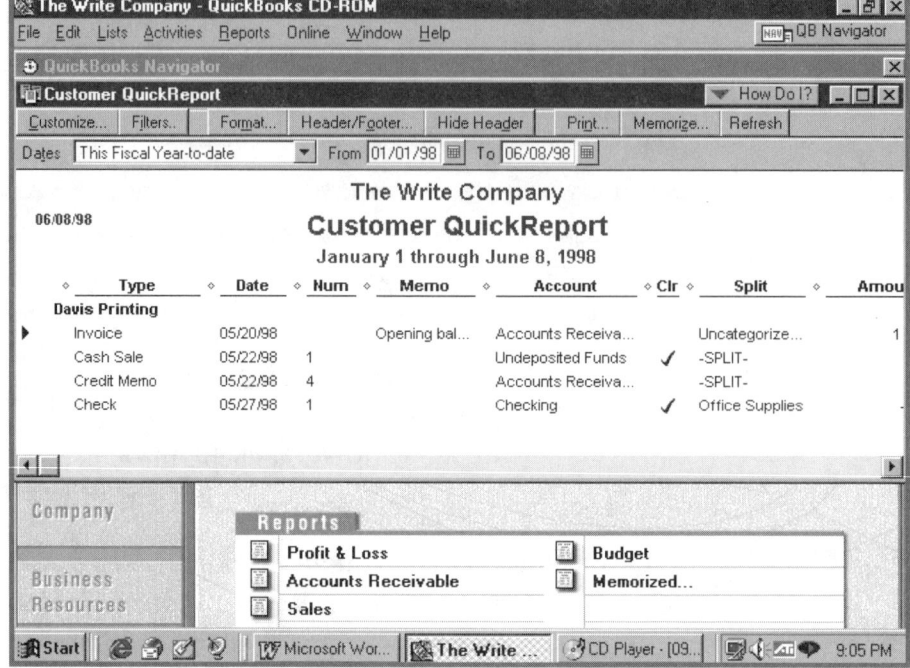

Figure 5.11

The QuickReport will use your current report settings and generate a fast report for the item you select.

section shows you how to create and quickly print a few reports that will help you get a feeling for how your business is doing and help others understand where you're coming from.

Producing a Profit and Loss Statement

Are you lost when it comes to profit and loss? The report sounds much more intimidating than it actually is to create. Any time you go to talk to a banker or any potential investor, the interested party will want to see both your profit and loss statement and your balance sheet.

◀ ◀
Your *profit and loss statement* shows you how your business is doing—big-picture-wise—in terms of income and expenses. Do the expenses eat up all the income? Vice versa?
◀ ◀

To create a profit and loss statement, follow these steps:

1. Open the Reports menu.

2. Choose Profit & Loss. A submenu appears. How do you want to show the data? The first choice, Standard, is probably your best bet unless you need to show a specific angle, such as how two periods in the current year to date compare with each other. For this example, choose Standard. Figure 5.12 shows the effect that the Standard selection has on the Profit & Loss statement.

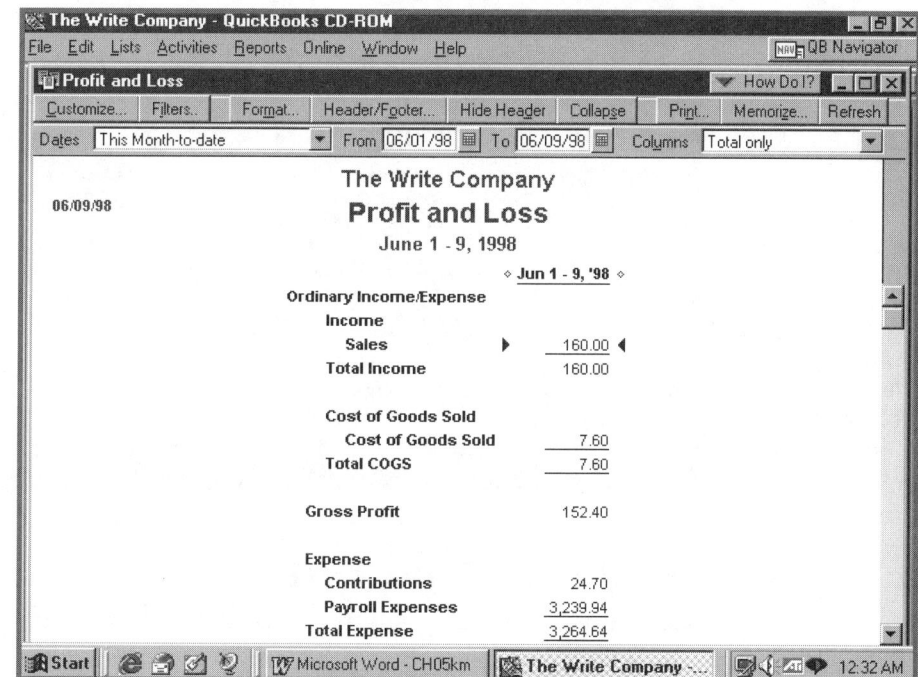

Figure 5.12

The Standard Profit & Loss statement shows ordinary income and expense information to give you a big-picture look at your company's financial situation.

Printing Your Balance Sheet

A balance sheet is similar to a profit and loss statement. The balance sheet lists your assets, liabilities, and equity, showing what you own and what you owe. To print a balance sheet, follow these steps:

1. Click on the Taxes and Accountant tab in the Navigator window.
2. In the Reports area, click on Balance Sheet. A pop-up menu appears.
3. Choose Standard. Figure 5.13 shows the resulting report.

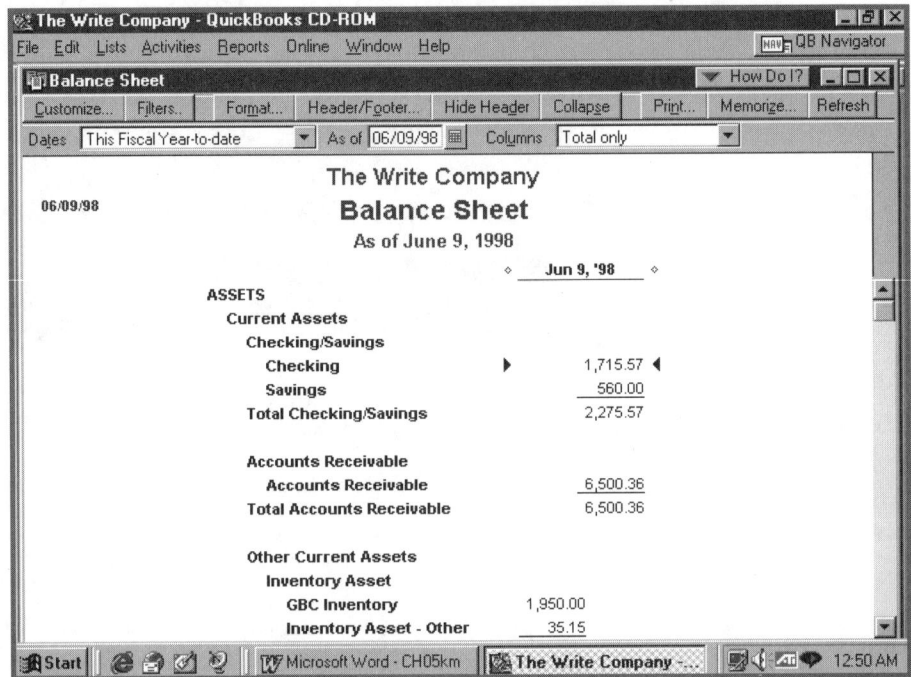

Figure 5.13

The Balance Sheet lists your business assets, liabilities, and equity.

Printing a Phone List

It may not be the first kind of report that rushes to mind, but a phone list can be a truly helpful thing. You may want to list the numbers of your employees, your vendors, or your customers. To print the phone list, follow these steps:

1. Display the list box of the item for which you want to print the phone list. (If you want to print the phone list for customers, for example, open the Lists menu and choose Customer: Job. To print a vendor phone list, choose the Vendors List box.)

2. Click on the Reports button. The submenu appears.

3. Click on the Phone List option. QuickBooks displays the list in the Report window (see Figure 5.14).

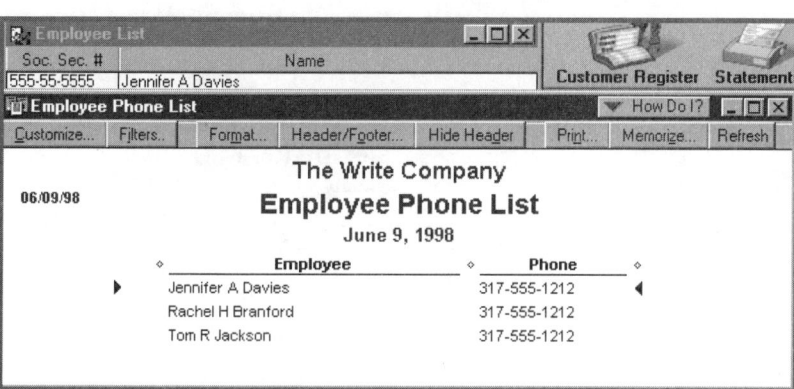

Figure 5.14

You can print a phone list from one of the List boxes by clicking on Reports and choosing Phone List from the submenu.

Creating a Sales Report

It's important, if you're going to make sales, to be able to track and understand the sales you've made. QuickBooks gives you a number of different sales reports you can use to review your sales results. Here are the steps:

1. Click on the Sales and Customers tab.

2. Click on the Items & Services icon. The Item List appears.

3. Click on the Reports button and choose Reports on All Items.

4. From the submenu that appears, choose Sales Reports and By Item Summary. Figure 5.15 shows the sales report selected.

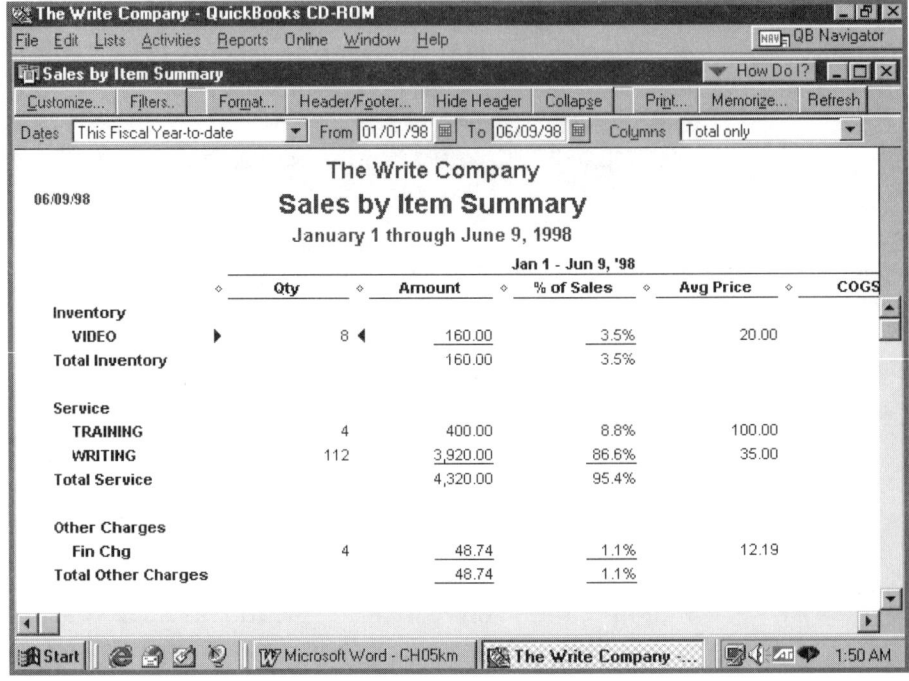

Figure 5.15

The Sales by Item Summary report breaks down sales figures for the period you specify.

Producing a Price List

The final report item you'll produce here is a price list. Especially if you offer a variety of services or products, having a price list handy is a great service for yourself and your employees as well as for your customers. To create the price list, follow these steps:

1. Click on the Sales and Customers tab.

2. Click on the Items & Services icon. Click on Reports.

3. From the submenu, click on Price List. Figure 5.16 shows the price list for The Writing Company.

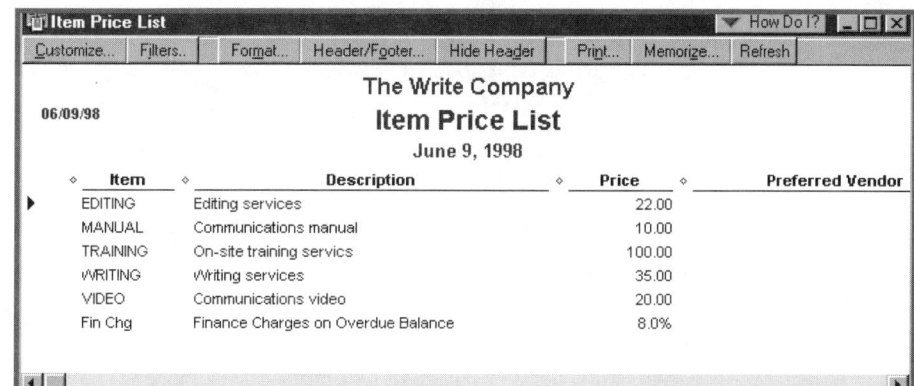

Figure 5.16

Print a price list by displaying a List box, choosing Reports, and clicking on Price List.

Take a Break

Is the whole reporting idea beginning to take shape for you? QuickReports are easy—they are great for those times when you need to see how things are going quickly. This is a good time to take a break; after you've had a chance to walk around a little and give your spouse and kids a quick hug, get something to drink and a snack or two (you know, those carrot sticks are better for you than those chocolate chip cookies...) and come on back to learn about customizing, memorizing, and filtering your QuickBooks reports.

Formatting Your Report

Now go back to the basic report. Suppose that you're creating a basic Profit & Loss statement for potential investors. You want it to look good. You want to make a few changes in the Reports window.

> **TIP**
> One of the most noticeable changes you can make is a change in font. The *font* controls the way the text looks—you might use big bold letters or small script-style letters. For best results, however, avoid the temptation to get fancy and mix a bunch of different font styles. You want your readers to be able to see clearly what you're trying to communicate, and using too many different fonts can actually detract from the effectiveness of your report.

Start by creating the report. When you've got it displayed in the Reports window, click on the Format button in the Reports toolbar. The Format Report dialog box appears, as shown in Figure 5.17.

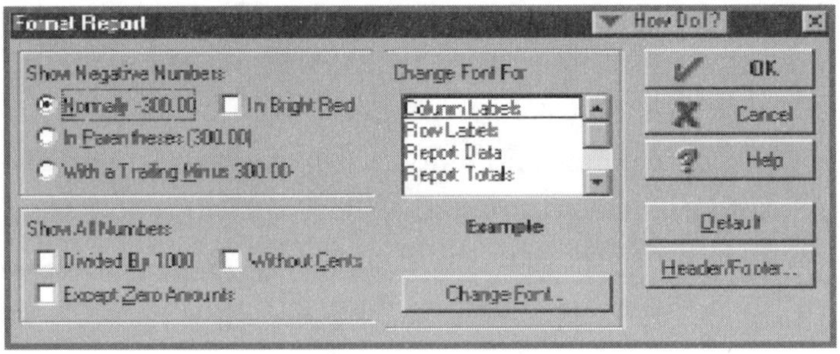

Figure 5.17

The Format Report dialog box enables you to choose a number format, change fonts, and more.

Changing Number Display

If you want to change the way negative numbers are shown, choose a different option in the Show Negative Numbers area of the Format Report dialog box. By default, QuickBooks displays a minus sign in front of the number. Other options include displaying the negative number in red, placing it in parentheses, or displaying a minus sign following the number.

You can change the number format by choosing one of the options in the Show All Numbers area. If you want the amounts to be shown rounded to the dollar, click on Without Cents.

Changing the Font

The first thing you need to do if you want to change the font used in your report is to select the item for which you want to change the font. In the Standard Profit & Loss report, you can choose Column Labels, Row Labels, Report Data, or Report Totals. Click on the item you want to change. For The Writing Company report, I selected Column Labels.

Click on Change Font. The Column Labels dialog box appears (see Figure 5.18). If you selected a different report element, the name of that element displays in the top of the dialog box.

To change the font, follow these steps:

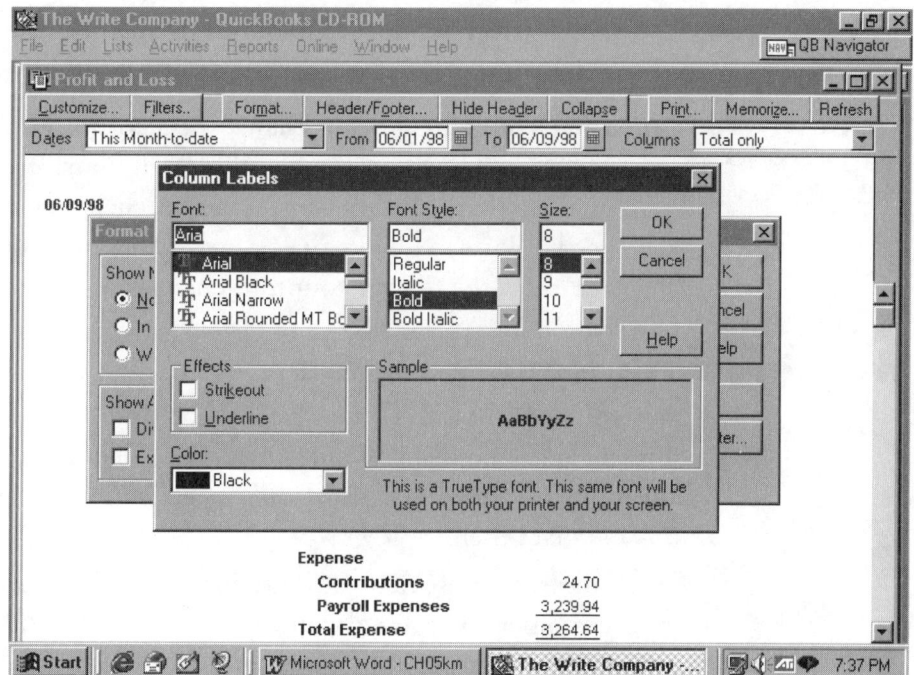

Figure 5.18

You can choose a new font, a new look, a new type size, or a new style for report text.

1. Choose the new font. Scroll through the list until you find a font name that interests you; click on it to see the text in the Sample window change. Press Tab.

▸▸▸▸▸▸▸▸▸▸▸▸▸▸▸▸▸▸▸▸▸▸▸▸▸▸

The technical definition for *font* is one size and style of a particular typeface, which means that 10-point bold Times Roman is one font, and 72-point italic Garamond is another.

▸▸▸▸▸▸▸▸▸▸▸▸▸▸▸▸▸▸▸▸▸▸▸▸▸▸

2. Choose the Font Style you want; press Tab.

3. Choose the Font Size. Remember that report text is generally 10- or 12-point. Anything smaller may be hard on your readers' eyes.

4. If you want to choose a font effect (Strikeout or Underline), click on the check box of the option you want.

5. You can change the color of the text if you want by clicking on the down arrow beside the Color box. Remember that unless you have a color printer, the changed color will appear only on the screen.

6. After you've made your changes, click on OK. A pop-up box asks whether you want to change all related fonts. If you want to change all fonts that are of the same typeface, click on OK. You are returned to the Format Report dialog box. Click on OK one more time to return to the report. Your font changes will appear.

Working with Report Filters

Now you know how to create a basic report and change the format to show different numeric displays and fonts. But what about those times when you want to change the actual *content* of the report, and not simply the look of what's there?

For example, suppose that your interior design firm wants to print a report of all customers who hired you to do jobs totaling $15,000 or more in 1997. There are several different considerations for creating a report like this. First, you need to rule out all the customers whose jobs were $14,999 or less. Next, you need to locate only the jobs done in 1997. If you simply printed a Customer report, you would get not only all customers showing all jobs with all amounts, but you'd get the transactions from all the years you've been in business (or at least, for all the years you've entered into QuickBooks).

Filtering takes care of this for you. Like the filter on your furnace, the QuickBooks filter catches all the stuff you don't want and discards it so you don't have to sift through it in a report. You set up a filter to make sure that everything that is *not* $15,000 or more gets filtered out. Similarly, another filter cuts out all the jobs from years *other than* 1997.

Filtering Ideas

How can you filter your reports? Here are a few ideas:

- **By date.** One common report involves showing specific data for a certain time frame.

- **By account.** You may want to produce a report of only income accounts and filter out all expense accounts.

- **By item**. If you want to see sales for a particular product or service, you can limit the report results to those showing the item you are interested in tracking.

- **By vendor.** You can create a report that shows transactions for a certain time, involving a certain item, with a certain vendor.

- **By customer.** You can limit your reports to a certain customer or selected customers.

- **Custom fields.** If you've added fields to your lists, as in the Additional Info tab of the New Customer, New Job, or New Vendor dialog boxes, you can use those fields as filters in your reports.

Applying Filters

To apply a filter to your report, display the report in the Reports window and click on the Filters button. The dialog box shown in Figure 5.19 appears.

The basic concept of filtering is simple, but you have a lot of choices to make. Here are the steps:

1. Choose the filter you want to apply. Scroll through the list, if necessary, to get to the filter you want to apply. Try clicking on a couple of

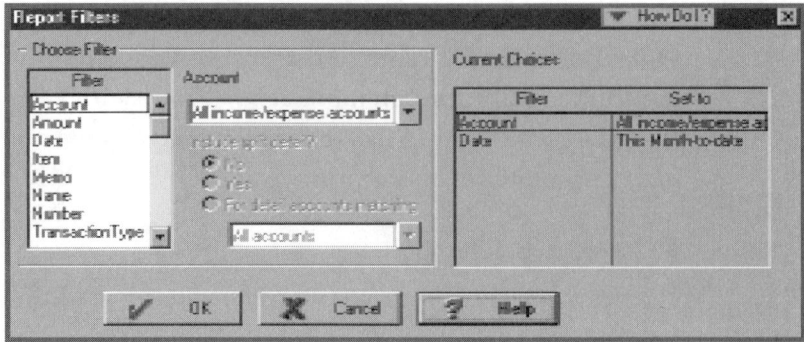

Figure 5.19

In the Report Filters dialog box, you choose the filter you want to apply to the report.

different filters. Notice that when you click on a different filter, the options to the right of the Filters list change. For example, Figure 5.20 shows the options that appear when you click on Billing Status.

2. Choose the secondary options. The Current Choices list reflects the filters you have applied.

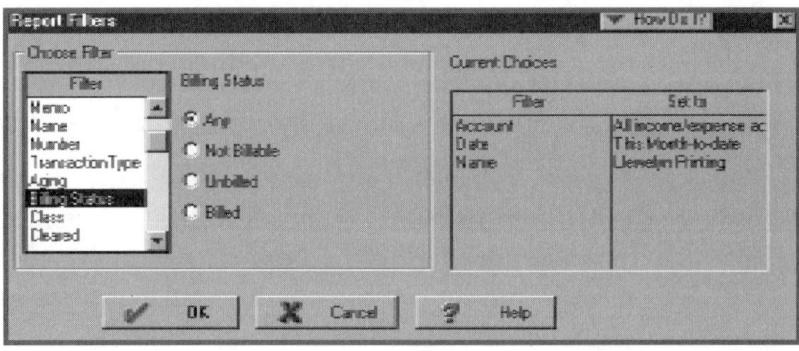

Figure 5.20

Different options appear in the Filters box depending on the filter you select.

 TIP If you want to remove a filter you added to the Current Choices list, simply click on it and press Delete. QuickBooks removes the filter from the list.

3. When you have the filters set the way you want them, click on OK. You return to the Reports window, and the report is filtered as you specified.

Memorizing Reports

Once you invest the time and trouble getting your report just the way you want it, you can have QuickBooks memorize the report so that you can run it again without recreating all the filters and special formats.

What would you want to memorize? Perhaps you do a monthly report showing the sales of a particular item by a particular employee. Maybe you need to do quarterly payroll reports with customized information for commissions and consignment sales. Whatever the need, QuickBooks makes it easy.

Saving a Memorized Report

To memorize a report you've created, follow these steps:

1. When the report is displayed in the Report window, click on the Memorize button. QuickBooks displays the Memorize Report dialog box (see Figure 5.21).

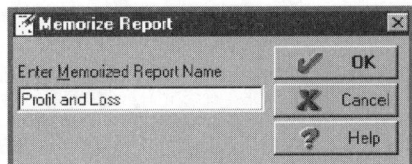

Figure 5.21

Enter a name for the report you want to memorize in the Memorize Report dialog box.

2. Enter a name for the report (use something descriptive that you'll remember later). Click on OK. The report is saved, along with all its filters and format settings.

Using a Memorized Report

Once you've saved the memorized report, you need to be able to select it when you want to use it. To choose a memorized report, simply open the Reports menu and choose Memorized Reports. The Memorized Reports list appears; click on the report you want and click on Generate Report.

Creating Custom Reports

Thus far, you've learned to create, preview, and print a basic report. You discovered how to change a report's format and how to filter out data you don't need. You also found out how to memorize a report you've modified. Another option QuickBooks gives you is the ability to customize your reports by changing the dates, the way the values are calculated, and the columns used.

To customize your report, follow these steps:

1. Display the report in the Report window.

2. Click on the Customize button. The Customize Report dialog box appears, as shown in Figure 5.22.

Figure 5.22

When you click on Customize in the Reports window, the Customize dialog box appears so that you can make more choices about the report elements displayed.

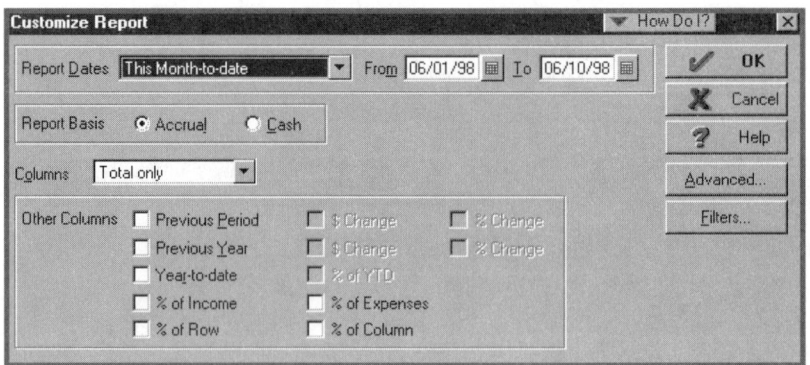

3. Choose the dates for the report in the Dates box. Press Tab.

4. Enter the From and To dates you want to see, pressing Tab after each.

5. Choose the Report basis (Accrual or Cash) you want to show.

▸▸▸▸▸▸▸▸▸▸▸▸▸▸▸▸▸▸▸▸▸▸▸▸▸▸▸
You use an *accrual* basis if you want to create the report based on the time the customer was billed; choose *cash* if you want to create the report based on income that has already changed hands.
▸▸▸▸▸▸▸▸▸▸▸▸▸▸▸▸▸▸▸▸▸▸▸▸▸▸▸

6. In the Columns field, choose the item you want to show in the report columns. Press Tab.

7. In the Other Columns area, click on the check boxes of any additional columns you want to show.

8. Click on the Advanced button. The dialog box shown in Figure 5.23 appears. You can choose whether to display all rows and columns, and you can choose the type of reporting calendar you want. Click on OK.

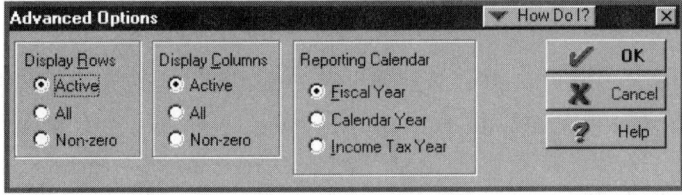

Figure 5.23

In the Advanced Options, you specify whether you want all the rows and columns to display.

TIP

If you want to further customize your report by adding filters, you can click on Filters in the Customize Report dialog box.

9. When you are finished entering customizing options, click on OK to return to the Reports window.

10. If you want QuickBooks to remember the report settings you entered, click on Memorize, enter a name for the report, and click on OK.

Adding Graphs

A graph can show in a glance what might take you a page or two to show in a report. When you need to see sales trends, get a picture of your purchases, track how your business is growing, or see how your expenses compare to your income, you can use a graph—a picture of your financial data—to show what's going on.

To create a graph in QuickBooks, start by opening the Reports menu. Choose Graphs. A submenu appears, listing six basic graphs to illustrate different types of data:

- Income & Expenses
- Sales
- Accounts Receivable
- Accounts Payable
- Net Worth
- Budget vs. Actual

To create the graph, simply choose the type you want. QuickBooks draws the graph and displays it in the QuickInsight window (see Figure 5.24).

In this figure, you actually see two graphs. The first shows a bar graph—Income and Expenses shown by the month—and the second shows a pie graph. A key on the right shows what the different colors represent.

TIP To find out the value of a particular item on the graph, position the magnifying glass pointer on the bar or element and right-click.

Modifying the Graph

You can change the way the data is displayed—and change the data that *is* displayed—by choosing different options in the QuickInsight window. Play around with this a little bit:

SUNDAY MORNING   **Tracking Results: Reporting Your Financial Data**

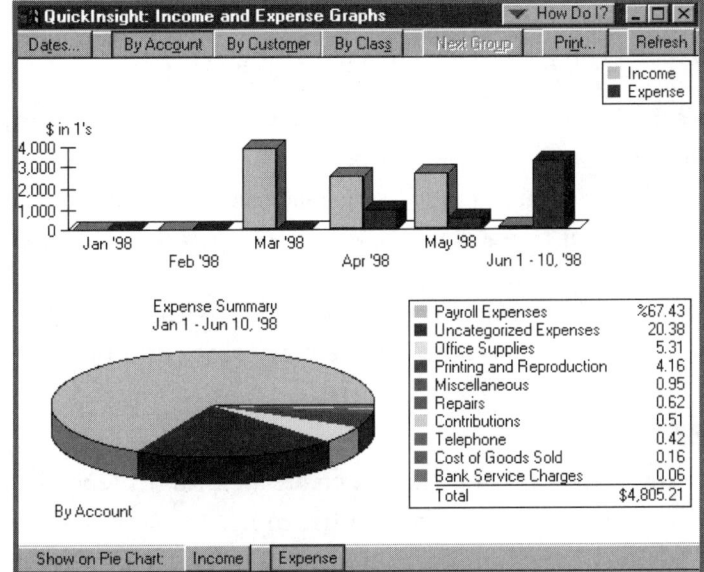

Figure 5.24

Creating a graph is as simple as opening the Report menu, choosing Graphs, and clicking on the type you want.

1. Click on the Dates button in the QuickInsight toolbar. The Change Graph Dates dialog box appears. Enter a new date (or select one from the list) and click on OK. The graph is updated to show data from the period you selected.

2. Click on By Customer. QuickBooks redraws the graph to show how everything looks when you compare the same data broken down according to individual customers. Which customers do the most business? This graph will tell you at a glance.

3. If you've used Classes to organize your data, you can click on By Class to see how QuickBooks redraws the graph.

4. At the bottom of the graph window, you can click on Income to see a graph of Income only (as opposed to Expenses, which is shown by default).

5. If you'd like to print a copy of the graph, click on Print and choose your print options. The graph will print in color only if you have a

color printer, of course. If you use a single-color printer, the graph will print colors in shades of gray.

 TIP Different graph types will have different options, but the process is the same from graph to graph. Experiment with the different types to get just the look you want.

6. When you're finished working with the graph, click on the Close button to return to the Navigator window.

What's Next?

Now that you know how to create all kinds of reports in QuickBooks, you are ready to move on to another topic. The next session today focuses on a relatively new but hot phenomenon in bookkeeping for both business and personal use: online banking. What have you heard about electronic transfers? Are they safe or not? Is money really "money"? How does online banking work? The next session helps you explore how to set up QuickBooks to work with your bank so that you can get in on the online banking craze. Specifically, you'll work through the following tasks:

- Understanding the online banking process
- Setting up QuickBooks for online banking
- Talking to your bank
- Getting help with online banking
- Transferring funds online
- Working with credit cards
- Getting software updates
- Using your Web resources

So take a rest, get something to eat, let the dust from reports and graphs settle in your head, and come back ready for some twenty-first century surfing with online banking.

SUNDAY AFTERNOON
Online Banking with QuickBooks

- ✪ Exploring Tax-Related Categories
- ✪ Preparing Your Tax Return from Quicken Reports
- ✪ Using Quicken with Tax Software
- ✪ The Tax Deduction Finder
- ✪ Planning for Next Year's Taxes

Online banking? Just a few years ago, this term didn't even exist in accepted vocabulary. Today it's possible—even expected. Why make a trip to the bank if you don't have to? Why wait in those lines in the lobby, or worse, in the drive-thru lane? QuickBooks makes it possible for you to pay bills, write checks, receive payments, and more—while sitting right there in front of your PC. Sound improbable? Or maybe unsafe? This session shows you how you can use online banking to accomplish more in less time—with less legwork—with QuickBooks. You'll tackle the following tasks in this work session:

- Setting up QuickBooks for online banking
- Talking to your bank
- Getting help with online banking
- Transferring funds online
- Working with credit cards
- Getting software updates
- Using your Web resources

You're closing in on the end of your QuickBooks weekend. After this afternoon, you have only one more session left. So finish up your lunch, clear your desk, and settle in for another learning-intensive afternoon. When you're finished, you'll understand how online banking can work for your business in QuickBooks.

Understanding Online Banking

Online banking is a relatively new phenomenon for small business. Send a check without *writing* one? How is that possible? Will your creditors actually *accept* a payment they can't hold in their hands? The world is changing quickly, and online connections are facilitating that change at an ever-increasing rate.

QuickBooks includes a number of features that help you do your banking right from your computer desk. This section introduces the various new concepts you will be navigating for the first time as you check out online banking possibilities.

What Can You Do with Online Banking?

Most of the transactions you handle at the drive-up window or in the bank lobby are available online. You can use QuickBooks to do the following tasks:

- E-mail your financial institution
- Make payments
- Transfer funds
- Check balances and transaction histories
- Pay taxes

Online Basics

At first, the idea of money flowing from one place to another—from payer to payee—without ever being in anyone's hands, seems odd. How do you know it's going where it's supposed to go?

It works like this: You arrange with your bank or with another financial institution that supports online banking (QuickBooks can help you with this) to create an online account. The bank gives you the necessary information to access, route, and secure your transactions. You dial up the bank using your Internet service provider; use QuickBooks to move funds, pay bills, and check balances; and then disconnect and use the data you have saved in your QuickBooks file.

SUNDAY AFTERNOON Online Banking with QuickBooks

You can use two different levels of online services with QuickBooks. The most comprehensive features involve *online account access*. This means that you can do all the same things online that you could do in the lobby of your neighborhood bank:

- Check account balances
- See a transaction history
- Find out which checks have cleared
- Transfer funds
- Pay bills
- Send e-mail to the bank
- Download transactions from savings, checking, credit card, or money market accounts

The lesser level is *online payments* only, which enables you to make payments by using QuickBooks to send a payment to your bank. Your bank then sends the payment out to the vendor using electronic funds transfers (EFTs). If your vendor is not set up to be able to receive online payments, the bank will print the check for you and mail it as needed.

 If you are aware that one of your vendors does not support online payments, be sure to allow five days between the time you pay and the time the bill is due. This gives the bank time to get the check printed and in the mail with enough time to beat the deadline.

Where Does Your Money Go?

When you access your account online, you are electronically transferring money from one account to the other. Of course, real money—dollar bills, that is—never changes hands. One account is debited and another is credited. The calculations and cross-checks are done. This type of transfer is called an EFT (electronic funds transfer), and it's the same kind of thing you use when you use a debit card to purchase gasoline or buy office supplies.

Issues and Worries about Online Banking

I'll admit it: I was leery of anything online for a good long while. Although I love the Internet and spend quite a bit of time researching and corresponding online, I was one of those people who distrusted the transmission of sensitive things like credit card numbers. I didn't like the idea that most information on the Internet was "interceptible" and that my charge card numbers could wind up in the possession of people with less-than-honorable motives. In fact, I still have a healthy sense of skeptical caution about online promotions, promises, and what appear to be unprotected practices. These, among other concerns, are typical issues being addressed by those working to enhance and improve online banking:

- **Loss of control.** For many people, the idea that their accounts are somehow "inside" their computers feels like a loss of control. If you are writing a check in your checkbook, you write it, tear it out, put it in an envelope, address it, stamp it, and take it to the mailbox. You know it's on its way. And usually we can be fairly confident that the U.S. Postal Service is going to get it to its destination. But if the accounts are somehow within the system unit of your PC and a bolt of lightning fries the hard disk, then what? And sure, the program says it's transferring funds from one account to another, but what if it doesn't really happen that way? Two different solutions can help this one: First, back up your QuickBooks files regularly. And I mean *regularly*. Like every third day, if not every day. Also, always use the same technique to do your online banking. (There are three different ways to start the banking process and send transmissions; I recommend that you use a single way until you are comfortable with what's happening and recognize the different phases of the transaction.)

- **"I can't 'see' it."** Similar to the feeling of losing control, that inability to actually *see* the transaction take place is a hard one to get over. Everything is automated; one computer talks to another and sends a transaction. To counteract this worry, keep a paper list for a while of your online transactions, just so you have something familiar to look at and refer to when you check that the transaction was in fact made.

- **How do I know they'll make the transfers when they say they will?** Part of this question will be answered simply by experience—after a few tries with online banking, you'll see that the transactions are happening the way they are supposed to. Another way to allay these concerns is by getting a transaction history; you can display a list of recent transactions and download cleared transactions to your QuickBooks file.

- **What if there's a problem?** Because the loss of personal contact can be an issue, you often don't know where to go if something doesn't appear to work correctly. When you are working with online banking, you have several avenues for help: the QuickBooks help files, your bank, and the Intuit Web sites.

- **Limited banks—limited options.** Because online banking is still a developing industry, isn't it possible that transactions—maybe *your* transactions—will fall through the cracks? What if your bank tried to send a payment to another bank that doesn't accept online banking? Yes, online banking is relatively new and yes, many places are just now getting on the bandwagon and making online payments possible. But your bank will be able to pick up the slack for companies that are not yet online. When you use online payments to pay bills electronically to a vendor who does *not* accept EFTs, your bank will actually print the check and mail it to the vendor as needed.

What about Security?

In the last few years on the Internet, things have taken a more protective turn. Now *encryption* and *authentication* are two words you see batted around Internet security discussions. QuickBooks uses both methods to safeguard your transmissions and your online accounts. *Encryption* is a method of encoding your data—literally turning it into something unreadable by human or computer eyes—that requires a key to decode the data back into something usable. A bank capable of online banking works with encryption invisibly—you don't need to do anything to your QuickBooks data in order for it to be encrypted, and therefore protected—on its way to the bank.

Authentication is another process used to keep your data safe and accurate. This is another transparent process that checks to be sure that the data packets that were sent are the same data packets received. No tricks, no errors, no surprises.

While you are online, QuickBooks is sensitive to any data being transmitted over the connection that can be seen by others. The program displays a Security Alert dialog box when this potential is at play (see Figure 6.1). You can choose to have QuickBooks display this alert each time sensitive information passes through a less-secure area of the Internet, or you can click on the In the Future check box to disable the feature.

Figure 6.1

QuickBooks displays a Security Alert when information may be passing through less-secure zones.

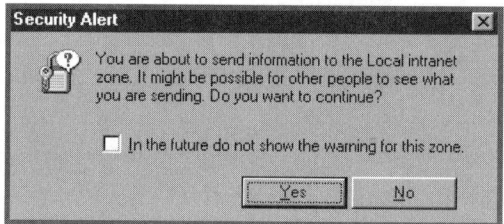

QuickBooks also includes password protection to safeguard your data files so that only you can get into and work with the files. Within QuickBooks, you can set up passwords for different users so that more than one individual can have access to QuickBooks data.

One final protective measure: When you set up your online account with a financial institution, you choose a PIN (personal identification number) that you enter at the beginning of each online transaction. As long as you keep your PIN secret, it's yours alone and no one else can have access to your data or your code.

What You Need to Get Started

Assuming you determine that online banking is something you want to try, what do you need to get started? Here's the list:

- Your PC, of course

SUNDAY AFTERNOON   Online Banking with QuickBooks

SETTING PASSWORDS IN QUICKBOOKS

Even though the standard version of QuickBooks 6.0 is available only as a single-user program (meaning one user can work with QuickBooks at a time), you can set up the program for use by multiple users at different times. You can set passwords for different users. Here's how:

1. In the Navigator, open the File menu.

2. Choose Set Up Users and Passwords.

3. From the submenu, choose Set Up Users. If this is the first time you've used QuickBooks' password feature, the Set Up QuickBooks Administrator dialog box appears. Enter the administrator's name and password; then type the password again to confirm it. The User list appears, with the administrator's name showing. (The administrator has access to all areas and operations in QuickBooks.)

4. Click on Add User, and when the Set Up User Password and Access window appears, type the new user name and password. Enter the password a second time to confirm. Click on Next.

5. Specify whether you want the user to have access to all of QuickBooks or to specific areas you select. If you click on selected areas, you will be asked to choose those areas as the wizard continues. Click on Next and follow the instructions in the rest of the wizard to choose the areas you want the user to have access to.

6. Click on Finish at the last screen. The User List dialog box is redisplayed, and the new user is added to the list.

- A modem (the faster the better: 33.6KBps or faster is a good investment)
- Internet access through a local provider or your network's LAN
- Advance arrangements with your bank to get the account information you need (you can select a financial institution using QuickBooks online features)

Talking to Your Bank

You have the option of setting up your QuickBooks online accounts through your existing bank. Any bank that offers checking services can accept online payments; whether or not your bank will allow you to do electronic fund transfers will depend on the bank.

So how do you find out what your bank supports? Call and find out. If you are using one of the banks on QuickBooks' financial institutions list, you start with the Online Banking Center, click on Getting Started, and click on the Financial Institutions button. You can then choose the name of the bank you want to work with from the list.

What do you say once you get through to the bank?

- Ask about online banking. What services does the bank support?
- Is there a monthly charge for online banking privileges, and if so, how much?
- How many days will it take for your account to be active? (Expect a wait of five to ten business days.)
- What does the bank need from you in order to set up the online services?
- Are there any limitations? For example, are certain types of accounts restricted? Is there a limit to the number of transactions you can do in a single session?
- What is the bank's routing number? What number will it assign to your accounts? (This number will probably be your social security number or Federal ID.)
- What is your next step? What kind of information does the bank need from you?

Setting Up QuickBooks for Online Banking

QuickBooks includes everything you need to get started online with a financial institution that supports online banking. You will have a few days'

wait, however, because your bank needs to send you an information packet through the mail, along with your PIN.

If your bank does not support online services, you can choose a bank from the list QuickBooks provides. In this section I'll show you that list, among other things. In fact, you'll go over the whole process of getting started with online banking. The whole shebang looks like this:

1. You first apply for online services, either through your own bank or through Intuit's Online Payment Service.

2. You create a QuickBooks online account using the Online Banking Center.

3. In QuickBooks, you set up the vendors and customers to whom you plan to send online payments.

4. You make the payment using one of three methods: by using the Write Checks window, by using the Pay Bills window, or by entering the payment into the online account register.

5. You send the transaction to your financial institution using QuickBooks. The sections that follow go through each of these steps in more detail.

Starting Out with Online Banking

The first stop in online banking is the Getting Started option in the Online menu. When you choose that option, a wizard begins to walk you through the process of setting up online services (see Figure 6.2).

As you can see, you have the option of learning more about the whole online banking ball of wax by clicking on Tell Me More. Using the options in this wizard, you can set up your Internet connection, select your financial institution, and apply for an online account. Finally, using the Getting Started Wizard, you can enable the online account you have set up.

Checking Out the Online Menu

When you are working in the QuickBooks Navigator, you can get to the online features by opening the Online menu. QuickBooks offers a number of online services, and you can use one, all, or any combination of the services that meet your business needs.

- **The Online Banking Center.** You use this center to work with your online accounts, make payments, check balances, and more.

- **The Payroll Service.** You use the Payroll Service to have QuickBooks figure your payroll, help with payroll taxes, and produce payroll reports.

- **The QuickBooks Update Service.** You can use this option to download updates to your registered version of QuickBooks.

- **The Intuit Web sites.** Use these Web sites to find additional information about Intuit products, get help online, find financial resources, and more.

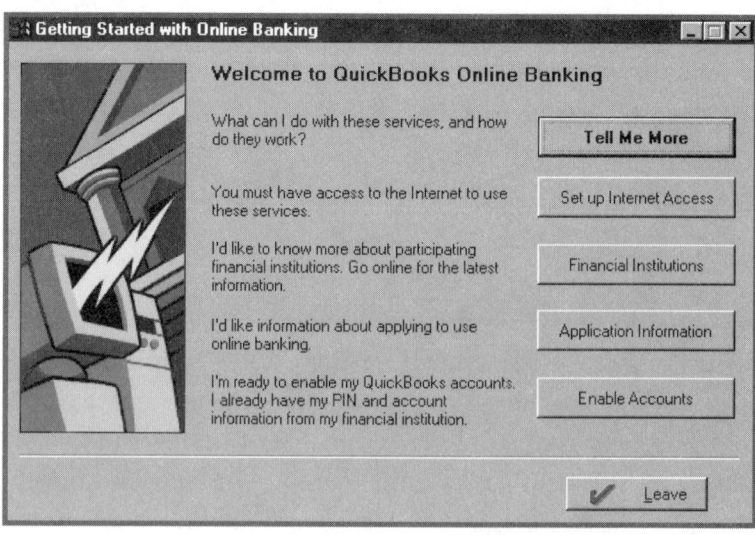

Figure 6.2

The first stop is the Getting Started Wizard. QuickBooks will help you set up your account and get going online.

Getting an Internet Connection

Obviously, you're not going to be doing much online banking if you don't have an Internet connection. QuickBooks can help you get online, even if you haven't connected to the Internet previously. Intuit works with Concentric, an Internet service provider, to help you get connected for the first time.

If you already have Internet service but want to check out Concentric anyway, you can visit the Web site at **www.concentric.net**.

In the Getting Started Wizard, click on Set Up Internet Access. The Internet Connection Setup window appears, as Figure 6.3 shows. The three different options allow for different ways to connect to the Internet:

- If you already have a connection to the Internet and want to use your current Internet service provider (ISP), click on the first option. QuickBooks then walks you through the process of setting itself up to work with your current Internet connection.

- If you access the Internet through a network, select the second option. QuickBooks asks you a number of questions about your current system so that you can reach the Internet through your network.

- If you do not have a current connection to the Internet but want to set one up, click on the third option. QuickBooks asks you questions and helps you get an account set up with Concentric, a leading Internet service provider.

Finding a Bank Online

After you've set up your Internet access, you can find a bank online. If you are planning to work through your existing bank, you don't need to do this step; you will simply contact your financial institution about online banking and wait for it to get you the necessary materials to log on to your account. If you need to find a bank other than your current one, however, you can rely on QuickBooks to help you find an online financial institution. Here's how:

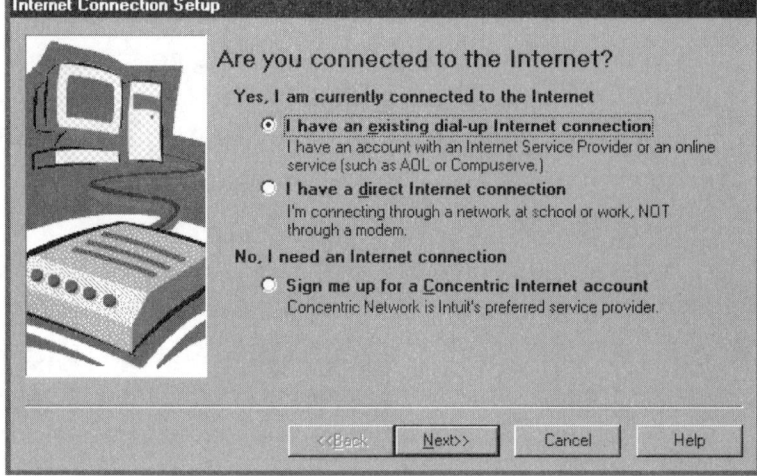

Figure 6.3

You have three options for setting up QuickBooks to work with an Internet account.

1. In the Getting Started Wizard, click on the Financial Institutions button. The Connect To dialog box appears, complete with the information you entered when you set up your Internet access (see Figure 6.4).

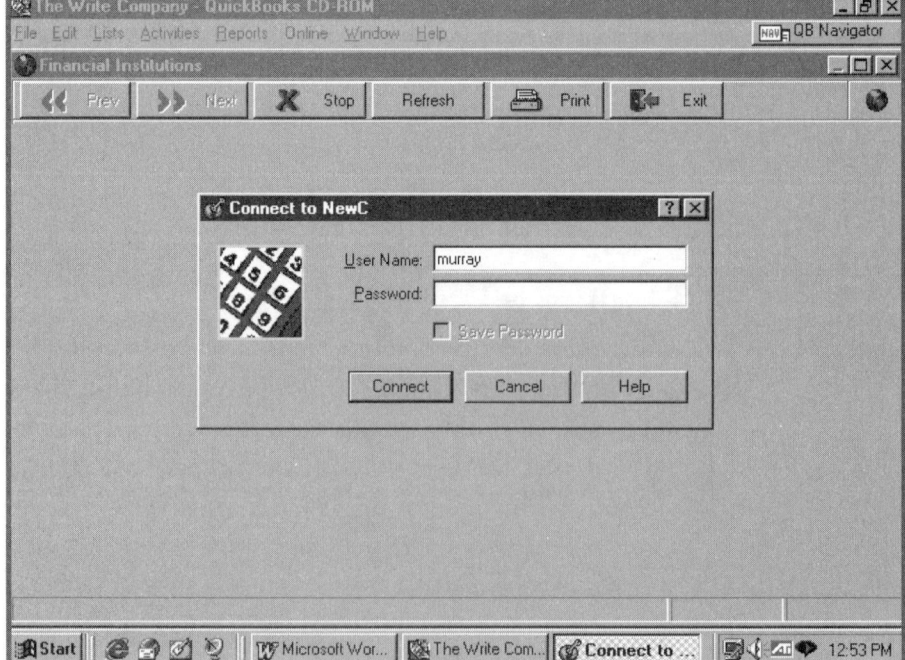

Figure 6.4

QuickBooks displays its own browser and brings up the Connect To box so that you can dial your Internet connection.

2. Enter your password and click on Connect. QuickBooks dials, sends your username and password, and connects to the Intuit Financial Institutions List page (see Figure 6.5).

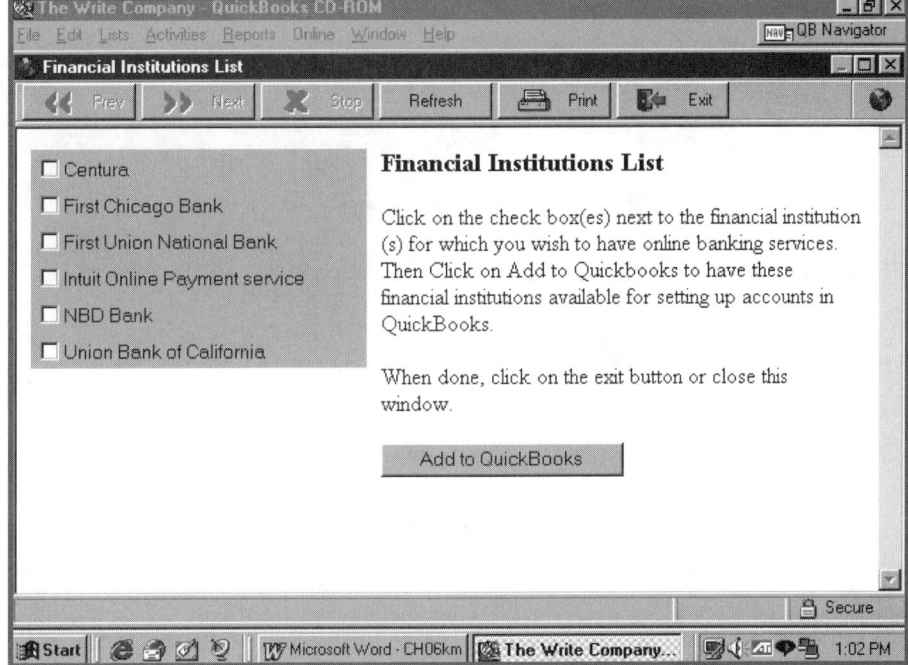

Figure 6.5

The Financial Institutions list provides you with a number of banks you can use to set up your online accounts.

3. Click on the institution you want to use to set up online accounts. You can choose more than one if you like. Click on the Add to QuickBooks button. The Security Alert dialog box appears to let you know that when QuickBooks downloads the bank's information to your hard drive, others may be able to see. Click on Yes if you want to continue. If you want to hide that message in the future, click on the check box displayed.

4. Click on Exit. QuickBooks downloads the bank information to your hard drive so that your version of the QuickBooks program will have access to the information (see Figure 6.6). When the download is complete, you are returned to the Getting Started Wizard.

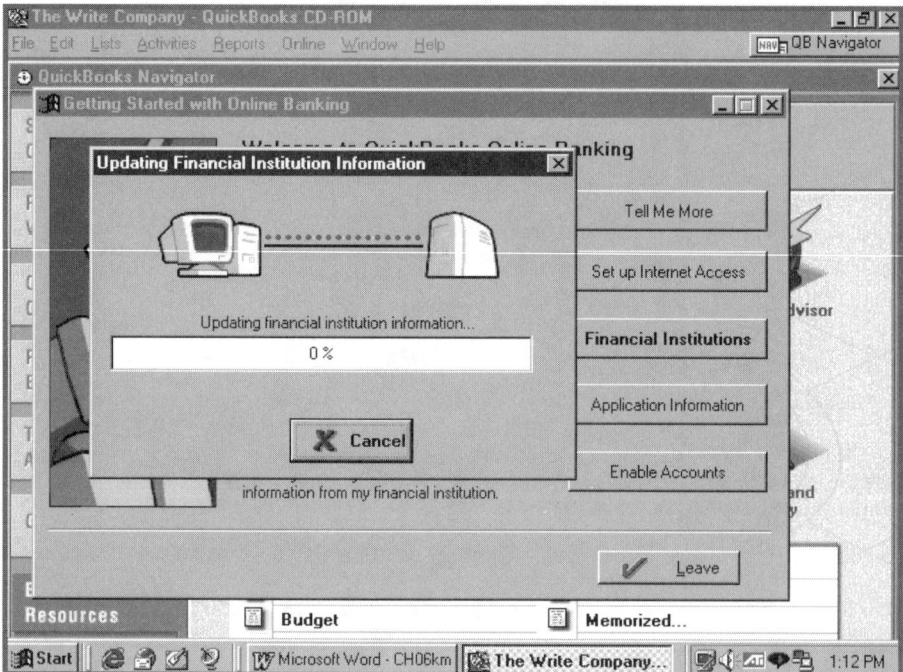

Figure 6.6

QuickBooks shows the progress of the banking information download.

Applying for Online Services

The next step in setting up online accounts is applying for the account. In the Getting Started Wizard, click on Application Information. The Online Banking Setup Interview window appears (see Figure 6.7). Click on Next to continue.

You can apply over the Internet, or you can apply directly to your financial institution. In this example, you'll apply directly over the Internet. Follow these steps:

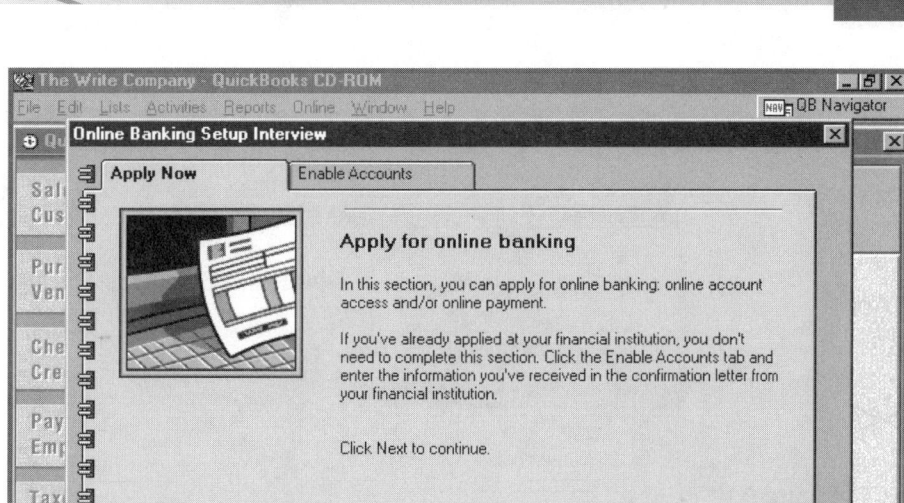

Figure 6.7

QuickBooks launches another interview—the Online Banking Setup Interview—to help you apply for your online accounts.

1. Click on the option I Would Like to Get Application Information over the Internet. Click on Next.

2. Click on the Apply Now button. Again, QuickBooks displays the Connect To box so that you can go online.

3. Enter your password and click on Connect. QuickBooks dials and connects through your Internet provider. The Financial Institutions Directory page is displayed. Here you see a number of questions and answers regarding online services (see Figure 6.8). Notice the small closed padlock in the lower-right corner of the window. This indicates that transfer of data at this point is secure.

4. If you want information for all services, click on the Any Services button in the upper-left corner of the window. If you want instead to receive only information regarding banking accounts, charge card accounts, or bill payment, click on the appropriate button.

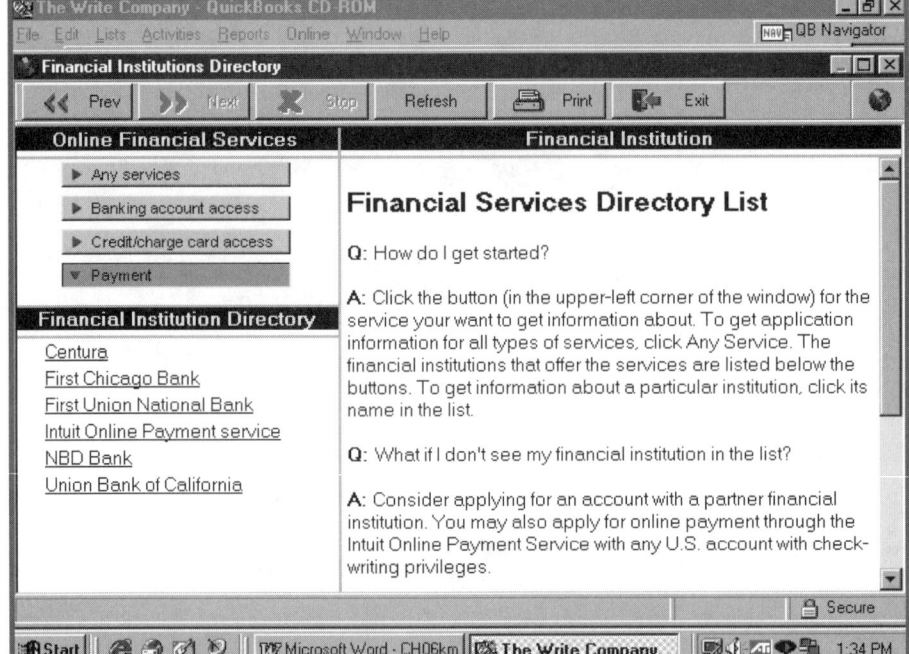

Figure 6.8

The Financial Institutions Directory list answers questions and gives you options for setting up online accounts.

5. Click on the bank you want to apply to in the financial institution directory. The information in the right side of the window changes to give you contact information for that bank (see Figure 6.9).

6. Complete the application process according to the bank you have selected. First Chicago Bank, the online bank I selected, offered three options for the application process: (1) Fill in the online application and mail the written authorization to the bank; (2) fill in the online application and have the bank call me to verify my applications; or (3) print the application and the authorization and mail them both. Make your choices and enter the information for your new business account as requested.

7. Submit the application.

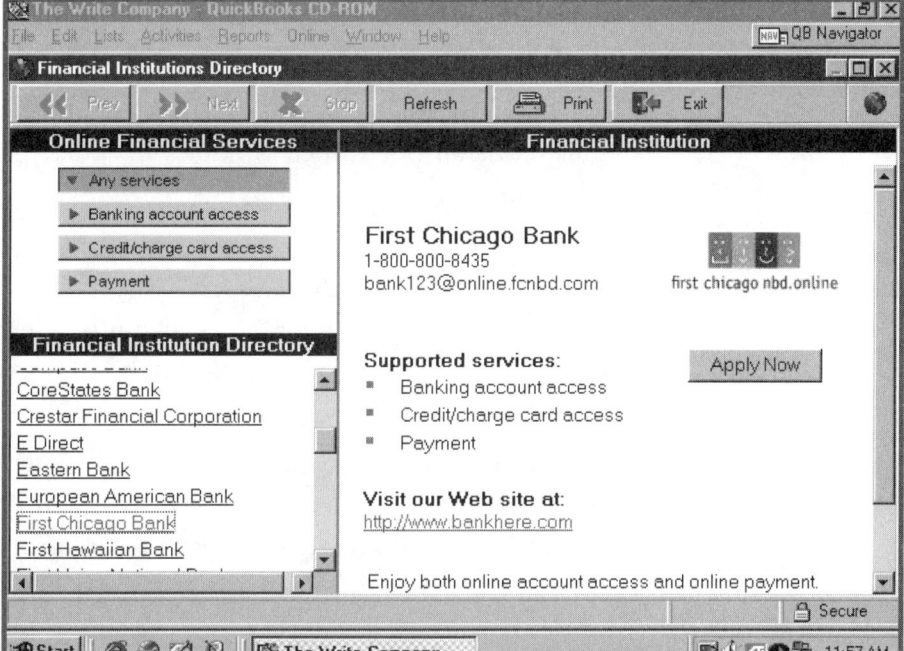

Figure 6.9

Information for the bank you selected appears; you can click on Apply Now to begin the process of applying for online banking services.

Congratulations! You just applied for online banking services. You will be notified with the routing and PIN numbers so that you can begin working with your online accounts.

> **NOTE** Although you can apply for your account directly over the Internet, you will not be able to begin using your online account today. The bank of your choice will need to send you information through the mail—for security purposes—and you will be able to log on using the PIN supplied in the mailed info.

Enabling Your Accounts

Do you have your account information and PIN? Once you do, you're ready to enable your accounts and start using the online services. Here are the steps:

260 Learn QuickBooks 6 In a Weekend

1. Open the Online menu, select Online Banking, and choose Getting Started.

2. Click on the Enable Accounts tab. QuickBooks alerts you that it must close all other open windows in order to run the interview. Click on OK.

3. The Online Banking Setup Interview dialog box appears with the Enable Accounts tab displayed. The list box is selected. If you are using a bank you set up online, click on the down arrow to choose the name of the bank from the list box (see Figure 6.10). Click on Next.

4. QuickBooks reminds you that you need the letter from the bank supplying your bank account information and PIN. If you have the letter, click on Yes. If you don't yet have it, click on No.

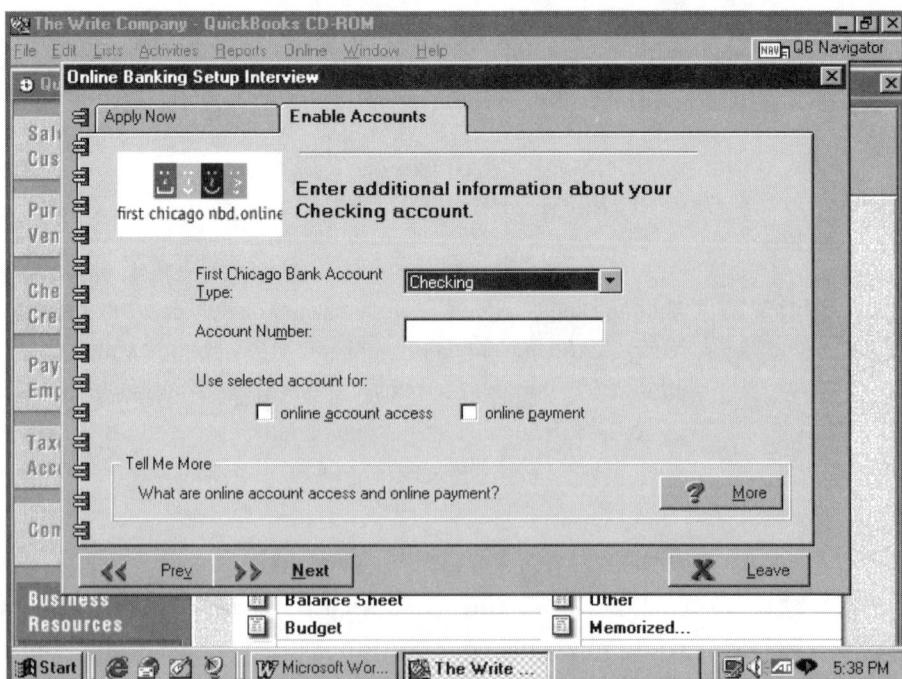

Figure 6.10

Choose the bank you plan to work with in the Enable Accounts tab.

SUNDAY AFTERNOON   Online Banking with QuickBooks   **261**

If you don't yet have your confirmation letter, click on No and then click on Leave. It's doubtful, in your weekend session, that you have been able to apply for and receive your online banking information and PIN, so you should continue with examples that show you how to use the basics of the online processes. Through the rest of this session, you get the online system set up and ready so that when you get your account information and PIN, you'll be ready to go online and start your banking transactions immediately.

5. If you answer Yes, QuickBooks asks you to enter your routing number and PIN in the available spaces. Type the information and click on Next.

6. Will you be using an existing account or starting a new one? If you want to work online with one of your existing QuickBooks accounts, select it from the list. If you want to start a new account, click on Create a New QuickBooks Account. Click on Next.

   For an existing account, choose the account type you want to use and enter the account number. Click on the appropriate check box to indicate whether you want online account access or just online payment enabled. Click on Next and review the information you've entered. Click on Next again and QuickBooks shows you the Service Agreement. Read through it and click on OK.

   For a new account, choose a QuickBooks account type and enter an account name (see Figure 6.11). If the account is a subaccount of another account, enter that information. Finally, enter an opening balance and a start date for the new account. Click on Next. Enter an account number and click on the online services you want (online account access or online payment only). Click on Next. Review your choices and click on Next again.

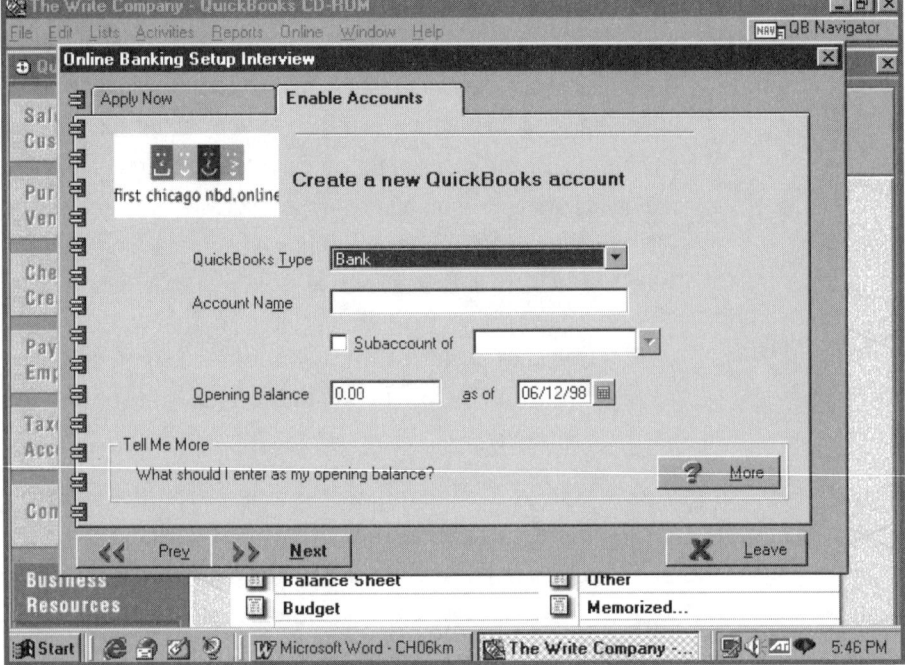

Figure 6.11

When you create a new account for your online banking, enter the account type and name, along with balance and start date information.

Who Will You Pay Online?

Now that you've got your account set up, you're ready to set up your vendor and customer accounts. This process is the same whether you are working with traditional or online payments, and you already worked through the steps in Saturday afternoon's session, "Writing the Check: Paying for Goods and Services," so you'll just review it quickly here. If you are entering a new vendor:

1. Open the Lists menu and choose Vendors. The Vendor List box appears.

2. Click on the Vendors button and select New. The New Vendor dialog box is displayed. Enter the name, address, and contact information for the new vendor.

3. Click on the Additional Info tab. Enter the account number by which the vendor will recognize you, along with the type and terms that apply to transactions with this vendor.

4. When you've finished entering the information, click on OK to close the dialog box. If you want to continue entering more vendor information, click on Next.

If you are editing vendor information:

1. Display the Vendor List box by opening the Lists menu and choosing Vendors.

2. Click on the Vendor button and choose Edit or press Ctrl+E. The Edit Vendor dialog box appears, and you can edit the information as needed.

3. Click on OK to save the edits and return to the Navigator window.

Not all the people and companies you issue payments to will be able to handle EFTs, or online payments. For those accounts, your bank will print the checks you send and mail them to the payee for you.

Using Online Banking

Okay. You've learned about the basics on online banking, and you have set up your Internet connection, found a financial institution, and applied for your online account. After you have received your online account number and your PIN through the mail and have enabled you online account(s), you are ready to make payments and send transactions using QuickBooks' online features.

Writing a Check

For the basic procedures like writing checks, online is no different from working on the desktop. You are still creating the transaction as usual. It's what you do with it that varies. When you send an online payment, the check is transmitted electronically from your modem, through your phone line, to your bank's system. The bank's system then either routes the payment to the payee's bank or prints and mails the check.

Here are the basic check-writing steps:

1. Click on the Checking and Credit Cards tab in the Navigator window.

2. Click on Checks in the graphic in the center of the window.

3. The Write Checks window appears. QuickBooks automatically enters the online delivery date for you. In the Bank Account list box, choose the account you want to use (in this case, Online). Click on the Online Payment check box in the top portion of the check, as Figure 6.12 shows.

4. Choose the vendor in the Pay to the Order Of field. Press Tab.

5. Enter the amount. Press Tab.

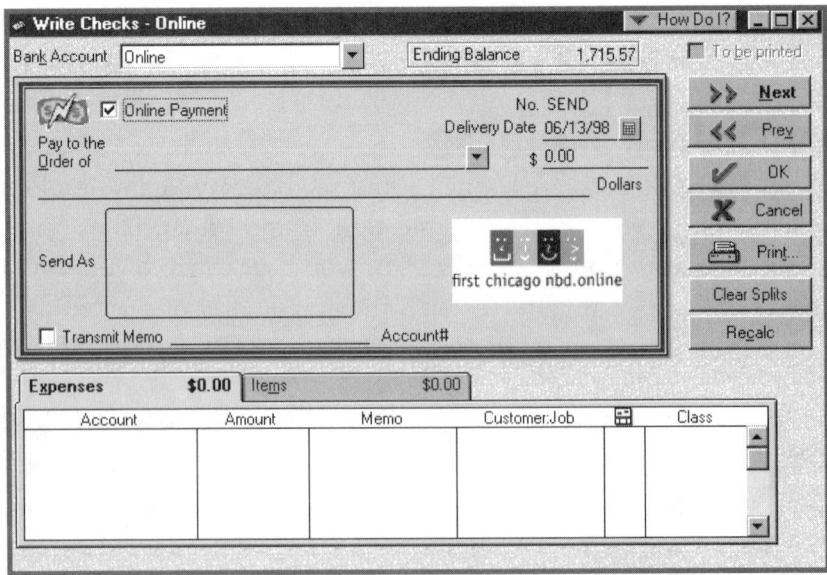

Figure 6.12

You write a check the traditional way by selecting the online account for online banking transactions.

SUNDAY AFTERNOON   **Online Banking with QuickBooks**   **265**

 If you have not entered complete payee information for that particular vendor, QuickBooks will alert you to this fact and give you the option of updating the information.

6. If you don't fill in complete address information, QuickBooks will prompt you to fill the address in completely. Otherwise the bank will have no way to mail checks that cannot be transmitted online to the vendor.

7. Choose the account for the check and click on Next if you want to write more checks or click on OK to close the Write Checks dialog box.

The check is prepared and saved, ready to be transmitted online. QuickBooks displays a message that the transaction has been placed in the Online Banking Center's Send list. You will soon learn how to send your transactions. For now, you'll take a look at paying bills online.

Paying Bills Online

If the bill you are paying is part of your QuickBooks bill-paying system, the program will alert you to this fact when you go to write a check to that vendor. When you want to pay bills online, follow these steps:

1. In the Navigator, click on the Purchases and Vendors tab.

2. Click on the Pay Bills graphic. The Pay Bills dialog box appears.

3. In the Pay By area, click on Online Payment. The Include Reference No. check box appears, already selected (see Figure 6.13).

4. Select the bills you want to pay online by clicking in the leftmost column.

5. Click on OK. QuickBooks records the bills as paid and places the transactions in the Online Banking Center Send list.

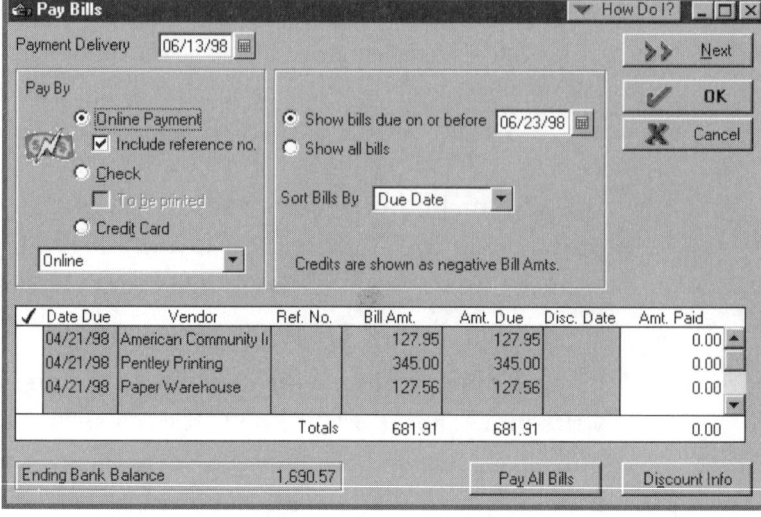

Figure 6.13

The process of paying bills online is a simple one—just display the Pay Bills window and click on Online Payment.

Working with the Register

Another way you can enter online transactions is by working directly in the online account register. To display this register, follow these steps:

1. Open the Lists menu and choose Chart of Accounts.

2. Locate the online account (mine appears at the top of the Chart of Accounts list). Double-click on it. The online account register shows the online transaction to the Paper Warehouse already entered and ready to send (see Figure 6.14).

3. Enter the transaction information as you would for a typical check. In the Type column, enter SEND instead of a check number or another identifier. Press Enter to save the transaction and move to the next line in the register. QuickBooks lets you know that you have just created an online transaction, and the transaction is saved in the Send list.

4. When you are finished entering transactions, click on the Close box.

SUNDAY AFTERNOON Online Banking with QuickBooks

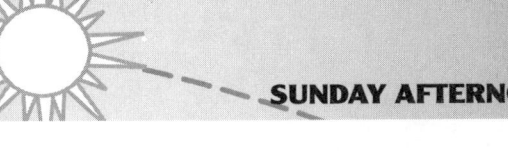

Figure 6.14

The online account register gives you another way of entering online transactions.

Sending Transactions Online

When you're ready to send the transactions you've created, follow these steps:

1. Open the Online menu.

2. Choose Online Banking; then select Online Banking Center. The Center appears on your screen, as Figure 6.15 shows.

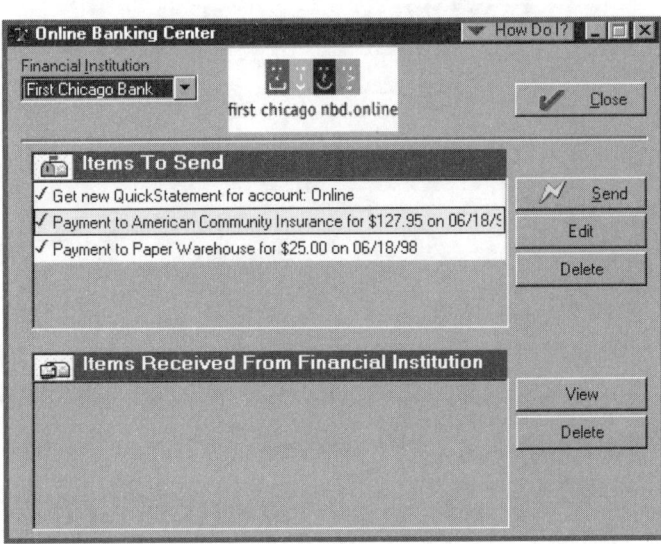

Figure 6.15

The Online Banking Center lists all the transactions you are ready to send as well as those you have received from your bank.

3. The bank you've chosen for online banking is displayed by default in the Financial Institution box, but if you have set up more than one account, click on the down arrow and choose the bank you want from the list.

4. The items ready to send are displayed in the Send box. They are already selected, meaning that if you click on Send, QuickBooks will make the Internet connection and send these transactions over the phone line. If you want to deselect the transaction to send later, click on it to remove the check mark. If you want to delete the transaction entirely, click on the transaction and then click on Delete.

5. Finally, click on Send. You may see a message that the bank you have selected requires you to change your online PIN. If so, click on OK; the Change Online PIN dialog box appears, as Figure 6.16 shows.

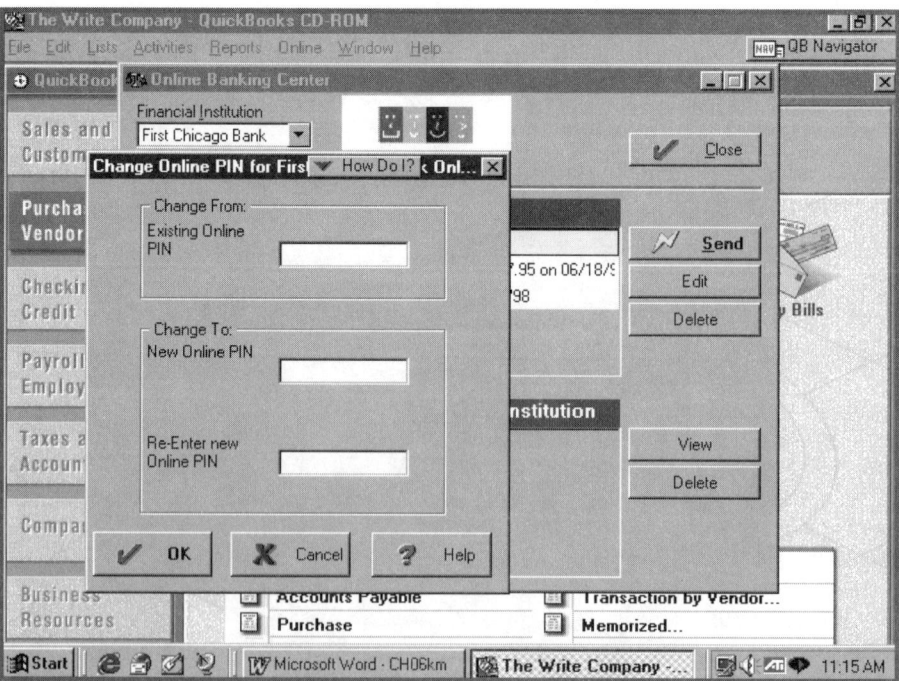

Figure 6.16

Your bank may request that you change your PIN/password right away for security purposes.

6. When you click on OK after changing your PIN, QuickBooks begins to dial your service provider. When the Connect To dialog box appears, enter your password and click on Connect.

QuickBooks dials the local access number you supplied for your Internet service provider. The transactions are sent, and any waiting transactions are downloaded to your system and displayed in the Items Received from Financial Institution box. To see one of the received items, click on it in the list and click on View.

Scheduling Your Payments

One of the great things about online payments is that you can keep money in your account as long as possible and pay out at the times you specify. If your rent is due on the first of the month, for example, and you know that the leasing company accepts online payments, you can schedule the payment for the first (or the night of the thirtieth if you're a cautious soul) and keep that money in your account right up until the time it needs to be sent. If you were mailing a traditional check, you would need to allow five to seven days' lead time.

As you learned in the preceding sections, you can make online payments using any of three different methods:

- You can use the Write Checks window
- You can use the online account register
- You can use the Pay Bills dialog box

When you schedule your online payments, you do so using the same three avenues. Here's how:

- In the Write Checks window, click in the Delivery Date field and type the date you want the payment transmitted.

- In the online account register, enter the delivery date in the Date column and make sure the transaction reads SEND in the Type column.

- In the Pay Bills dialog box, click on the Payment Delivery box and specify the date you want the payments to be sent.

TIP

Remember also that you can control whether or not an item is actually sent by enabling or disabling it in the Online Banking Center's Send list. If you click on a selected item in the Items to Send box, the item is deselected and won't be sent until you select it for a future transmission.

Transferring Funds Online

Uh-oh. It's payday and you're running short in your payroll account. You need to dash off to the bank, but you're expecting a client any minute and the bank is across town (and it's lunchtime). What can you do? If you're set up to use the online banking features, you can let QuickBooks transfer funds from one account to another.

NOTE

The only catch with transferring funds online is that both accounts have to be at the same financial institution. QuickBooks cannot move funds from an account at Bank A to an account at Bank B.

You can use two different methods to transfer funds from one account to another:

- Open the Activities menu and choose Transfer Money.
- Enter the transaction directly in the register for that account.

Using the Activities Menu

Okay, start in the menu bar. Follow these steps:

1. Click on Activities. A submenu appears; click on Transfer Money. The Transfer Funds between Accounts window appears, as Figure 6.17 shows.

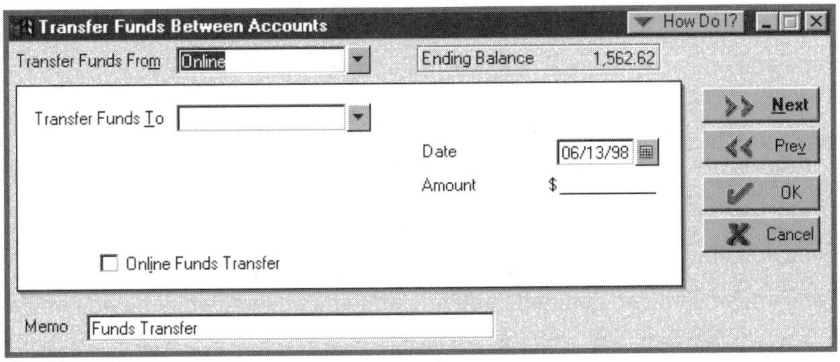

SUNDAY AFTERNOON   Online Banking with QuickBooks

Figure 6.17

You can make online transfers of funds between accounts if both accounts are online at the same bank.

2. In Transfer Funds From, choose the online account from which you want to transfer the money.

3. In Transfer Funds To, select the online account to which you want the money to go.

4. Choose the date you want the transaction to take place.

5. Enter the amount.

6. Click on the Online Funds Transfer check box.

7. Click on OK.

The next time you do online banking, QuickBooks will send this fund transfer and move the funds from one account to the other.

Using the Register

First, start by displaying the register for your online account. Do this by opening the Lists menu, choosing Chart of Accounts, and double-clicking on the online account in the list. Then enter the transfer by following these steps:

1. Make sure that the register for the account you want to send funds *from* is open on your screen.

2. In the Type column, enter SEND.

3. Enter nothing in the Payee field. Click in the Payment column and enter the amount of the transfer.

4. In the Account field, enter the account to which you want to transfer the funds. Press Enter to save the transaction.

5. When you're ready to send the transfer, open the Online menu and choose Online Banking. Next, click on Online Banking Center and click on Send.

TIP To check your online balance, click on Online, Online Banking Center, and Send.

Sending Online Messages

Another benefit of online banking is that you can easily correspond with your bank about transactions, balances, loans, and more. When you want to send a message to your financial institution, follow these steps:

1. Open the Online menu and choose Online Banking. Click on Create Message. A submenu appears.

2. Choose Online Banking Message. The Home Banking Message dialog box appears, as Figure 6.18 shows.

3. Enter a subject for the message and select the correct account in the Regarding Account box.

4. Click in the Message area and type your message.

5. If you want to print a copy of your message, click on Print; otherwise, click on OK. QuickBooks then saves the message in the Send list and will transmit it when you open the Online menu, choose Online Banking, select Online Banking Center, and click on Send.

Getting Help with Online Banking

Later in this session, you will learn how to get help from the various Intuit sites for all kinds of challenges. But what about those times when you just

SUNDAY AFTERNOON Online Banking with QuickBooks **273**

Figure 6.18

Along with your transactions, you can send messages to your bank to request information about your account transactions or payment history.

need a simple answer to a quick question or you don't understand a basic process you've got to master? QuickBooks gives you several ways to get help with online procedures:

- Click on the How Do I? buttons in the Online Banking Center or related dialog boxes to find out more about specific online procedures.

- Press F1 when a set of options is displayed that you want to know more about. The help window that appears will list the various options and give you links to more complete information.

- Use the Help Index. Try entering the following online-related terms to discover more about online banking: *online banking, online payroll,* and *online payments.*

Take a Break

Are you getting the hang of online payments? This whole arm of the banking industry is relatively new, but it's clearly not going away. With the blossoming of Internet commerce and the potential of remote-site bank ing, more and more dollars will flow through the pipeline, and greater and greater numbers of people will be demanding and expecting the ultimate in security measures. Once you get set up to do online banking in QuickBooks, you can leave the hassle to your PC—just point and click and make those payments.

After the break, you learn about how to transfer funds online and work with credit card payments. Additionally, you'll find out how to use your online resources to get the latest software updates and get help when you need it.

So take a few minutes and wander around, stretch, yawn, get a soda, and come back to your desk ready to climb back into the wires for another look around the online world.

Using the Payroll Service

QuickBooks offers an online payroll service that can take care of autodepositing your employees' checks and preparing and filing your federal and state payroll tax forms. The service can also prepare Forms W-2 and W-3 for you.

How do you get started? First, check out the video on your QuickBooks CD that gives you the highlights of the payroll service. Here are the steps:

1. Open the Online menu. Choose Online Payroll Service.

2. From the submenu, choose About Online Payroll. The QuickBooks Online Payroll Service window appears.

3. Make sure that the CD-ROM is in the drive. Click on Help.

4. When the Help window appears, click on SHOW ME to see the video.

TIP To apply for the Online Payroll Service, call 1-800-332-4844 Monday through Friday during regular business hours. To get help with the Payroll Service, call 1-888-712-9702.

SUNDAY AFTERNOON   Online Banking with QuickBooks

When you call to sign up for the Payroll Service (1-800-332-4844), you will need the following information:

- Your company's legal name, address, and contact info
- Your federal employer identification number (EIN)
- The owner's name, social security number, and contact info
- Bank account and routing numbers
- The frequency with which you pay federal taxes
- The contact person at your company
- A credit card number for the application fee

The QuickBooks representative who takes the information will give you a Payroll Service application number, which you then enter during the signup interview (that's the next step). Be sure to write the number down in a safe place so that you have it to refer to later.

Not Yet for Everyone

QuickBooks 6.0 is the first release in which the Online Payroll Service is offered, and as a new feature, it still has some areas and features that are unsupported. For example, if you or your employees live or work in any of the following states, the full features of the Payroll Service are not currently available to you:

- Indiana
- Kentucky
- Florida
- New Jersey
- Ohio
- Pennsylvania
- Puerto Rico

Also, if you are an agricultural employer (which means you file Form 943), a Medicare Qualified Government Employer (MQGE), or a household employer (filing Schedule H, Form 1040), the Payroll Service will not be fully able to handle all your reporting needs.

Subsequent releases and updates will make more of these features available, however, so check with the Intuit Online Payroll Service number (1-888-712-9702) periodically to see what is supported.

Using the QuickBooks Updates Service

All software products are evolving products. Every major program goes through a new release every so often that introduces new features and responds to changes in the industry. QuickBooks 6.0 is the most recent upgrade of the QuickBooks program. But between those major releases, manufacturers issue what they call *maintenance releases*, which may fix small problems users find in their versions of the program. You can download maintenance releases for free from Intuit.

Here's how:

1. Open the Online menu.

2. Choose QuickBooks Update Service. The Update Service dialog box appears (see Figure 6.19). You can use the service to go online and find out what updates are available; then you can download the updates to your computer.

3. Click on Go Online. QuickBooks displays the Connect To dialog box, and when you supply your password and click on Connect, QuickBooks dials your ISP and makes the connection. The program searches for and then downloads program updates that have been made available since the last time you used this feature (see Figure 6.20).

When the download is complete, QuickBooks will prompt you to restart QuickBooks so that the new changes can take effect. When you exit and then restart the program, QuickBooks asks whether it is okay to go ahead and install the program changes. When you click on Yes, QuickBooks installs the update, and the newest program fixes will be in place. The updates that were received are listed in the QuickBooks Update Service dialog box along with the dates they were received, so the next time you check for updates, you can see what you've already received (see Figure 6.21).

SUNDAY AFTERNOON   Online Banking with QuickBooks   **277**

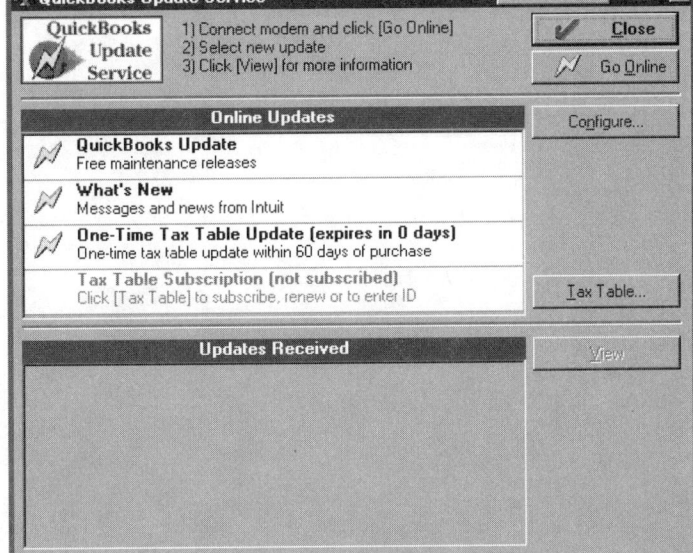

Figure 6.19

The QuickBooks Update Service enables you to get the latest program updates from Intuit.

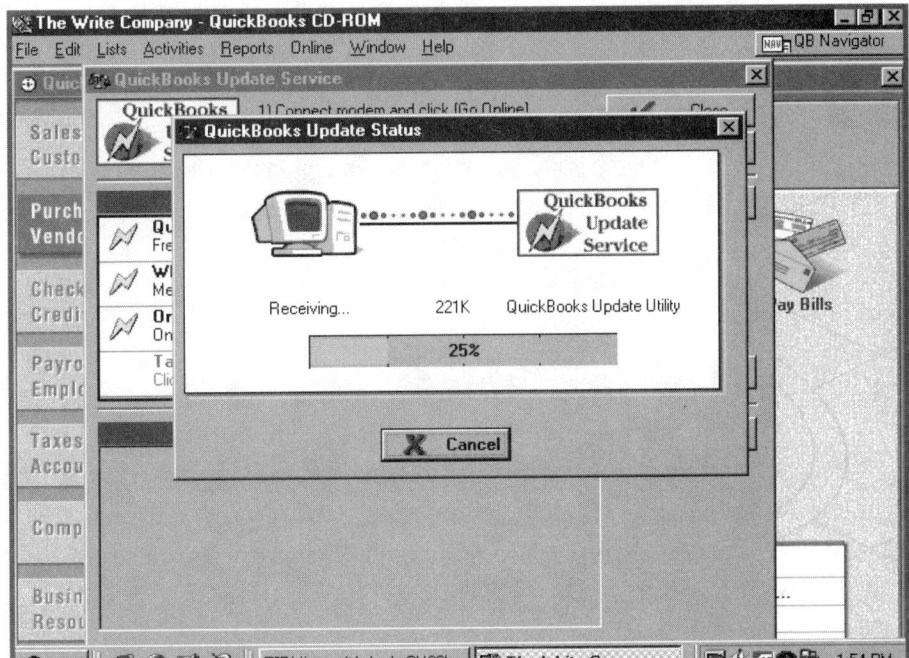

Figure 6.20

QuickBooks sends the update files to your computer as soon as you connect.

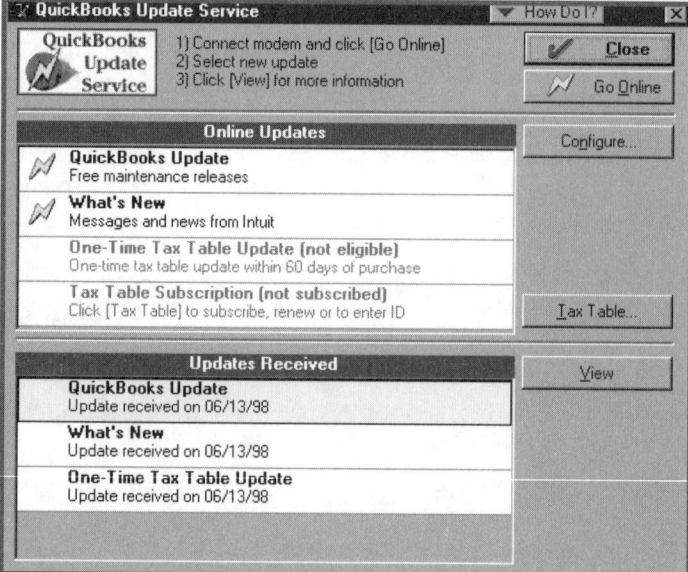

Figure 6.21

The QuickBooks Update Service dialog box shows which updates you have received after you've updated at least once.

TIP Through the update service, you can also get tax table updates, which include the most current tax forms and withholding tables. For the first 60 days after you purchase QuickBooks, you can go online and download one tax table update free of charge; after that there is a subscription fee, and Intuit will allow you to download tax tables (or send them to you automatically) on a regular basis. To subscribe to the QuickBooks Tax Table Update service, call 1-800-644-8371.

Getting New Tax Tables

Another option on the Online menu gives you access to tax tables and updated tax information. Click on Online and then click on Payroll Tax Tables. QuickBooks displays the Connect To dialog box. Enter your password and click on Connect. QuickBooks dials into your ISP and then logs on to the Intuit Web site (see Figure 6.22).

Figure 6.22

You can have access to updated tax tables through the QuickBooks subscription tax table service.

Notice that the two columns in Figure 6.22 both address subscription issues. If you are not yet a subscriber, you can use the links on the right to find out more about the tax service and to subscribe to the service. If you are currently a subscriber, you can renew your subscription, download new tax tables, check your current tax tables, and more.

Click on the links you want, download what you need, and when you're ready to return to QuickBooks, click on Exit.

NOTE Yes, you're really on the Internet. The browser you're looking at when QuickBooks logs onto the tax table site is QuickBooks' built-in browser.

Using Your Web Resources (Intuit Web Sites)

One more feature that goes along with the whole "online" motif in this session is the collection of Web resources QuickBooks houses in the Online menu. By opening the Online menu, selecting Intuit Web Sites, and choosing the Web site you want, you can glean information from each of the following sites:

- **QuickBooks.com**, which takes you to the QuickBooks home page and gives you access to the latest information about the product as well as tips and tricks from experts and other QuickBooks users. You can also purchase companion products as well as checks and forms, and you can get technical support from this site.

- **SmallBusiness by Quicken.com**, which is a Web site with all kinds of information for owners and operators of small businesses. From articles on how to set your rates to tax information to classifieds, SmallBusiness includes a huge variety of information that will help you run your business more effectively.

- **Cashfinder.com**, which helps you find money for your business (no kidding!).

- **QuickBooks technical support**, giving you access to technical advice and troubleshooting.

- **The Intuit Home Page**, which is the mothership of all the Intuit product Web sites. Here you can find out more about the company, order supplies, and even look into getting a job with Intuit.

- **The Intuit Market**, which is the shopping point for things like checks, invoices, purchase orders, and receipts.

Take some time and check out each of these resources next time you're online with QuickBooks. Bookmark sites that are particularly useful to you and return to them periodically to see whether they have been updated.

What's Next?

You're almost there! One more QuickBooks work session and you're done. This session has been all about QuickBooks' online features—from online bank transactions to getting program upgrades to downloading tax tables and using your Web resources. The next session winds up the book by delving into that no-man's land of taxes, taxes, taxes. Luckily, QuickBooks includes a number of features that make tax time easier and help you communicate with your accountant in a language he'll understand. Specifically, the next session focuses on the following tasks:

- Setting up a tax system
- Working with tax information in QuickBooks
- Using the Journal
- Handling payroll taxes
- Preparing tax reports
- Preparing an accountant's review

Feel like taking a break? Go ahead and stop, take a little time for yourself, and clear your head. When you're ready, come back for the finale of your QuickBooks intensive weekend. It's not long now!

S U N D A Y   E V E N I N G

Organizing Tax Information

- ✿ Finding Out about Journal Entries
- ✿ Handling Business Taxes
- ✿ Reporting Payroll Taxes
- ✿ Working with Sales Tax
- ✿ Using the Accountant's Review

Taxes. Does the word make you break out in a sweat? Do you have the picture of your least-favorite IRS agent tacked up to the center of your dart board? Or conversely, maybe you just *love* paying taxes. Most of us fall somewhere in the middle. QuickBooks includes a number of features to help you get organized and ready for tax season—for *all* the tax seasons—that hit throughout the year. Whether you are a sole proprietor paying only quarterly taxes or a corporate employee responsible for hundreds of payroll checks each week, QuickBooks can help you get the hang of tracking, organizing, and reporting your taxes.

And because we all need more than a little help now and then and rely on the expertise of accountants to make those calls we cannot, QuickBooks includes the Accountant's Review feature—a reporting mechanism that helps you create reports in a language and form your accountant will understand. You don't have to speak accounting—QuickBooks will take the normal QuickBooks data and translate it to accountantese. This session shows you how to prepare your QuickBooks data for the tax man and for the person who represents you to the tax man—in one swoop.

Use QuickBooks along with a companion tax-preparation program such as TurboTax to get the maximum benefit for your business with the least hassle (not to mention a reduced margin of error).

One of the few tabs you haven't explored in the QuickBooks Navigator is the Taxes and Accountant tab. Click on that tab to display items related to organizing and filing taxes and preparing information for your accountant (see Figure 7.1).

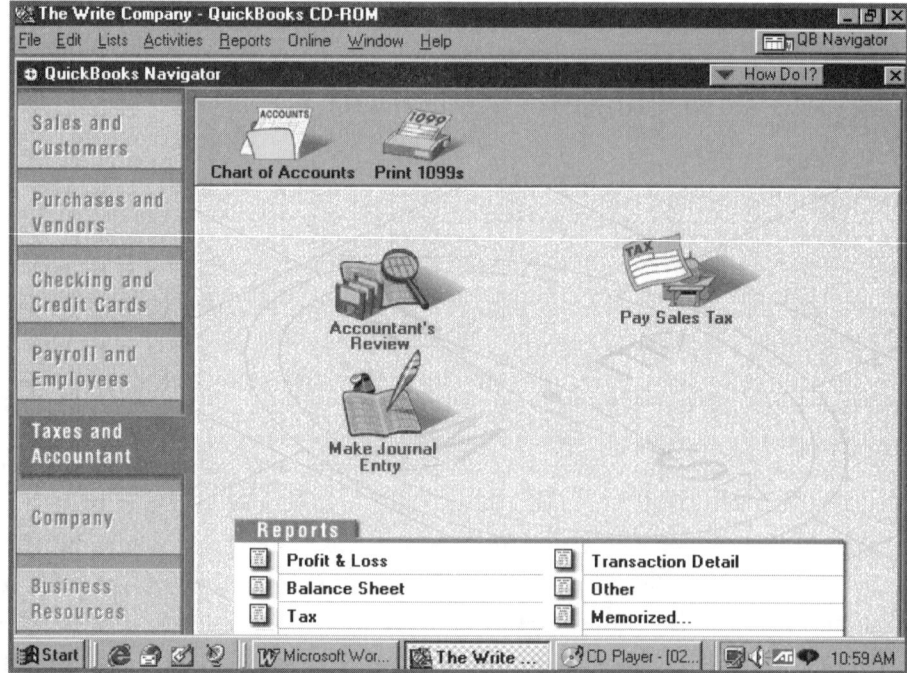

Figure 7.1

QuickBooks displays tax and accounting preparation features in the Taxes and Accountant tab.

Finding Out about Journal Entries

Journal entries may be something you never need to worry about, if you're not an accountant and don't ever plan to become one. A *journal entry* is the traditional accounting term for entering a transaction (debit in one column and credit in the other) in a general ledger. For most routine daily operations, you use features in QuickBooks, such as the check register, purchase orders, invoices, and bills, to track the transactions in your business. In special cases, you might use QuickBooks' General Journal feature to enter a transaction that is different from the norm.

NOTE QuickBooks recommends that you avoid making adjustments to your accounts using the General Journal unless you really know what you are doing, accounting-wise.

To use the Journal Entry feature, follow these steps:

1. Display the Taxes and Accountant tab.
2. Click on the Make Journal Entry icon. The General Journal Entry dialog box appears, as shown in Figure 7.2.

Figure 7.2

In the General Journal, you can enter specialized transactions if you are familiar with traditional accounting practices.

3. Correct the date if needed; press Tab.
4. Provide an Entry number for your own records.
5. Choose an account for the transaction by typing it or by clicking on the down arrow and selecting it from the list. Press Tab.
6. Enter the debit/credit information; the name for the customer, vendor, or job; and the class, if applicable.
7. If you want to create another journal entry, click on Next; otherwise, click on OK to return to the Navigator window.

Handling Business Taxes

Even though most people don't eagerly await the tax season, preparation is getting easier than it used to be. Today there are computers, computer programs, angels called *online advisors*, and the person to whom the first business check goes every month (the accountant) to help set up and maintain business taxes.

QuickBooks includes a number of features that help you not only with income tax but also payroll and sales tax, as well. Each of these tax types are covered in this session.

> ### A Dependent Government
>
> This morning as I was having my first cup of coffee and waiting for the cobwebs to clear out of my head, I turned on the television for a quick look at the weather report (here in Indiana we are expecting a "Build the ark!" command sometime soon) and happened to find an old episode of the Burns and Allen show. Gracie Allen was having a chat with the tax man. (How appropriate, I thought.) Her question to him was: "Our tax dollars support the government and all its employees, right?" The tax man agreed. She looked at him quizzically. "Then why can't we claim them as dependents?"

Setting Up for Business Taxes

The process of setting up for tracking business taxes, if you are using the Chart of Accounts QuickBooks provides, is basically done for you. QuickBooks tracks income and expenses and helps you figure the amounts that flow through to the appropriate lines in your tax forms.

You can then use QuickBooks with a tax-preparation program, such as TurboTax (also from Quicken) to further work with, print, and file your completed tax forms.

TIP Although you need to "turn on" sales tax by using the Preference menu, the data for your business taxes is part of QuickBooks and is tracked for you as you enter daily transactions of sales and purchases.

SUNDAY EVENING Organizing Tax Information **289**

PREPARING TAX FORMS: THE PROCESS

The overall process for preparing your tax forms is pretty simple, although you may have a myriad of details to work with, depending on the nature of your business. When you want to prepare tax information with QuickBooks, the steps are these:

1. Make sure your accounts are assigned to the correct lines on the tax form you are using.
2. Figure out how much income your business made from sales and returns.
3. Determine your expenses for purchases.
4. Fill out the tax forms your company files.

What's Your Tax Form?

You may not even be aware that QuickBooks assigns the accounts you use to affiliated lines on the tax form you selected. Don't remember selecting a tax form? You did—way back in the EasyStep Interview.

When you set up your business, you entered your company name and selected the type of your business during the EasyStep Interview. Figure 7.3 shows the Company Info tab page that gives you the option of choosing your tax form.

TIP You can change the tax form for your business at any time by opening the File menu, choosing EasyStep Interview, and going through the Company Info tab until you get to the page displayed in Figure 7.3. Then simply select the tax form you need and click on Leave to exit the Interview and return to the Navigator window.

If you are unsure which tax form you need for your business, you can search the IRS's Web site for more information at **www.irs.gov**.

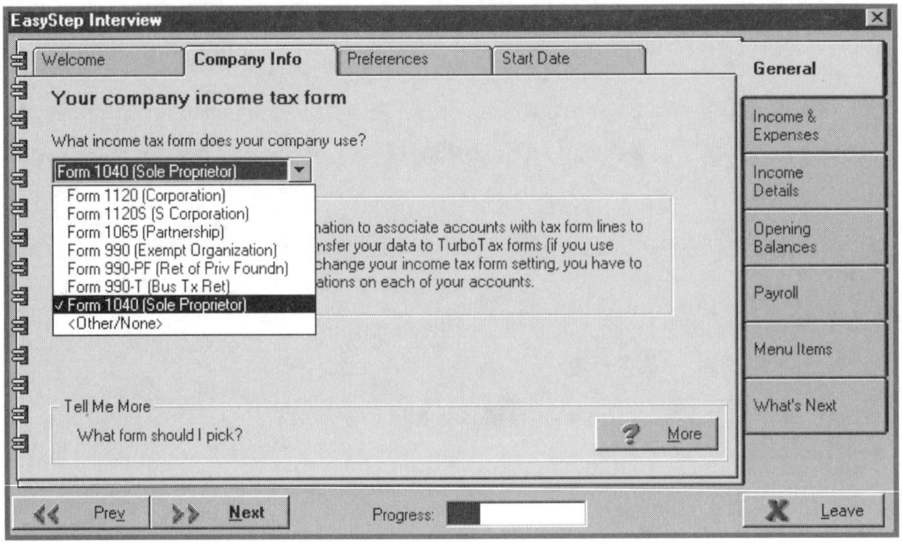

Figure 7.3

During the EasyStep Interview, you selected the tax form your business uses to report income. QuickBooks uses this form to assign tax line numbers for your accounts.

Checking Tax Line Assignments

Now that you know where the tax line assignments come from, take a look at what you—or QuickBooks—have assigned to the accounts you've created. To see which accounts you've got assigned to which tax lines, you need to create an Income Tax Transaction list. Here are the steps:

1. Display the Chart of Accounts by opening the Lists menu and choosing Chart of Accounts.

2. Click on the Reports button.

3. From the submenu, choose Income Tax Preparation List. A report similar to the one shown in Figure 7.4 appears.

Wait a minute. There are an awful lot of <Unassigned> accounts in that list. What's going on?

When you create accounts the QuickBooks way, meaning when you allow QuickBooks to create the accounts for you during the EasyStep Interview, QuickBooks assigns a tax line to the account. When you create a new ac-

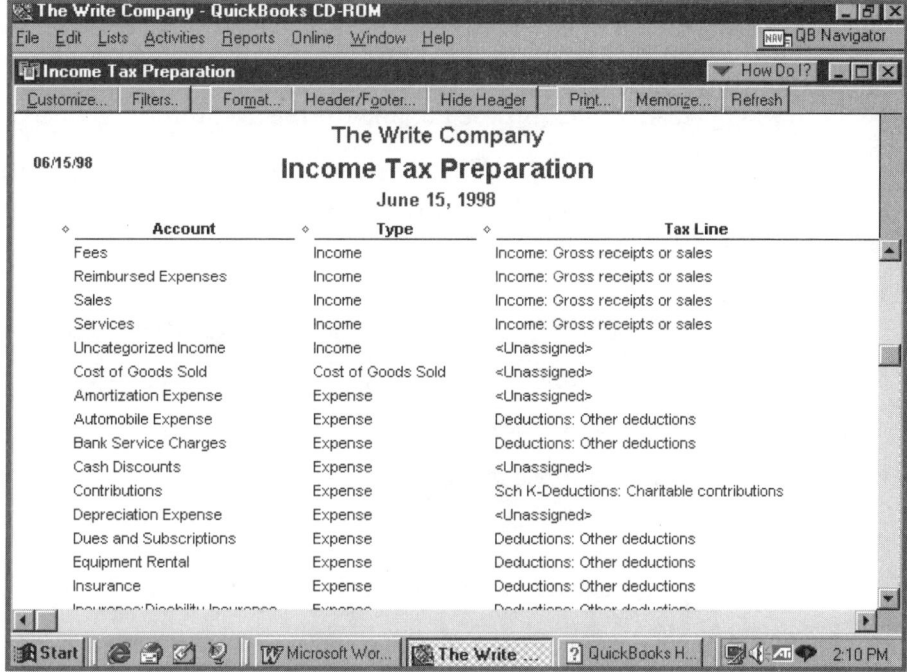

Figure 7.4

You can display an Income Tax Preparation list to determine what the tax line assignments are.

count using Quick Add or New Vendor, you have the option of assigning the account to a particular tax line. If you clicked on OK without assigning a tax line (as I did in several cases), the item will show up on the Preparation List as <Unassigned>.

Okay, so how do you assign an unassigned account? That's the subject of the next section.

Assigning a Tax Line to an Account

When you have <Unassigned> lines in the Preparation list and you want to assign a tax line to the account, follow these steps:

1. Make sure the Preparation list is displayed.
2. Move the mouse to the line and double-click on the line in the Tax Line column. The Edit Account dialog box appears.

3. Click on the down arrow in the Tax Line field. A list of tax line descriptions appears (see Figure 7.5).

4. Click on the tax line for the account.

5. Click on OK. When you return to the item in the Preparation list, the tax line is displayed there.

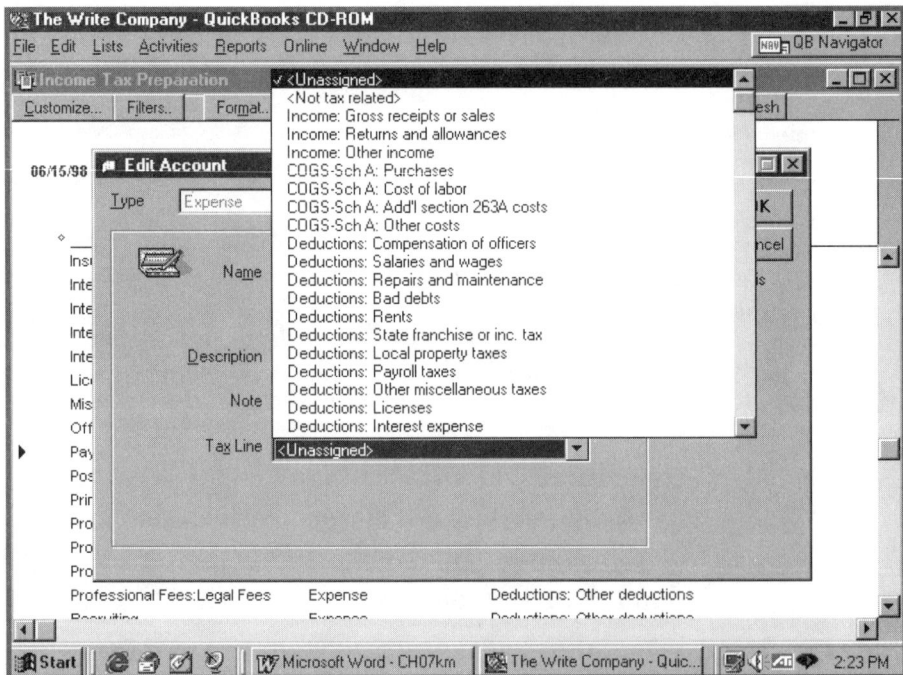

Figure 7.5

You can assign tax lines in the Edit Account dialog box.

 TIP You can also display the Edit Account dialog box by displaying the Chart of Accounts, selecting the account, and pressing Ctrl+E.

SUNDAY EVENING Organizing Tax Information **293**

Verifying Account Totals

Although the Preparation list displays the tax line assigned to each account, in order to put the amounts in the appropriate spaces on the tax forms, you need totals of each tax item. You can display an income tax summary that breaks the totals out according to tax line. To do this:

1. Open the Reports menu and choose Other Reports.

2. From the submenu that appears, choose Income Tax Summary. A report similar to the one shown in Figure 7.6 appears.

3. Click in the Dates field and make sure you have selected the correct time frame for the report. If you are preparing taxes for the previous year, choose Last Tax Year. QuickBooks recalculates the report based on the period you selected.

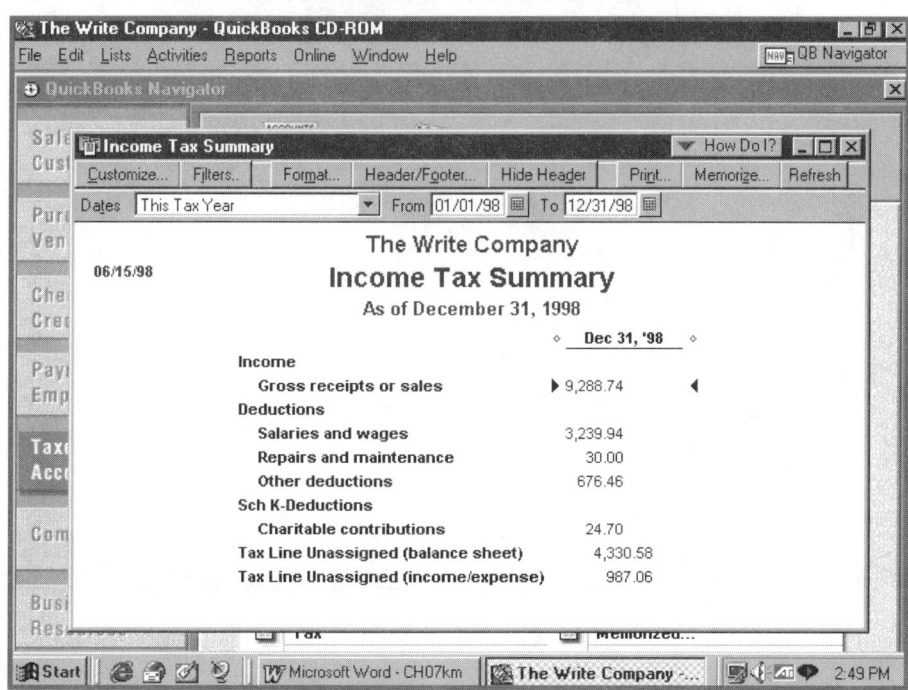

Figure 7.6

The Income Tax Summary report shows you the totals you have attributed to each tax category.

4. Modify and/or enhance the report as needed. Click on Print to display the Print Reports dialog box so that you can preview and then print your report.

Modifying the Income Tax Summary Report

Something doesn't look right? You can display a QuickReport on a suspicious-looking item by double-clicking on it. QuickBooks displays the Tax Line by Account report, as shown in Figure 7.7. Click on the Close box after you've checked the totals, or click on Print to display the Print Reports dialog box.

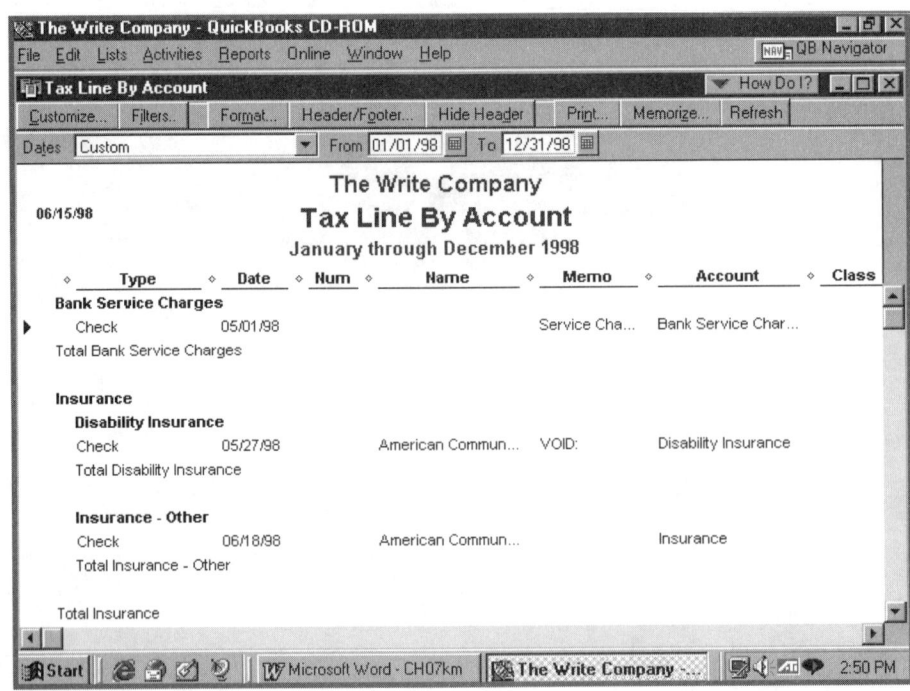

Figure 7.7

The Tax Line by Account report itemizes the transactions that make up the totals in the Income Tax Summary report.

Finding Sales Income Amounts

Now that you know you've got your tax lines assigned correctly (or you've corrected those that needed it), you need to determine your net sales for

the year. Again you use the Income Tax Summary report to find that amount. Here's how:

1. Display the Income Tax Summary report by opening the Reports menu, choosing Other Reports, and clicking on Income Tax Summary.

2. Specify the Dates you want (for last year, choose Last Tax Year). QuickBooks creates the report.

3. Write down the amounts for the following accounts:

    Gross receipts or sales

    Returns and allowances

4. Subtract the amount in returns and allowances from gross receipts or sales.

5. If your business did not have returns or credits, the amount you get as a result of the subtraction is your company's net sales. You can write that on your form and you're finished!

If your business *did* have returns or credits, however, you're not quite finished. Follow these steps to determine the net sales amount for your company:

1. With the Income Tax Summary still displayed on the screen, double-click on the gross receipts or sales account. QuickBooks creates a QuickReport showing you all the transactions that fall under that category.

2. Click on the Customize button in the Reports toolbar. The Customize Report dialog box appears (see Figure 7.8).

3. In the Columns list, click on Debit and Credit to add both those columns. Click on OK.

4. Scroll to the right to see the Debit and Credit columns (they are added close to the far-right end of the report).

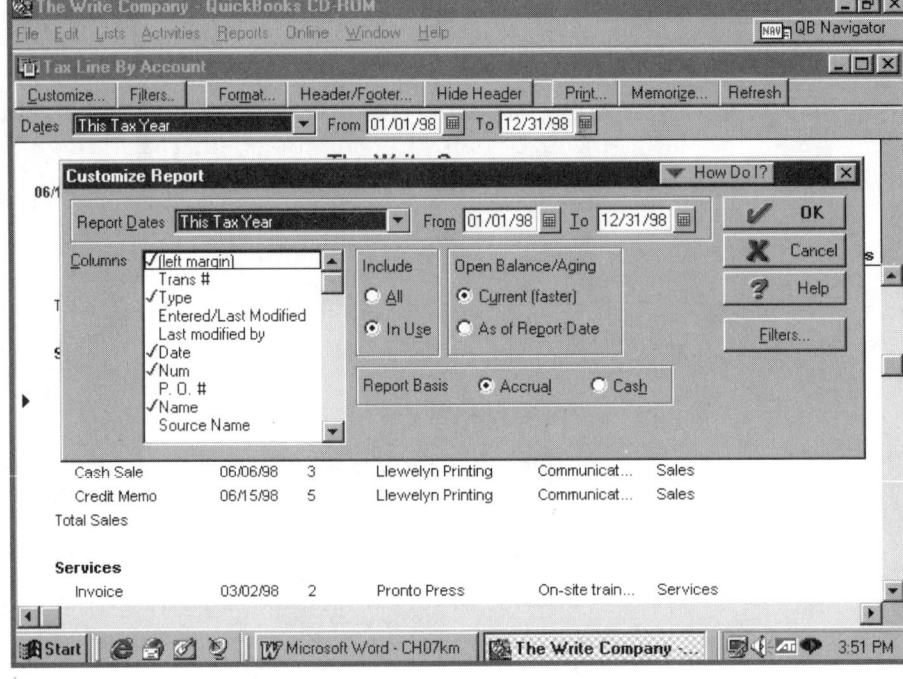

Figure 7.8

When you double-click on gross receipts, QuickBooks shows you all the transactions that contribute to that item.

5. Scroll down to see the totals of the columns (see Figure 7.9). Write the totals down on a scrap of paper.

◄ ◄

Gross receipts or sales is the total of your sales for the year, including any returns that were entered as credits or refunds.

◄ ◄

6. Use the Credit amount as your gross sales on your tax form.

7. Fill in the Debit amount in the line for returns and allowances.

8. Subtract the Debit amount from the Credit amount. That is the net sales amount that you can use on your tax form.

SUNDAY EVENING   Organizing Tax Information   **297**

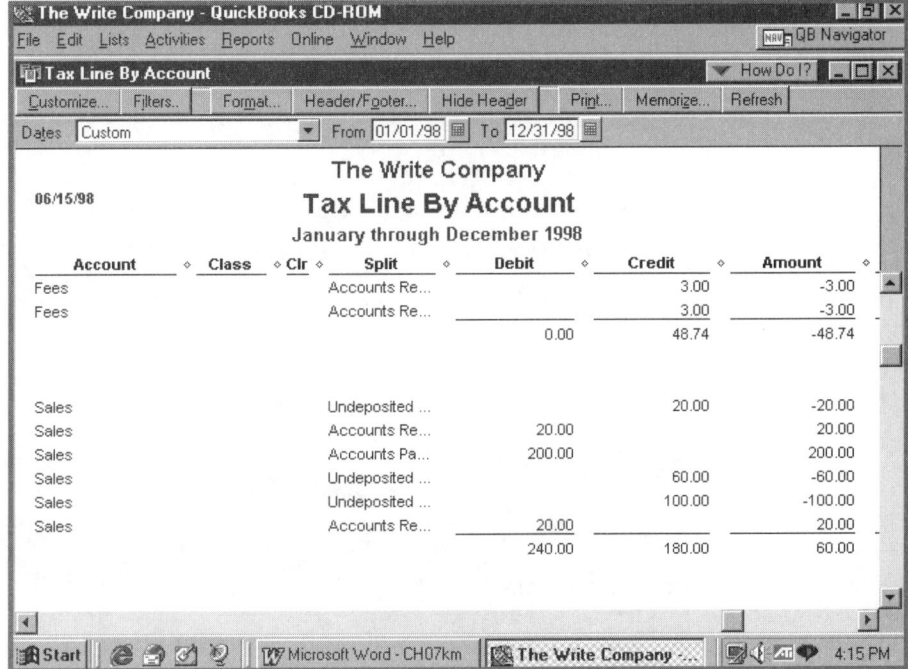

Figure 7.9

Record the Debit and Credit totals so that you can subtract them from gross receipts.

◀ ◀

Returns and allowances totals all the discounts you allowed as part of sales and will be subtracted from your gross sales to get net sales.

◀ ◀

Determining Your Total Purchases

Your next step in filling out your tax forms involves finding how much you bought during the previous tax year. This involves finding the total of all your purchases and creating another tax report called the Purchases by Item Summary report. Here are the steps:

1. Open the Reports menu and choose Purchase Reports.
2. From the submenu, choose By Item Summary.

3. Click on the Dates field and choose the tax period you're reporting on (if it's for last year's taxes, select Last Fiscal Year).

4. Write the TOTAL amount in your tax form's Cost of Goods Sold line (see Figure 7.10).

5. Format and enhance the report as needed. Click on Print to display the Print Reports dialog box to preview and print the report.

6. Close the report and return to the QuickBooks Navigator window by clicking on the Close button.

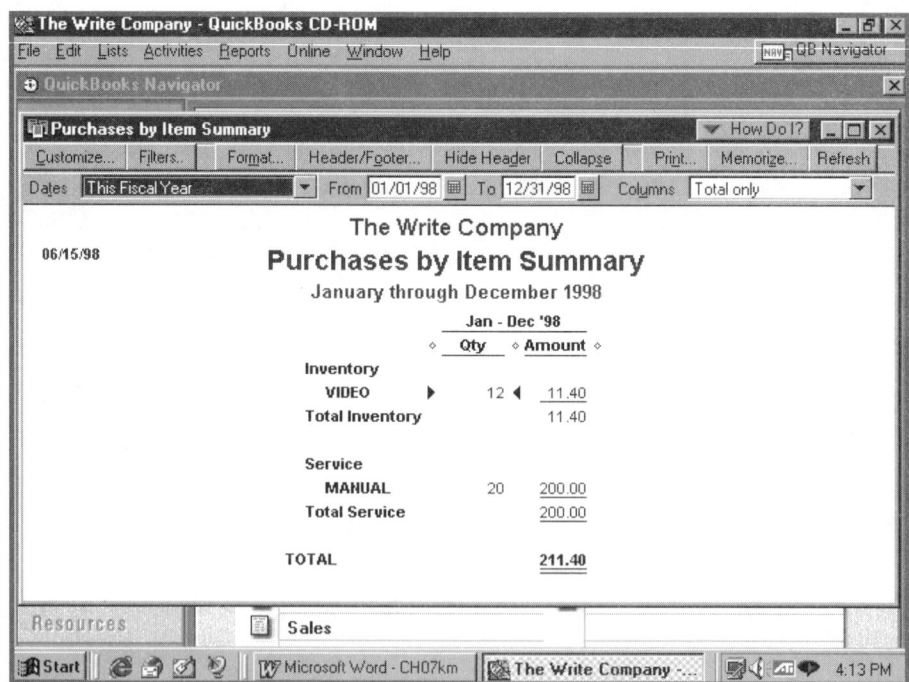

Figure 7.10

Your total purchases are recorded in the Cost of Goods Sold line on your tax form.

Filling Out Additional Forms

Depending on the type of company you have (sole proprietorship, corporation, or other), you may have additional forms to fill out. Two such forms

that QuickBooks can help you with are Forms 1120 and 1120S, which deal with corporate salaries.

In the Payroll Expenses account, QuickBooks does not distinguish between corporate officers and employees, but according to the IRS, you must report the two amounts separately. You need to take the payroll expenses total and divide it into the amount paid to your officers and the amount paid to your employees. You can use the Windows calculator to do the figuring. To display the calculator from QuickBooks:

1. Open the Activities menu and choose Other Activities.

2. From the submenu, choose Use Calculator.

3. Enter your calculations:

    Add the adjusted gross income of your corporate officers and put the total on the Compensation of Officers line on Form 1120 or 1120S.

    Add the adjusted gross income of your employees and place the total on the Salary and Wages line of the form.

4. When you're finished with the calculator, click on the Close box.

Preparing Your Tax Forms

The final step in preparing your business taxes is to fill in the forms. You've been doing that gradually, if you're writing in the amounts by hand as you figure them. You already have amounts for the following items:

- Gross receipts or sales
- Returns and allowances
- Net sales
- Compensation of officers
- Salary and wages

You can see how the accounts in QuickBooks correlate with the tax lines on your forms. Using your Income Tax Preparation list and your Income Tax Summary report, fill in the amounts line by line on your form.

Exporting Tax Information to a Tax Program

Another option for filling out your tax forms involves exporting your QuickBooks data to a tax-preparation program such as TurboTax. Three tax programs—TurboTax, TurboTax for Business, and ProSeries—can all use your QuickBooks data file as it is. To use QuickBooks data in a tax-preparation program such as the ones I mentioned here, simply start your tax program, select the Import command (it's probably in the File menu of your tax program), and open the QuickBooks file.

TIP To learn more about Intuit's TurboTax, visit www.intuit.com/.

Take a Break

Eeesssh. Even in the best-case scenario, taxes aren't a fun topic to dwell on. That's why the world needs accountants. When you get my accountant talking about tax reform, his eyes light up and he begins to get animated; his normally quiet, studious demeanor takes on an ethereal glow of energy; his hands gesture and he begins laying out this great plan for how he would fix the whole tax system for the IRS if they'd let him. I, on the other hand, fall asleep. Differences in personalities, I guess.

But hopefully you are still with me and are learning how QuickBooks truly can make your tax job easier and less intimidating. You can even submit taxes online, a topic you'll cover after the break. So take ten and get refreshed. See you in a few minutes.

Reporting Payroll Taxes

At this point, you're going to do only a quick review of payroll basics because half of Saturday evening's session ("Keeping Track of Inventory and

SUNDAY EVENING Organizing Tax Information

Managing Payroll") covered the various aspects of payroll and payroll tax reporting. Here it is in a nutshell:

The Payroll Process Revisited

The process of setting up and working with payroll looks like this:

1. Enable payroll features.
2. Enter your employee information.
3. Track payroll information.
4. Enter deductions.
5. Print checks.
6. Report payroll and pay payroll taxes.

Even though it looks as if payroll taxes don't come in until the end of the process, QuickBooks actually has you working with tax information the entire time you're tracking employee data. From the initial hire, you are working with W-4 information, including withholding and deductions and exemptions. By the time you prepare the reports, you have been entering and maintaining the data and can rely on QuickBooks to do the figuring for you.

Creating Payroll Subaccounts

Earlier in this session, you learned that the IRS insists that you separate corporate officers' pay from employee wages. You set up subaccounts in your Payroll Expenses account to handle these different payroll types. Here's how:

1. Open the Lists menu and choose Chart of Accounts.
2. Click on the Account button and click on New. The New Account window appears.
3. In the Type field, click on the down arrow and choose Expense.
4. Enter a name for the account (for example, "Compensation of officers," to correlate with the term on the tax line).

5. Click on the check box to the left of Subaccount Of.
6. Click on the down arrow and choose Payroll Expenses.
7. Enter a description, if you'd like.
8. Choose the tax line (in this case, Compensation of officers). Figure 7.11 shows the completed dialog box.
9. Click on OK.

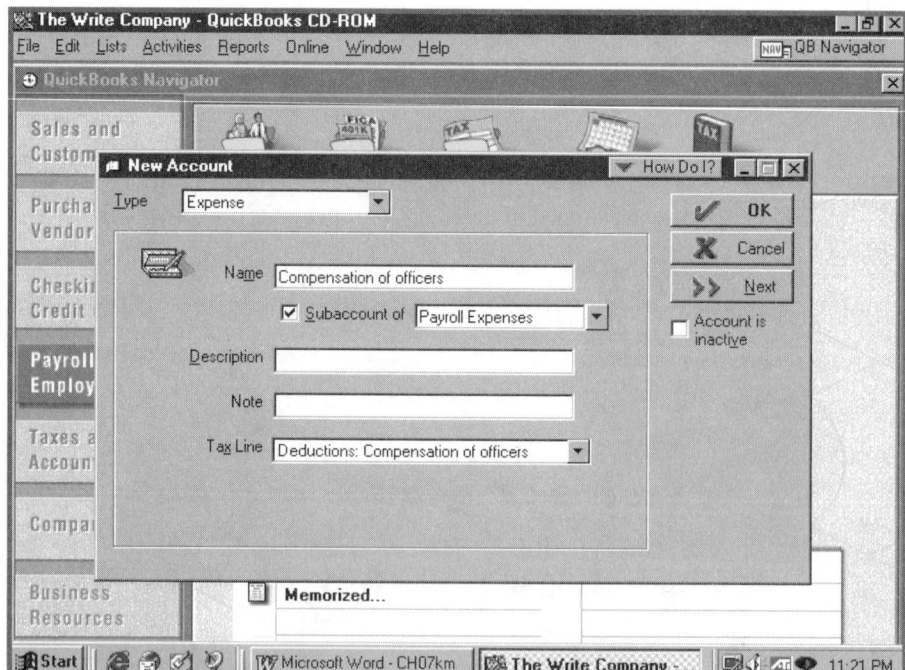

Figure 7.11

In the New Account dialog box, you set up the subaccounts you need in Payroll Expenses to track corporate salaries and wages separately.

 **NOTE** To complete the process of setting up the categories for both compensation of officers and salary and wages, repeat this process and create a subaccount of Payroll Expenses, this time entering "Salary and wages" as the subaccount name.

Payroll Reports: An Overview

In Saturday's session, you learned about the various reports you can create with QuickBooks. These are the forms you can generate from within the program:

- Form 941 is a form you submit quarterly showing the amount of federal tax, social security tax, and Medicare you paid for the quarter.

- Form 940 is the form you submit at the end of the year on which you report your company's FUTA (Federal Unemployment Tax) liability.

- W-2 is the form you supply to each employee showing the gross amount earned and the amount of federal, state, and local taxes that have been deducted from the gross.

- W-3 is a form that summarizes all the individual W-2 forms you create for your employees.

To create the reports, you simply click on the Payroll and Employees tab in the Navigator window and then click on the graphic of the report you want to generate.

Working with Sales Tax

The final tax you'll cover in this session is sales tax. Throughout QuickBooks, you've seen various check boxes and options that ask "Is the customer taxable?" Setting up sales tax is simple to do and easy to track. This section introduces you to the process.

Here's the general process of working with sales tax:

1. Turn on the sales tax feature.
2. Choose sales tax preferences.
3. Set up sales tax accounts.
4. Identify taxable items.
5. Record the sales tax.

> ### QUICKBOOKS' ONLINE PAYROLL SERVICE
>
> QuickBooks' Online Payroll Service can take care of automatically depositing your employees' checks and preparing and filing your federal and state payroll tax forms.
>
> To apply for the Online Payroll Service, call 1-800-332-4844 Monday through Friday during regular business hours. The service rep at the other end of the line will ask you for the following things:
>
> - Your company's legal name, address, and contact info
> - Your federal employer identification number (EIN)
> - The owner's name, social security number, and contact info
> - Bank account and routing numbers
> - The frequency with which you pay federal taxes
> - A contact person at your company
> - A credit card number for the application fee

6. Pay the sales tax.
7. Create a sales tax report.

The sections that follow explore each of these parts of the sales tax process.

Turning On Sales Tax

The first thing you need to do is to let QuickBooks know that you do, in fact, want to track sales tax. Here are the steps:

1. Open the File menu; choose Preferences. The Preferences dialog box appears.
2. Select Sales Tax in the scroll box on the left.
3. Click on the Company Preference tab (see Figure 7.12).
4. In the Do You Charge Sales Tax? area, click on Yes.

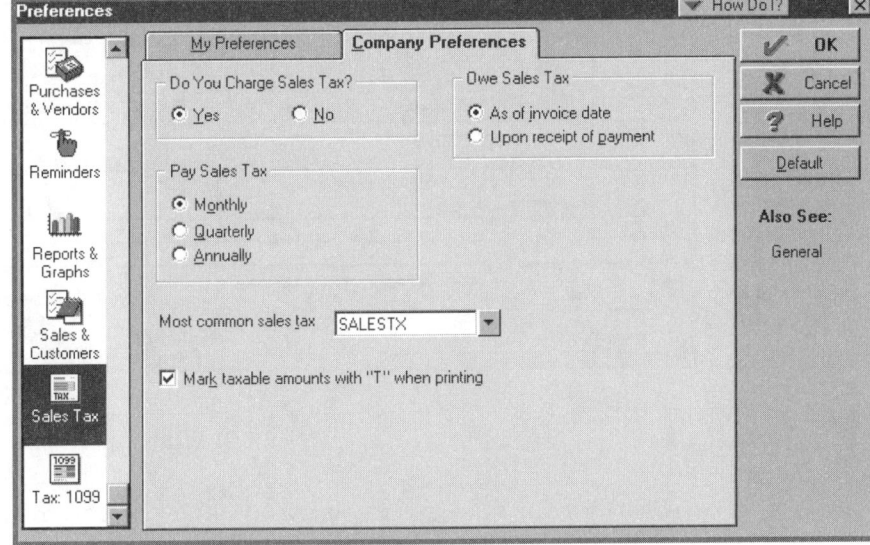

Figure 7.12

To turn on the sales tax feature, click on Yes in the Do You Charge Sales Tax? area.

5. In Owe Sales Tax, choose when you want the sales tax to be due.

6. In the Pay Sales Tax area, select whether you want to pay your sales tax liability monthly, quarterly, or annually.

7. Choose an account name for the sales tax.

8. If you want accounts that are taxable to be identified with a T when you print them, click on the check box in the bottom-center portion of the dialog box.

9. Click on OK.

QuickBooks turns the sales tax feature on, and you can begin entering sales tax information in invoices, purchase orders, receipts, credit memos, and more.

Setting Up Sales Tax

When you first begin tracking sales tax, you will need to enter a starting amount that corresponds with your QuickBooks start date. How much sales tax did you owe when you started using QuickBooks?

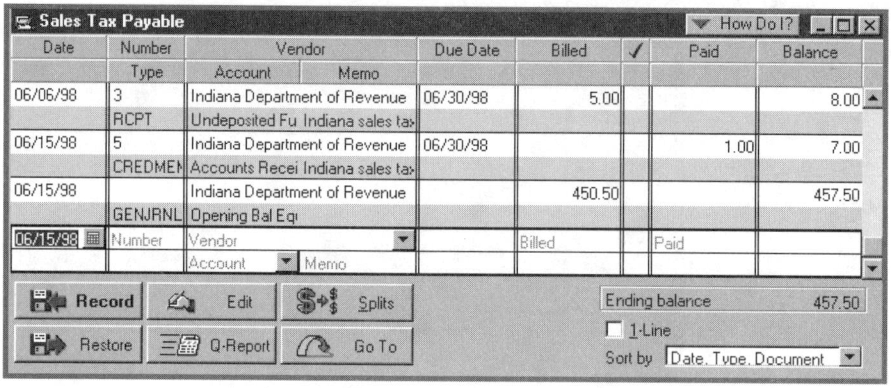

Figure 7.13

You enter the opening sales tax amount in the Sales Tax Payable register.

To set up your sales tax account and enter the current balance as of your start date, follow these steps:

1. Open the Lists menu and choose Chart of Accounts. The Chart of Accounts dialog box appears.

2. Select the Sales Tax Payable account; click on Activities and then click on Use Register. Click in the first available blank line in the register.

3. Enter the QuickBooks start date in the Date column.

4. Enter the tax agency to whom you pay the sales tax in the Payee field.

5. Enter the amount of sales tax in Billed.

6. Select Opening Bal Equity as the account. Figure 7.13 shows the completed sales tax opening balance transaction.

7. Repeat the process as necessary for different tax agencies.

8. Close the register by clicking on the Close button.

Identifying Taxable Items

Obviously, you are going to have some items that are taxable and some that are not. You need to distinguish for QuickBooks which items are taxable. If you selected the option Mark Taxable Amounts with "T" When Printing, QuickBooks will display a T beside a taxable item on sales forms you create. Then when QuickBooks does the calculations on the form, the program automatically includes all the taxable items in the calculation. Here's how to set up an item as taxable:

1. Open the Lists menu and choose Items. The Item List box appears.
2. Press Ctrl+N if you are entering a new item; select the item and press Ctrl+E if you want to edit an existing item. The Edit Item dialog box appears, as shown in Figure 7.14.
3. Click on the Taxable check box to select it.
4. Click on OK.

Figure 7.14

The Edit Item dialog box allows you to set up an item as taxable.

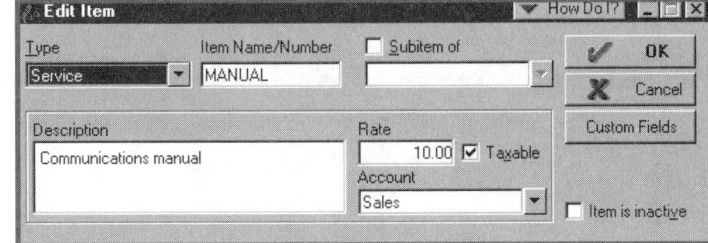

Recording a Tax Item

You can add a new item to track sales tax individually. This helps you distinguish between taxable and nontaxable items on your invoices and sales forms. To create a new tax item, follow these steps:

1. Open the Lists menu and choose Items. The Item List box appears.
2. Press Ctrl+N. The New Item dialog box is displayed.

3. Click on the Type down arrow and choose Sales Tax Item (see Figure 7.15).

4. Type a name for the sales tax item.

5. Type a description for the tax. (Note: This description will be printed on your sales forms.)

6. In the Rate box, enter the tax rate.

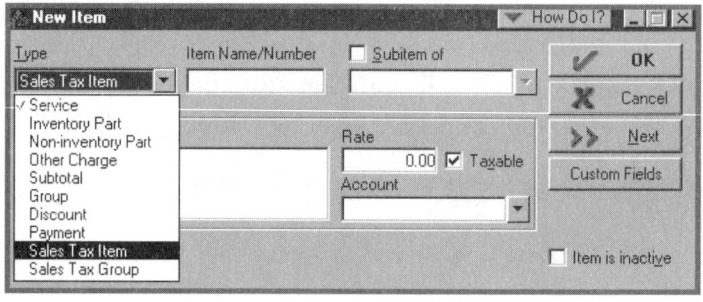

Figure 7.15

You can create a new sales tax item by displaying the Item List box and pressing Ctrl+N.

TIP You don't need to enter a percentage symbol after the value in the Rate field; just enter the number as a decimal amount. For example, enter 6.9% simply as 6.9.

7. In the Tax Agency field, enter the agency to whom you pay the tax.

8. Click on OK to create the item and return to the Item List box.

Paying Sales Tax

You're almost done with the sales tax issue. But collecting sales tax is only part of the picture—now you've got to pay it to your tax agency. Here's how:

1. Open the Activities menu and choose Pay Sales Tax. The Pay Sales Tax dialog box appears, as Figure 7.16 shows.

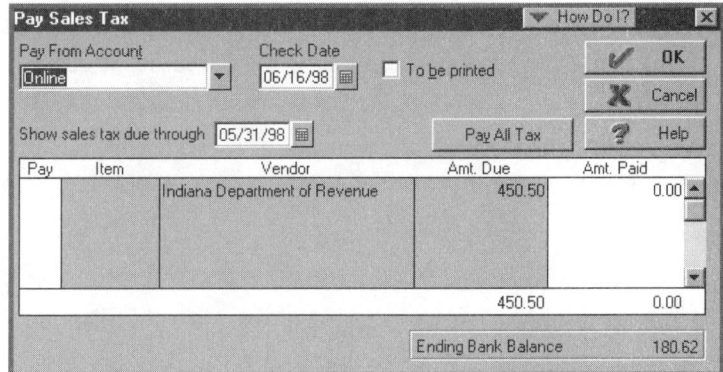

Figure 7.16

The Pay Sales Tax dialog box enables you to make sales tax payments to your tax agency.

2. Choose the account you want to use for payment by clicking on the Pay From Account down arrow and clicking on the account you want to use.

3. Enter the correct date.

4. In Show Sales Tax Due Through, enter the date of the latest tax transaction you want to display.

 TIP If you have several tax payments listed and want to pay all tax liabilities at once, click on the Pay All Tax button in the Pay Sales Tax dialog box.

5. Click on the items you want to pay by clicking on the item in the Pay column.

6. Click on OK to record the payments. QuickBooks then writes the check on the account you selected and adds the entry to your Sales Tax register and your check register for the selected account. When you are ready to print the checks, simply open the File menu, choose Print Forms, and select Print Checks.

TIP If you are sending your payment online, the transaction is queued for delivery electronically. The next time you open the Online menu, choose Online Banking, Online Banking Center, and click on Send.

Creating a Sales Tax Report

One final sales tax stop: creating a tax report. This is something you'll want to create for your accountant and also for your own records, so you'll know how much you're paying out to various tax agencies. To create a sales tax report, follow these steps:

1. Click on the Taxes and Accountant tab in the Navigator window.

2. In the Reports area, click on Tax. When the submenu appears, click on Sales Tax Liability Report. A report similar to the one shown in Figure 7.17 appears.

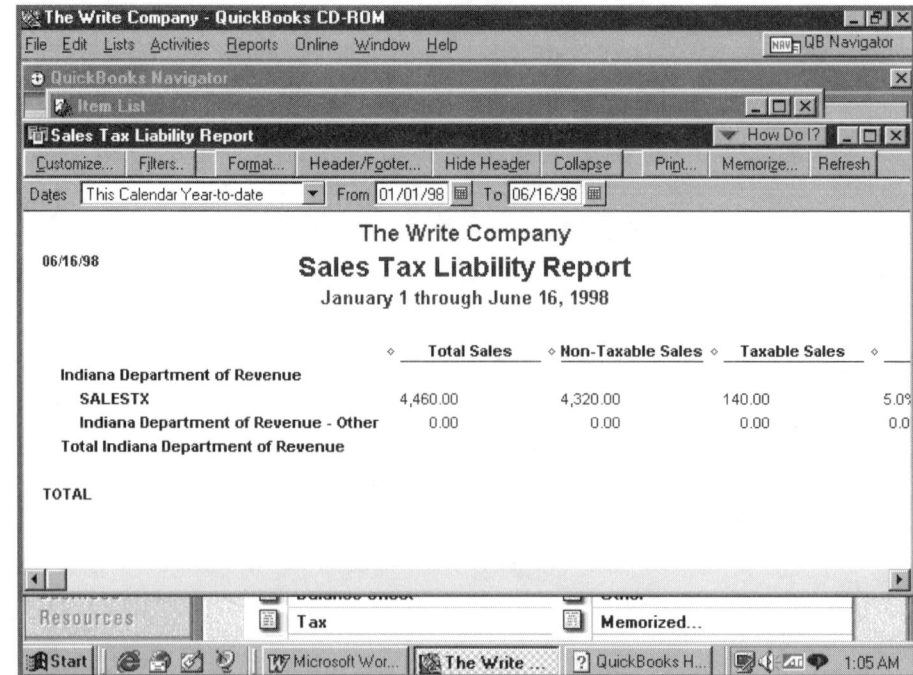

Figure 7.17

The Sales Tax Liability report shows the breakdown of taxable and nontaxable sales.

SUNDAY EVENING Organizing Tax Information

3. Change the Dates setting, if necessary.

4. Customize and enhance the report as desired.

5. Click on Print to display the Print Reports dialog box and preview the report before printing.

Using the Accountant's Review

Having an accountant is a good thing. Having a *good* accountant is even better. But having an accountant who is versed in QuickBooks is the coup de grâce—not only can you provide information he wants in an easy-to-use format, but you can provide him with a review copy of your QuickBooks files to work in while you continue your day-to-day operations.

QuickBooks includes a feature known as the *Accountant's Review*. This review is for those times when your accountant needs to look over your books and you cannot bear (or afford) to give them up. The review enables you to give a copy to your accountant and keep working in your file. The accountant can make changes in his copy and return it to you; you can then merge any changes into your master file.

Sound complicated? It's not too tough. And the benefit far outweighs the challenge. Take a look at the process:

1. Click on the Tax and Accountant tab in the Navigator window.

2. Click on Accountant's Review. The Accountant's Review Activities dialog box appears, as Figure 7.18 shows.

3. Click on OK to begin generating the review. QuickBooks tells you that it must close all open windows in order to run the review. Click on OK.

4. The Online Backup message box appears next, giving you the option of backing up your QuickBooks data. Click on Yes if you need to back up; click on No if it's not necessary.

5. In the Save Accountant's Copy To dialog box, choose the folder in which you want to store the file (see Figure 7.19). Enter a name for

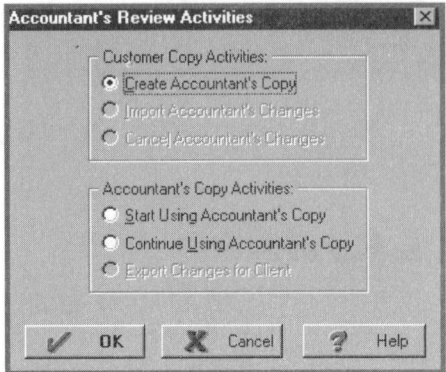

Figure 7.18

The Accountant's Review Activities dialog box shows you the tasks you can perform during the review.

the review copy in the File Name field. Click on Save. QuickBooks displays a message telling you the copy has been created. Click on OK to continue.

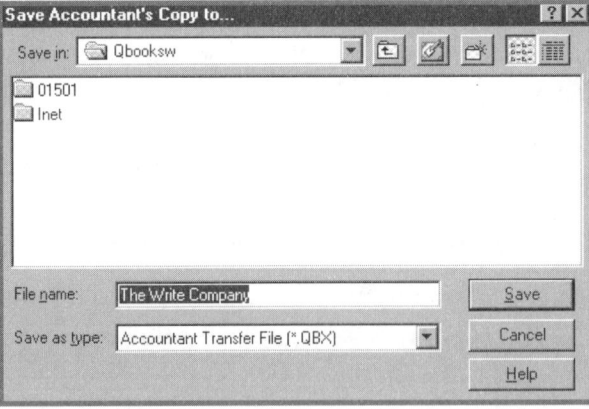

Figure 7.19

You use the Save Accountant's Copy To dialog box to save a copy of your QuickBooks data so that your accountant can view and work with the file, even while you continue to work on it.

TIP You will probably want to save the copy to a floppy disk, unless you're planning on sending the file over the Internet. If you save the file to a floppy disk, your accountant can insert the disk and work from that copy while doing the review.

Working with the Accountant's Copy

The next step involves getting the copy to your accountant. While he completes his review and makes any necessary adjustments, you are able to work in your master copy of the file without interruption. When he returns the copy to you, you merge the changes into your master copy using this process:

1. Display the Taxes and Accountant tab in the Navigator window.

2. Click on Accountant's Review. Once again, the Accountant's Review Activities dialog box appears.

3. This time, click on Start Using Accountant's Copy; then click on OK. The Open Accountant's Copy dialog box appears, as Figure 7.20 shows.

4. Click on the file name for the Accountant's Copy and click on Open.

5. QuickBooks alerts you that you need to rename the Accountant's Copy. Click on OK.

6. Enter a new name for the Accountant's Copy and click on Save. QuickBooks opens the accountant's copy. It looks similar to your working copy, except that "Accountant's Copy" appears in the title bar.

Merging the Accountant's Data

Finally, you can export the changes your accountant made so that you can use the changes in your own master file. To export the data, you display the Taxes and Accountant tab, click on Accountant's Review, and choose Export Changes for Client. QuickBooks prompts you that it must close all

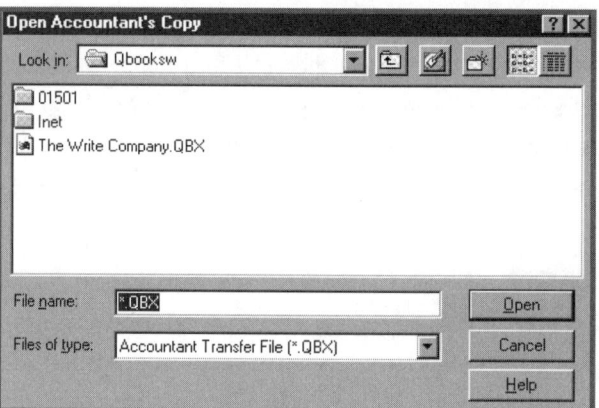

Figure 7.20

When you choose Start Using Accountant's Copy, QuickBooks displays a dialog box so that you can select the file.

open windows in order to carry out that procedure. Click on OK. The Save Export Changes To dialog box appears so that you can enter a name for the export file. It will be saved with an .AIF extension. Enter a name for the file and click on Save. After a moment, QuickBooks lets you know that the file has been created and is ready for you to merge the changes with the original data file.

You can merge the changes your accountant made into your master file by following these steps:

1. Put the disk with the exported changes (saved in the .AIF format as mentioned in the previous paragraph) in the disk drive.

2. Open your QuickBooks master file if you haven't already done so.

3. Open the File menu and choose Accountant's Review.

4. From the submenu, choose Import Accountant's Changes. Click on OK to back up your file data. When the Import Changes from Accountant's Copy dialog box appears, display the contents of the disk drive and choose the file you need.

5. Click on Open to merge the changes.

What's Next?

Well, technically, there's nothing *next*. You've done it! In a single weekend, you have gone through most of the basic-but-powerful features QuickBooks has to offer. Take a look at this list of tasks you've accomplished and feel good about how far you've come in just two-and-a-half days. You:

- Took the EasyStep Interview
- Set up your checkbook in QuickBooks
- Learned to create an invoice
- Entered customer information
- Printed mailing labels and invoices
- Recorded cash sales
- Used the To Do feature
- Set QuickBooks preferences
- Wrote checks
- Balanced your checkbook
- Figured out the Chart of Accounts
- Worked with Accounts Payable
- Set up a billing system
- Entered, edited, and deleted bills
- Organized an inventory system
- Set up and worked with payroll

- Created reports in QuickBooks
- Used QuickReports to show data fast
- Designed and printed custom reports
- Set up online banking
- Made transactions over the wire
- Transferred funds electronically
- Found updates for your QuickBooks software
- Got your taxes organized in QuickBooks
- Checked up on payroll taxes
- Took care of sales tax
- Created an Accountant's Review

Congratulations on a job well done! Not only will your business benefit as you use the many features and facets of QuickBooks, but you will find that your data is both more organized and more accurate, which translates into less worry and perhaps more free time for you!

Now that you've spent the weekend working, you're entitled to some time off, don't you think? Who's up for a trip to the beach?

APPENDIX A
Installing QuickBooks 6.0

This last bit of the book may be the first place you look if you haven't yet installed QuickBooks. The installation procedure is pretty simple–you just plug in the CD and follow along–but this appendix helps you prepare, lets you know what you need to have ready, and walks you through the installation process. Specifically, you will learn the following:

- How to install QuickBooks
- How to register QuickBooks
- How to upgrade the program

What Do You Need to Install QuickBooks?

First things first. Make sure you've got the right system to run QuickBooks 6.0. Here's the necessary hardware:

- An IBM PC-compatible with a 486/66 or higher processor (Intuit recommends a Pentium system)
- A VGA or SVGA monitor with a screen resolution of 800 x 600
- At least 16MB of RAM, 32 recommended
- 45MB of hard disk space (plus 40MB more if you also install Internet Explorer)
- Windows 95 or Windows NT 4.0 or higher

Options: Multiple floppy disks, a Zip drive, or a tape for data backup (you'll need to do backups regularly). You'll also need a printer if you plan to print checks, forms, reports, and such. Any printer that is Windows 95–compatible will work in QuickBooks 6.0.

Getting Ready to Install

Before you install any new program–and QuickBooks is no exception–you need to back up your PC, including all program and data files that are of any consequence to you or your business.

You can use several different methods to back up your data:

- If you are using a previous version of QuickBooks, use the backup utility in the program to back up your data files.
- Use the Windows 95 Backup utility to back up important files.
- Use any other commercial backup utility–including those provided along with Zip drives (from Iomega) or with your tape backup unit. It can be used to get a copy of important data and preserve it.
- Copy individual files out to disk and put them away in a safe place.

APPENDIX A   Installing QuickBooks 6.0

 **NOTE** Many people get in a big hurry when it comes time to install something. "Oh, I made a backup a couple of weeks ago," you shrug. "Besides, nothing will happen." But the first time something *does* happen—your system hangs and chokes on a chunk of important data—you will think differently about those sixteen or so minutes it takes to run a backup of your system.

Simple Installation

After you make backups of your important files, you're ready to roll. Here are the steps for installation:

1. Put the QuickBooks 6.0 CD in the drive. The program starts automatically (given that you've set up Windows that way) and displays the window shown in Figure A.1.

Figure A.1
QuickBooks launches the install program as soon as you put the CD in the drive.

 Because I have already installed QuickBooks and QuickBooks knows it, the program lists the last option as "Re-Install QuickBooks." Your screen will show "Install QuickBooks" the first time you install.

2. The Welcome to QuickBooks Setup window appears. Click on Next.

3. Read through the license agreement and click on Yes to agree.

4. Next, enter the registration number that came with your version of QuickBooks.

5. QuickBooks displays the name of the folder to which it will copy the QuickBooks files. If you want to change the folder, click on Browse and select a new folder.

6. QuickBooks then asks you how you want the program to appear in Windows 95; choose the name you want and click on OK.

7. The program checks for available disk space and then displays a review of information. Check to make sure your registration number, the folder for the program files, and the program group for the program appear correctly. Click on Next and the program is copied to your hard disk.

8. When installation is complete, the program will greet you with congratulations and an electronic handshake. (Okay, maybe not a handshake.) You're ready to begin working with the program.

 You can type the name of a folder that doesn't exist if you want QuickBooks to create it for you.

> **WHEN MIGHT YOU NEED TO REINSTALL?**
>
> Things happen. Sometimes weird things happen. You might be getting errors that say that files are missing or corrupt. Your program might be locking up for no predictable reason. Whenever you've sleuthed out a problem and can't find a provable cause, you may want to consider reinstalling as a last resort. As a matter of course, QuickBooks should work fine with no surprises—even the product in its testing stages was more sound than many released products put out by other companies. But knowing when—and how—to reinstall gives you that "just in case" option—just in case.

Reinstalling QuickBooks

If at some point you need to reinstall your version of QuickBooks, simply repeat this process. Your data files will remain intact. (This *doesn't* let you off the hook for backing up your data, however.)

Put the CD back in the drive and click on Re-Install when the initial screen appears. Complete the installation as usual and QuickBooks will overwrite any needed files.

About Upgrades

QuickBooks includes a feature in version 6.0 that enables you to get maintenance updates periodically.

◄ ◄

A *maintenance update* is a between-releases update that fixes a program glitch or solves a problem.

◄ ◄

To get maintenance updates in QuickBooks, follow these steps:

1. Open the Online menu.

2. Choose QuickBooks Update Service. The Update Service dialog box appears (see Figure A.2).

3. Click on Go Online. The program makes the connection, locates the updates as needed, and downloads them.

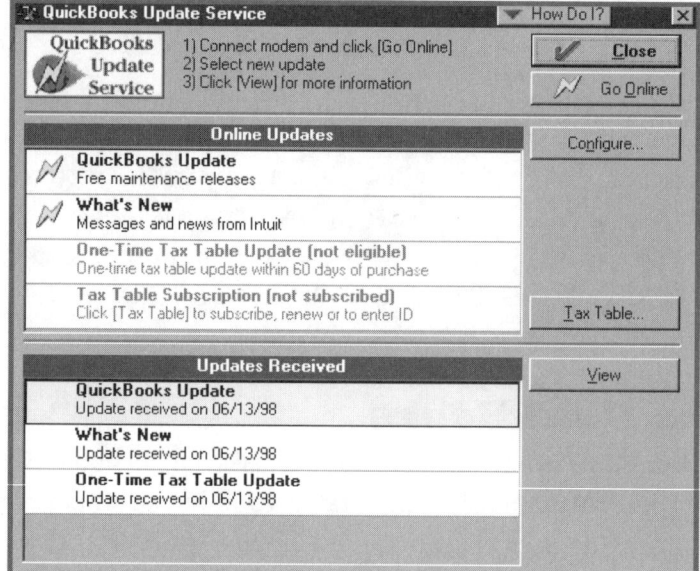

Figure A.2

You can use the QuickBooks Update Service to get the latest maintenance releases of the program.

APPENDIX B

QuickBooks Pro

Intuit offers another version of QuickBooks, which includes a few added features. If you work in a corporate environment and need a multiuser system with network capabilities, QuickBooks Pro is your program. Pro takes the basic features of QuickBooks and adds network features, a task manager, and a few other bells and whistles to make it an easy-to-use but extremely powerful bookkeeping package for businesses of all sizes.

Program Highlights

QuickBooks Pro is a multiuser version of the standard QuickBooks program, which you've been learning about throughout this book. *Multiuser* means that more than one person can work with the program—and the data—at the same time. QuickBooks Pro supports up to five users. Here are some of the other features QuickBooks Pro offers:

- A special Setup Wizard takes you through the many parts of QuickBooks Pro and helps you set up a new user for multiuser access.

- A user-tracking feature enables you to see who logged onto QuickBooks and at what time.

- An audit tracking feature helps you see when changes were made to the files and by whom.

- A job-costing feature helps you break down the various costs involved in each job.

- A project-tracking feature builds on the basic features in QuickBooks Pro to offer you full project-scheduling and management features.

What Do You Need to Run QuickBooks Pro?

Even though QuickBooks Pro is set up to run on networked systems, the overall hardware requirements are not much different from those needed for standard QuickBooks:

- An IBM PC-compatible with a 486/66 or higher processor (Intuit recommends a Pentium system)

- A VGA or SVGA monitor with a screen resolution of 800 × 600

- At least 16MB of RAM, 32 recommended

- 55MB of hard disk space (plus 40MB if you also install Internet Explorer and 9MB if you plan to install Timer)

- Windows 95 or Windows NT 4.0 or higher

- For multiuser functionality, Windows 95/NT peer-to-peer networking, Windows NT server, or a Novell NetWare network

Program Availability

FIND IT ONLINE

QuickBooks Pro is available through retail outlets and mail-order software houses. You can also purchase QuickBooks Pro directly from Intuit by visiting its QuickenStore Web site at **www.intuit.com/quicken_store/** or by calling 1-888-2-INTUIT.

GLOSSARY

Accountant's Review. A feature that prepares a set of your QuickBooks data files so that you can work uninterrupted while giving your accountant the data he needs.

Accounts payable. An accounting category that tracks where the money goes in your business.

Accounts receivable. An accounting category that tracks the income flowing into your business.

Accrual. Use an accrual basis if you want to create a report based on the time the customer was billed; choose cash if you want to create the report based on income that has already changed hands.

Assets. Current assets are assets you will convert to cash within a calendar year; fixed assets are those assets you will not be converting to cash within a year.

Authentication. A transparent process that checks to be sure that data packets sent match data packets received.

Balance sheet accounts. These accounts allow you to categorize your various expenditures so that you can easily see where the money goes.

Budget report. If you want to see whether your actual expenses and income are close to what you planned, print a Budget report.

Chart of Accounts. The Chart of Accounts shows you all the accounts you have set up in your business, according to the type of account you've set up.

Control. A control is a specific item you select—an icon, a tab, a radio button, a command button—to cause a specific action.

Credit memo. This is a form that lets customers know that you are crediting their accounts.

Current assets. These are assets you plan to turn into cash within a 12-month period; examples include cash and outstanding invoices.

Custom fields. These are fields you create and add to the Additional Info tab in the New Vendor, New Customer, or New Job dialog box.

Customer Register. The Customer Register enables you to view the data related to a particular client.

Depreciation. This is the decline in value of a fixed asset over time.

Electronic funds transfers. Also known as EFTs, these are online transactions.

Encryption. Encryption is a method of encoding your data—literally turning it into something unreadable by human or computer eyes—that requires a *key* to decode the data back into something usable.

Equity. This represents the net worth of your company.

Expense accounts. Expense accounts track the expenses through which money goes out of your business. Your expenses might include such items as Payroll, Rent, Materials, and Postage.

Federal ID Number. This is a number assigned to your business by the Federal government.

Fiscal year. Your fiscal year is the twelve-month period during which you track your financial information. Many businesses follow the calendar year for their fiscal year, but you can set up your fiscal year in the way that works best for you.

Fixed Assets. These are assets that will not be turned into cash within a 12-month period, such as a building, a car, or equipment.

Font. A font is one size and style of a particular typeface. For example, 10-point bold Times Roman is one font; 72-point italic Garamond is another.

Income accounts. Income accounts track the ways in which money comes into your business.

Income and expense accounts. Income and expense accounts track the money that comes into and flows out of your business.

Inventory account. An inventory account is an account set up in your Chart of Accounts that records inventory information.

Invoice. An invoice details a specific service or the sale of a particular product and requests an amount due.

Item. An item is a method QuickBooks gives you for filling in information quickly—you define an item and then can fill in complete information for a vendor, customer, or job by typing the name of the item.

Layout Designer. This is a feature in QuickBooks that helps you create a custom design for your forms.

Lists. One of the key organizing tools in QuickBooks, lists give you access to your vendors, customers, jobs, items, and more.

Maintenance updates. QuickBooks publishes software updates between major releases to fix program errors that users report.

Navigator. The main window of QuickBooks, the Navigator enables you to perform various operations by clicking on the organizing tabs and items on the graphic.

Net worth. This is the total value of your business, if all your assets were liquidated and all your liabilities were paid off.

Notepad. QuickBooks' Notepad feature enables you to attach notes to a customer file.

Online account access. With this type of access, you can do all the same things online that you could do in the lobby of your neighborhood bank: check account balances, transfer funds, write checks, review transactions, and more.

Online banking. An online component in QuickBooks, this feature enables you to do both traditional banking and bill paying online.

Online Banking Center. This is a window you display from the Online menu that enables you to send and receive transactions.

Online payments. The online payments feature enables you to make payments by using QuickBooks to send the money to your bank.

Point and click. The easiest method of choosing an option is to point at it and click the mouse button.

Preferences. You can set your preferences for the way QuickBooks operates by opening the File menu and choosing Preferences.

Profit & Loss report. If you want to show whether your business is profitable, do a Profit & Loss report.

Purchase order. This is a sales order you fill out when you order goods or services.

Reconciling. Reconciling is another term for balancing your checkbook.

Sales report. If you want to show the results of company sales over time, create a sales report.

Split transaction. This is a transaction that is applied to two or more vendors, customers, or jobs.

Start date. The start date you enter in QuickBooks is the day you start entering your transactions.

Statement. A statement is simply a report of activity on a particular client's account.

Subaccounts. Within each expense account, you can create subaccounts to further break down your expenses.

Tax year. This is the twelve-month period during which you track your tax liabilities. If you set up your fiscal year to be different from the calendar year, your tax year will coincide with your fiscal year.

Tech support. QuickBooks' technical support number is 1-888-320-7276.

GLOSSARY

Template. This is a predesigned form complete with fields and labels that you can modify to suit your needs.

To Do list. The To Do list is a list of reminders QuickBooks displays when you start the program. To add an item to your To Do list, open the Lists menu and choose To Do Notes.

Transaction report. If you want to show the transactions in a specific account, create a Transaction Detail report.

Vendors. Vendors are companies that sell you either supplies or services.

Wizard. This term is Microsoft-speak for an automated process that helps you create or configure something by asking you a series of questions.

INDEX

A

Accountant's Review, 311-315
    copy of report to accountant, 313
    merging accountant's data, 313-314
Accountant's Review Activities dialog box, 311, 312
accounts. *See also* bank accounts; Chart of Accounts; expense accounts; income accounts
    adding, 63
    asset accounts, 26
    choosing, 8-10
    customer tracking by, 80
    deleting accounts, 62
    deposits, making, 110-111
    editing accounts, 61-62
    equity accounts, 26
    filtering reports by, 233
    inactivating accounts, 62
    reactivating inactive accounts, 62-63
    renaming accounts, 61
    subaccounts, 16
    working with, 60-63
accounts payable, 147-148
    defined, 140

Accounts Payable register, 148
Accounts Payable report, 210
accounts receivable. *See* Income Details
Accounts Receivable report, 210
accrual basis accounting, 237
Activities menu, 42, 65
    transferring funds online with, 270-271
address information, 7
    employee addresses, 33
advisors, 55-56
    online tax advisors, 287-288
agricultural employers, 275
.AIF file extension, 314
asset accounts, 26
AuditTrail report, 214
authentication, 247-248

B

backing up, 58-59
    installation disk, 320
    for online banking, 246
Backup icon, 58

balance sheet accounts, 60
Balance Sheet reports, 210
    producing, 225-226
balancing checkbook, 132-134
    errors, correcting, 135
bank accounts. *See also* online banking
    opening balances, 25-26
billing system, 136-137
    accounts payable, 147-148
    cash, paying with, 145-146
    deleting bill payments, 149
    editing bill payments, 148
    entering bills, 137-138, 143-144
    goods and bill together, receiving, 142-143
    goods first, bill later, 141-142
    with online banking, 265-266
    paying bills, 145-147
    purchase orders, creating, 139-140
    receiving goods, 140-144
    setting up, 12-13
    tips for, 144
    vendors, adding, 138
    voiding bill payment, 149
budgeting, 38
Budget report, 210
Business Resources tab. *See* Navigator

C

cash
    bills paid with, 145-146
    sales, 108-110
cash basis accounting, 237
Cashfinder.com, 280
Cash Flow Forecast report, 213
charitable contributions, 29, 127

Chart of Accounts, 59-63
    accounts payable in, 147-148
    Check Register, accessing, 67
    Inventory Asset account, 157, 162
    working with, 60-63
Check Detail report, 213
Check Register. *See also* billing system
    adjustments, making, 134-135
    balancing checkbook, 132-134
    canceled checks, entering, 70
    charitable contributions, 127
    Chart of Accounts, accessing from, 67
    closing, 70
    dates on checks, entering, 68
    displaying, 66-68
    editing transactions, 129-130
    employees, one-time checks to, 127
    entering checks, 68-70
    memo field, 125
    Number column, 124-125
    past transactions, entering, 70
    payroll checks entered in, 195-196
    reminder feature, 131-132
    setting up, 14
    single check, printing, 123
    splitting transactions, 128-129
    transactions, entering, 124-125
    vendors, adding, 126-127
    voiding checks, 130
    writing checks, 121-123
checks. *See also* Check Register; online banking
    from Intuit, 117-118, 123
    Navigator tracking, 40-41
    online ordering, 197
    ordering computer checks, 117-118, 123

Index

paying bills with, 118-119
payroll checks, issuing, 193-197
setting up, 14
classes for business, 13-14
closing
   Check Register, 70
   Navigator, 50
COGS (Cost-of-Goods) account, 162
collapsing report subitems, 218
Column Labels dialog box, 231
columns for reports, 222
commissioned employees, 28
company file, creating, 8
Company Info section, 6-10
Company Name, 6
Concentric, 253
Connect To dialog box, 254-255
contacting QuickBooks, 55
contributions, payroll, 29-31
controls, 47
Create Item Receipts dialog box, 141
Create Purchase Orders dialog box, 139-140
credit cards. *See also* online banking
   Navigator tracking, 40-41
   opening balances for, 24-25
credit limit, 20
credit memos, 111-112
Custom Cash Sale template, 104
Custom Credit Memo template, 104
Customer Info
   editing, 86
   starting with, 76-77
Customer:Job list, 77
   adding customers, 84
   inactivating customers, 88

notes on customers, 86
printing customer list, 89-90
report list available with, 211
Customer lists. *See also* New Customer dialog box
   adding customers to, 77-83
   editing customer information, 86
Customer Register, 112-113
customers
   adding customers, 77-83
   deleting jobs, 89
   filtering reports by, 233
   inactivating, 87-89
   jobs, adding, 83-85
   Navigator tracking, 40
   notes on, 86
   online banking account for, 262-263
   organizing customer data, 78-81
   printing list of, 89-90
   split transactions, 128-129
custom fields
   filtering reports by, 233
   for inventory, 163-164
   New Customer dialog box, adding with, 81-83
Customize Report dialog box, 218
custom reports, creating, 236-237

D

dates and times
   Check Register, entering in, 68
   filtering reports by, 233
   in graphs, 239
   for reports, 220-221
day-care contributions, 29-31
DBA (doing business as) company, 6
deductions of employees, specifying, 191-193

deleting
    accounts, 62
    bill payments, 149
    customer jobs, 89
    filters from reports, 234
    report filters, 234
Deposit Detail report, 213
deposits to accounts, 110-111
dialog boxes, working with, 45-47
direct Deposit, 34
discounts, setting up, 108
drop-down text boxes, 48

E

EasyStep Interview, 4-10. *See also* employees; payroll
    Menu Items, 38
    preferences, choosing, 10-14
    preparations for, 5
Edit Account dialog box, 292
Edit Customer dialog box, 86
editing
    accounts, 61-62
    bill payments, 148
    Check Register transactions, 129-130
    customer information, 86
    graphs, 238-239
    payment information, 111
    templates, 104
Edit Item dialog box, 155
Edit menu, 42
electronic fund transfers (EFTs), 245
Employee List box, 181-182
employees. *See also* payroll
    adding employees, 33-34
    Employee Template, 180
    Navigator tracking, 41
    one-time checks to, 127
    records, setting up, 31-33
    sick leave, tracking, 32-33, 186
    vacation time, tracking, 33, 186
    YTD amounts for, 34-36, 187-190
Employee Template, 180
encryption, 247-248
Enter Bills dialog box, 123, 137-138, 142
Enter Cash Sales dialog box, 108-109
equity accounts, 26
estimates, setting up for, 12-13
exiting QuickBooks, 71
expense accounts
    Chart of Accounts including, 60
    setting up, 16-17
    subaccounts, 16
expenses
    invoices including information on, 94
    setting up expensed items, 13
exporting
    Accountant's Review, 314
    tax information to tax program, 300

F

federal employer identification number (EIN), 275
Federal ID number, 6, 7
Federal unemployment tax (FUTA), 28
File menu, 42
filters
    for customized reports, 237
    for reports, 218, 232-235
finance charges, 94-97
    assessing, 96-97

Index

figuring, 94
setting up, 95-96
template for, 104
Finance Charge template, 104
Financial Institutions button, 250, 254
Financial Institutions Directory, 257-259
Fine Alignment dialog box, 103
fiscal year, 7
start date and, 15
fixed assets, 26
folders, creating, 322
fonts
defined, 232
for mailing labels, 101
report fonts, 230, 231-232
footers for reports, 218
Form 940, 198, 200-201, 303
Form 941, 198, 199-200, 303
Form 1120/1120S, filling out, 299
Format Report dialog box, 230
formatting reports, 218, 229-232
Form W-4, Employee's Withholding Allowance Certificate, 183

G

General Journal feature, 286-287
General Ledger report, 213
Getting Started Wizard, 251, 252
Application Information, 256
Connect To dialog box, 254-255
Financial Institutions button, 254
graphs, 238-240
editing graphs, 238-239
printing, 239-240
gross receipts/sales, 296

Group with Other Undeposited Funds option, 108
deposits, making, 110-111

H

headers/footers for reports, 218
help, 50-51
How Do I? button, 51-52
with online banking, 272-273
online help, 57
Qcards, 53
reports, help for, 219
Help Index, 51
for online banking, 273
Help menu, 42
History report, 213
Home Banking Message dialog box, 272, 273
hourly employees, 28
household employers, 275
How Do I? button, 51-52
in Online Banking Center, 273

I

icons
Backup icon, 58
selecting, 45
inactivating customers, 87-89
inactive accounts, 62
reactivating, 62-63
income accounts
Chart of Accounts including, 60
setting up, 15-17
subaccounts, 16
Income by Customer Summary report, 215
Income Details
entering, 17-21

item types, 18-20
income taxes. *See* taxes
Income Tax Summary report, 213
    modifying, 294
    sales income amounts, finding, 294-297
installing QuickBooks, 318-323
    hardware for, 319-320
    preparation for, 320
    reinstalling, 322
    simple installation, 320-322
Internet. *See* online banking; online services
Internet Connection Setup Wizard, 56, 253
Internet Service Providers (ISPs), 253
Intuit Market, 280
Intuit Web sites, 56, 252
    Home Page, 280
    information on, 280
inventory, 10, 153-154
    adding items to, 159-164
    adjusting information, 169-171
    analyzing data with reports, 174
    Chart of Accounts Inventory Asset account, 157
    creating accounts, 156-159
    cross-checking, 165
    custom fields, setting up, 163-164
    reports on, 176
    Edit Item dialog box, information in, 155
    future items, setting up for, 163
    Inventory Asset account, 162
    Item List box items, 159-160
    master printout of, 168
    ordering stock, 172-173
    Physical Inventory Worksheet, 165-166
    purchase order description, 161
    QuickReport, 166, 169

    receiving items into, 173-174
    Reminders list for, 172-173
    selling stock in, 171-172
    stock report, printing, 177
    taking inventory, form for, 165-166
    tips on, 167-169
    troubleshooter role, 168
    turning on feature, 155-156
    Valuation Summary report, 175-176
    vendor status reports, 177-178
    warning about, 157
Inventory and Purchase Orders Are Active option, 157
Inventory Items, 21
Inventory reports, 210
invoices
    creating, 90-94
    effective invoice features, 91
    formats for, 11-12
    printing, 93, 103-105
    statements and, 18
    templates for, 92
IRS Web site, 8
Item List box, 159-160
item types, 18-20

J

jobs. *See also* Customer:Job list
    split transactions, 128-129
journal entries, 286-287
Journal report, 213

L

labels. *See* mailing labels
landscape orientation, reports in, 216

Legal Name, 6
list boxes, 47-50
  buttons in, 49
List menu, 42
lists, 64-66
  displaying, 65
loans
  opening balances for, 25
  tracking, 25
local area networks (LANs), 249

M

mailing labels
  aligning, 101-103
  creating, 98-101
  printing, 98-101
  selected names, printing for, 99
maintenance updates, 323
Make Deposits dialog box, 111
Medicare Qualified Government Employer (MQGE), 275
memorizing reports, 219, 235-236
Menu Items, 38
menus. *See also* specific menus
  selecting items on, 43-44
  submenus, displaying, 44
  working with, 43
merging accountant's data, 313-314
mileage reimbursement items, 28
Missing Checks report, 213
modems, 249
multiple jobs, tracking, 23
multiple tax rates, 11
multiuser, defined, 327

N

Navigator, 39-41
  backing up data, 58
  Business Resources tab, 41, 54
  advisors, using, 55-56
  Checking and Credit Cards tab, 40-41
  closing/reopening, 50
  Company tab, 41
  Payroll and Employees tab, 41
  Purchases and Vendors tab, 40
  Reports area in, 208-209
  Sales and Customers tab, 40
  Taxes and Accountant tab, 41, 286
  working with, 44-50
New Customer dialog box, 77, 78
  Additional Info tab, 79-81
  fields, adding, 81-83
  jobs, adding, 83-85
New Employee dialog box, 184
New To Do dialog box, 87
New Vendor dialog box, 121
non-inventory part item, 20
notes. *See* loans
number display for reports, 230

O

online account access, 245
online advisors, 287-288
online banking. *See also* Payroll Service
  accessing account online, 245
  account register, 267
  applying for services, 256-259
  authentication, 247-248
  bill paying, 147, 265-266
  confirmation letter, 260-261

customer account, setting up, 262-263
enabling accounts, 259-262
encryption, 247-248
existing account, working with, 261
existing bank, setting up with, 250
finding a bank, 253-256
Getting Started option, 250-251
Getting Started Wizard, 251, 252
help with, 272-273
Home Banking Message dialog box, 272, 273
Internet connection, 253
messages online, sending, 272
new account, creating, 261
passwords for, 248
Pay Bills dialog box, 266
payroll, 186
PIN (personal identification number), 248
register, transferring funds with, 271-272
routing number of bank, 250
scheduling payments, 269-272
security issues, 247-248
sending transactions online, 267-269
service charges, 250
setting up for, 250-263
taxes, filing, 198
transaction history, 247
transactions handled with, 244
transferring funds online, 270-272
vendor account, setting up, 262-263
Write Checks dialog box, 264
writing checks with, 263-265
Online Banking Center, 250, 252
How Do I? button, 273
list of transactions, 267

Online Banking Setup Interview dialog box, 256, 257
enabling accounts through, 260
Online menu, 42, 252
online payments accounts, 245
Online Payroll Service. *See* Payroll Service
online services. *See also* Intuit Web sites; online banking; Payroll Service
QuickBooks Update Service, 276-278
sales tax, paying, 310
Open Check Register dialog box, 124
opening balances
adjusting, 134
for bank accounts, 25-26
for credit cards, 24-25
on Customer Register, 113
of customers, 81
entering, 21-26
for loans, 25
multiple jobs, tracking, 23
outstanding balances, customers with, 22
with vendors, 24
Open Purchase Orders dialog box, 142-143
overtime rates, 28

P

passwords, 248
for online banking, 248
setting passwords, 249
Pay Bills dialog box, 145-146
for online banking, 266
scheduling online payments, 270
Pay Liabilities dialog box, 197-198
payments. *See also* online banking
deposits, making, 110-111

Index

Group with Other Undeposited Funds option, 108
receiving payments from invoices, 106-108
Payments to Deposit dialog box, 111
payroll, 178-179. *See also* employees
    adding employees, 183-186
    Additional Info tab, 183
    additions, 28
    changing employee information, 186-187
    Checkbook Register, entering checks in, 195-196
    class, tracking by, 191
    contributions, 29-31
    customer and job, tracking by, 191
    day-care contributions, 29-31
    deductions, specifying, 191-193
    direct deposit, 34
    documents for setting up, 180-181
    employee information, entering, 181-193
    expenses of payroll, tracking, 190-191
    Federal unemployment tax (FUTA), 28
    filing taxes online, 198
    Form 940, 198, 200-201, 303
    Form 941, 198, 199-200, 303
    issuing checks, 193-197
    mileage reimbursement items, 28
    Navigator tracking, 41
    New Employee dialog box, 184
    online payroll, 186
    Pay Liabilities dialog box, 197-198
    payments, entering, 36-38
    Payroll Expenses account, 301-302
    Payroll Info tab, 183, 184
    preferences, choosing, 179-180
    Preview Paycheck dialog box, 194-195
    prior payments, entering, 36-38
    reporting taxes, 300-303
    setting up, 12-13, 27-38, 301
    sick leave information, 186
    subaccounts, creating, 301
    Taxes dialog box, 185-186
    turning on features, 179
    unemployment rate information, 27
    vacation information, 186
    W-2 forms, 198, 201-202, 303
    W-3 forms, 198, 202, 303
    YTD amounts, setting up, 34-36
    YTD (year-to-date) adjustments, 187-190
Payroll Expenses account, 301-302
Payroll Info tab, 183, 184
Payroll Item list, 192
Payroll reports, 210, 303
Payroll Service, 252, 274-275
    applying for, 304
    starting, 274
Payroll Tax Tables, 278-279
Pay Sales Tax dialog box, 309
phone list, printing, 226-227
Physical Inventory Worksheet, 165-166
PIN (personal identification number), 248, 251
    confirmation letter using, 261
    sending transactions, use with, 268-269
portrait orientation, reports in, 216
preferences
    choosing, 10-14
    payroll preferences, 179-180
Preferences dialog box
    Finance Charges item, 95-96
    working with, 45-47
preset accounts, 8, 9
previewing
    Preview mode, 102

reports, 216-217
Preview Paycheck dialog box, 194-195
price list, producing, 228-229
printers for reports, 214
printing. *See also* reports
   customer lists, 89-90
   graphs, 239-240
   invoices, 93, 103-105
   mailing labels, 98-101
   phone list, 226-227
   Preview mode, 102
   single check, 123
Print Invoices dialog box, 105
Print Labels dialog box, 101
Print Reports dialog box, 215-217
Product Invoice template, 92, 104
Professional Invoice template, 92, 104
Profit & Loss report, 210
   producing, 224-225
project tracking, 13
purchase orders, 20. *See also* billing system
   creating, 139-140
   duplicate purchase order number option, 157

Q

Qcards, 53
QuickBooks.com, 280
QuickBooks Pro, 9-10, 325-328
   hardware requirements, 327-328
   running, 328
QuickBooks Update Service, 252, 276-278, 323
   tax forms and tables with, 278
QuickenStore Web site, 328
QuickReports, 222-223, 224
   inventory QuickReport, 166, 169

R

Receive Items tab, 141-142
Receive Payments dialog box, 106, 107
Reconcile dialog box, 133
recording tax items, 307-308
refreshing screen, 219
refunds, credit memos for, 111-112
reinstalling QuickBooks, 322
reminder feature, 131-132
Reminders list, 14
   inventory stock, ordering, 172-173
renaming accounts, 61
reorder point, 21
Report Filters dialog box, 234
reports. *See also* inventory; QuickReports; specific reports
   accrual basis reports, 237
   available reports, 208-209
   cash basis reports, 237
   choosing reports, 212-213
   collapsing subitems in, 218
   column content for, 222
   creating reports, 214-223
   custom reports, creating, 236-237
   dates for, 220-221
   From and To dates for, 220-221
   filters for, 218, 232-235
   finding reports, 209-212
   fonts for, 230, 231-232
   formatting, 218, 229-232
   graphs in, 238-240
   help, 219
   ideals for filtering, 233
   memorizing reports, 219, 235-236
   number display, changing, 230

Index

orientation for printing, 216
phone list, printing, 226-227
printing, 215-217
    quick/customized reports, 176
project reports, creating, 223-229
sales tax reports, 310-311
Reports button, 65
Reports menu, 42, 211
Reports toolbar, 218-219
Report window
    formatting report in, 229-232
    information in, 217-222
    printing in, 215
    title bar, 217
resale numbers, 80

S

salaries. *See* payroll
sales
    cash sales, 108-110
    gross receipts/sales, 296
    inventory stock, 171-172
    Navigator tracking, 40
    price list, producing, 228-229
Sales report, 210
    creating, 227-228
sales tax, 307-311
    current balance, entering, 306
    online payment, 310
    paying, 308-310
    rate items, 308
    recording tax items, 307-308
    reports, creating, 310-311
    setting up, 11-12, 305-306
    turning on, 288, 304-305

working with, 303-306
Save Accountant's Copy To dialog box, 311, 312
Save Export Changes To dialog box, 314
saving
    backup files, 59
    memorized report, 235
scheduling online payments, 269-272
screen, 42-50
Security Alert dialog box, 248, 255
security of online banking, 247-248
Select Invoices to Print dialog box, 104, 105
Select Mailing Labels to Print dialog box, 99
Select Names dialog box, 99
Select Name Type dialog box, 127
Service Invoice template, 92
service items, 18-19
Setup Wizard for QuickBooks Pro, 327-328
sick leave information, 186
    tracking, 32-33
single tax rates, 11
SmallBusiness by Quicken.com, 280
Small Business Web page, 57, 58
social security number, 250
sounds, disabling, 126
split transactions, 128-129
Standard Statement template, 104
start date, 14-15. *See also* opening balances
    fiscal year and, 15
state disability insurance (SDI) rates, 181
statements
    invoices and, 18
    profit and loss statement, 224-225
    Standard Statement template, 104
state taxes
    state disability insurance (SDI) rates, 181

state unemployment tax (SUI), 181
withholding tax, 28
state unemployment tax (SUI), 181
state withholding tax, 28
subaccounts, 16
submenus, displaying, 44

T

taxes, 287-300. *See also* Accountant's Review; payroll; sales tax
assigning tax lines to accounts, 291-292
credits and returns, handling, 295-296
customer information, 20
Edit Account dialog box, 292
exporting information to tax program, 300
Form 940, 198, 200-201, 303
Form 941, 198, 199-200
Form 1120/1120S, filling out, 299
Form W-4, Employee's Withholding Allowance Certificate, 183
identifying taxable items, 307-311
journal entries, 286-287
Navigator tracking, 41
online advisors, 287-288
online filing, 198
Payroll Tax Tables, 278-279
preparing tax forms, 299-300
QuickBooks Update Service, forms and tables with, 278
recording tax items, 307-308
sales income amounts, finding, 294-297
selecting tax forms, 8
taxes, 287-300
time for filing forms, 202
total purchases, determining, 297-298

verifying account totals, 293-294
W-2 forms, 198, 201-202, 303
Taxes dialog box, 185-186
tax line assignments, 290-291
Tax Line By Account report, 294
Debt/Credit totals, 297
tax tables
Payroll Tax Tables, 278-279
QuickBooks Update Service, tax tables with, 278
tax year, 7
technical support, 57, 280
telephone list, printing, 226-227
templates
editing, 104
Employee Template, 180
invoice templates, 92
viewing templates, 104
tips
Accountant's Review, saving, 313
accounts
categories for, 17
choosing type of, 62
asset accounts, 26
backup files, saving, 59
billing system, 138
Check Register
Chart of Accounts, accessing from, 67
dates on checks, entering, 68
new transaction, moving to, 70
split transactions, amount of, 129
Customer Register, 113
customers, adding, 84, 85
customized reports, 237
To Do list, adding bills to, 119

Index

EasyStep Interview, completing, 6
employee information, 31
Enter Bills dialog box, 123
Federal unemployment tax (FUTA), 28
finance charges, 94
folders, creating, 322
General Journal, using, 287
graphs, 238-240
    options for, 240
Group with Other Undeposited Funds option, 108
help information, using, 51
individual companies, setting up, 7
installation disk, backing up, 320
inventory
    cross-checking, 165
    editing inventory part item, 163
    Inventory Asset account, 162
    Physical Inventory Worksheet, 165-166
    Reminders list for, 172-173
invoices
    notes on, 93
    printing, 105
    several invoices, printing, 93
lists, 65
mailing labels
    aligning, 103
    Print Mailing Labels button, 104
    selected names, printing for, 99
    testing print, 101
online banking
    balance, checking on, 272
    confirmation letter, 261
    vendors supporting, 245
opening balance information, 22

payments
    editing information, 111
    Group with Other Undeposited Funds option, 108
pay period, choosing, 37
payroll
    changing employee information, 187
    checking employee information, 183
    Employee list, displaying, 183
    unemployment rate information, 27-28
Payroll Service, applying for, 274
preferences, 10
printing quick/customized reports, 176
Print Mailing Labels button, 104
QuickBooks, contacting, 55
QuickBooks Update Service, 278
QuickReports, 223
Receive Items tab, 142
reports
    available reports, displaying, 208
    filters, removing, 234
    fonts in, 230
    print orientation, 216
sales tax, 288
    online payments, 310
    paying, 309
    rates, 11, 308
start date, fiscal year and, 15
taxes, Edit Account dialog box, 292
TurboTax
    QuickBooks with, 280
    Web site, 300
Vendor dialog box, Additional Info tab, 121
vendors, 24

W-3 forms, 198, 202, 303
Write Checks dialog box, 122
To Do list, 38
   bills added to, 119
   new to do, adding, 87
Transaction Journal report, 213
transferring funds online, 270-272
Trial Balance report, 213
TurboTax, 288
   QuickBooks with, 280
   Web site for, 300

U

undoing deletions, 89
unemployment rate information, 27-28
updates, 323. *See also* QuickBooks Update Service
   maintenance updates, 323
User List dialog box, 249

V

vacation information, 186
   tracking, 33
Valuation Summary report for inventory, 175-176
Vendor button, 65
Vendor dialog box, Additional Info tab, 119-121
Vendor List box, 65
vendors, 24
   adding vendors to list, 119-121
   billing system, adding to, 138
   Check Register, adding to, 126-127
   filtering reports by, 233
   inventory, vendor status report in, 177-178
   Navigator tracking, 40
   online banking account for, 262-263
   opening balances with, 24
   split transactions, 128-129
voiding checks, 130

W

W-2 forms, 198, 201-202, 303
W-3 forms, 198, 202, 303
Warn About Duplicate Purchase Order Numbers option, 157
Warn If Not Enough Inventory to Sell option, 157
warning symbol, 6
Window menu, 42
wizards, 45
   Getting Started Wizard, 251, 252
   Internet Connection Setup Wizard, 56
   Setup Wizard for QuickBooks Pro, 327-328
   YTD Amounts Wizard, 187, 188
Write Checks dialog box, 121-123
   for online banking, 264
   scheduling online payments, 269
   single check, printing, 123

Y

year-to-date amounts, setting up, 34-36, 187-190
YTD Amounts Wizard, 187, 188
YTD (year-to-date) adjustments, 34-36, 187-190

Z

Zoom In/Out, 102

Prima's fast & easy Series

Relax. Learning new software is now a breeze. You are looking at a series of books dedicated to one idea: To help you learn to use software as quickly and as easily as possible. No need to wade through endless pages of boring text. With Prima's FAST & EASY series, you simply look and learn.

Windows® 98
1-7615-1006-0
$16.99 (Can. $23.95)

Microsoft® Word 97
0-7615-1007-9
$16.99 (Can. $23.95)

Microsoft® Excel 97
0-7615-1008-7
$16.99 (Can. $23.95)

Internet Explorer 4.0
0-7615-1191-1
$16.99 (Can. $23.95)

ACT!™ 4.0
0-7615-1412-0
$16.99 (Can. $23.95)

FrontPage® 98
0-7615-1534-8
$16.99 (Can. $23.95)

SmartSuite® Millenium
0-7615-1699-9
$16.99 (Can. $23.95)

Microsoft® Office 97
0-7615-1162-8
$16.99 (Can. $23.95)

Also Available

Access 97
0-7615-1363-9

Publisher® 98
0-7615-1513-5

Netscape Navigator® 4.0
0-7615-1382-5

WordPerfect® 8
0-7615-1083-4

Outlook 98
0-7615-1405-8

WordPerfect Suite® 8
0-7615-1188-1

Coming Soon

Internet Explorer 5.0
0-7615-1742-1

Lotus Notes
0-7615-1393-0

Quicken Deluxe 99
0-7615-1787-1

www.primapublishing.com

Call now to order
(800)632-8676, ext. 4444

Prima Publishing and Fast & Easy are trademarks of Prima Communications, Inc. All other product and company names are trademarks of their respective companies.

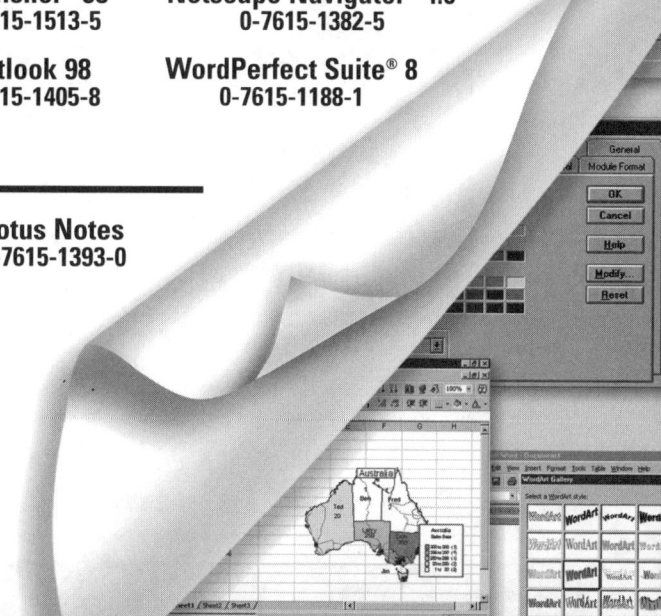

Prima's In a Weekend™ Series

Learn Windows 98 In a Weekend
0-7615-1296-9
$19.99 (Can. $27.95)

Learn HTML In a Weekend
0-7615-1293-4 • CD-ROM
$24.99 (Can. $34.95)

Increase Your Web Traffic In a Weekend
0-7615-1194-6
$19.99 (Can. $27.95)

Create FrontPage® 98 Web Pages In a Weekend
0-7615-1348-5 • CD-ROM
$24.99 (Can. $34.95)

Organize Your Finances with Quicken Deluxe 98 In a Weekend
0-7615-1186-5
$19.99 (Can. $27.95)

Also Available
- Learn Access 97 In a Weekend
- Learn Word 97 In a Weekend
- Create PowerPoint Presentations In a Weekend
- Learn the Internet In a Weekend
- Learn Publisher 97 In a Weekend
- Create Your First Web Page In a Weekend, Revised Edition
- Upgrade Your PC In a Weekend

Coming Soon
- Learn Digital Photography In a Weekend
- Organize Your Finances with Quicken Deluxe 99 In a Weekend

GOOD NEWS! You can master the skills you need to achieve your goals in just a weekend! Prima Publishing's unique IN A WEEKEND series offers practical fast-track guides dedicated to showing you how to complete your projects in a weekend or less!

www.primapublishing.com

Call now to order (800) 632-8676, ext. 4444

Prima Publishing and In a Weekend are trademarks of Prima Communications, Inc. All other product and company names are trademarks of their respective companies.